Travels on the St. Johns River

UNIVERSITY PRESS OF FLORIDA

Florida A&M University, Tallahassee
Florida Atlantic University, Boca Raton
Florida Gulf Coast University, Ft. Myers
Florida International University, Miami
Florida State University, Tallahassee
New College of Florida, Sarasota
University of Central Florida, Orlando
University of Florida, Gainesville
University of North Florida, Jacksonville
University of South Florida, Tampa
University of West Florida, Pensacola

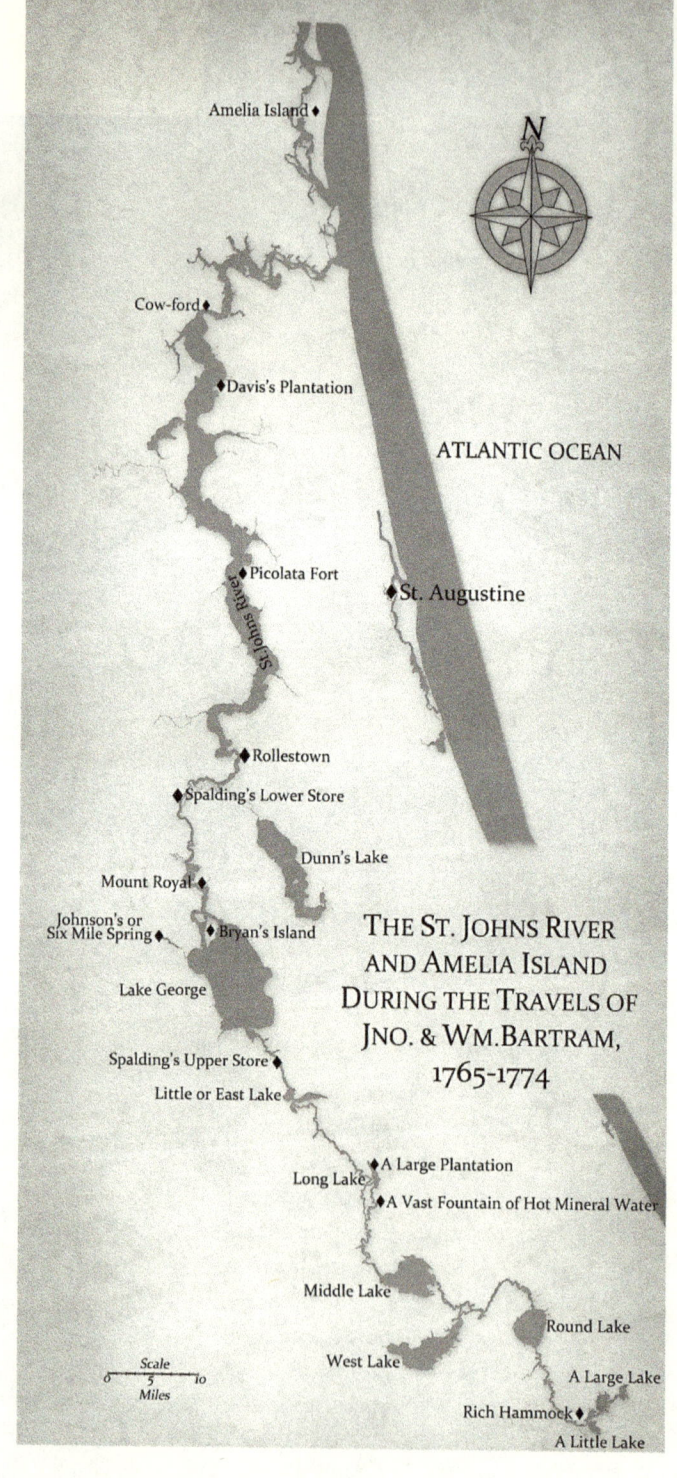

# Travels on the St. Johns River

John Bartram and William Bartram

EDITED BY
THOMAS HALLOCK AND RICHARD FRANZ

UNIVERSITY PRESS OF FLORIDA
Gainesville / Tallahassee / Tampa / Boca Raton
Pensacola / Orlando / Miami / Jacksonville / Ft. Myers / Sarasota

COPYRIGHT 2017 BY THOMAS HALLOCK AND RICHARD FRANZ
All rights reserved
Maps created by Dean Campbell
Published in the United States of America

First cloth printing, 2017
First paperback printing, 2023

28 27 26 25 24 23    6 5 4 3 2 1

Library of Congress Cataloging-in-Publication Data
Names: Bartram, John, 1699–1777, author. | Bartram, William, 1739–1823, author. | Hallock, Thomas, editor. | Franz, Richard, (professor) editor.
Title: Travels on the St. Johns River / John Bartram and William Bartram ; edited by Thomas Hallock and Richard Franz.
Description: Gainesville : University Press of Florida, 2017. | Includes bibliographical references and index.
Identifiers: LCCN 2016035944 | ISBN 9780813062259 (cloth) | ISBN 9780813080444 (pbk.)
Subjects: LCSH: Florida—Description and travel. | Saint Johns River (Fla.)—Description and travel. | Saint Johns River Valley (Fla.)—Description and travel. | Bartram, John, 1699–1777—Correspondence. | Bartram, John, 1699–1777—Travel—Florida. | Bartram, William, 1739–1823—Travel—Florida. | Natural history—Florida.
Classification: LCC F314 .B29 2016 | DDC 917.5904/64—dc23
LC record available at https://lccn.loc.gov/2016035944

The University Press of Florida is the scholarly publishing agency for the State University System of Florida, comprising Florida A&M University, Florida Atlantic University, Florida Gulf Coast University, Florida International University, Florida State University, New College of Florida, University of Central Florida, University of Florida, University of North Florida, University of South Florida, and University of West Florida.

UNIVERSITY PRESS OF FLORIDA
2046 NE Waldo Road
Suite 2100
Gainesville, FL 32609
http://upress.ufl.edu

## Contents

List of Illustrations vi
Foreword vii
BILL BELLEVILLE

Introduction 1
THOMAS HALLOCK

### Part I

1. *Diary* 13
JOHN BARTRAM

2. *Travels* 43
WILLIAM BARTRAM

3. Correspondence 115

### Part II

4. Through Their Eyes: The Bartrams Explore the St. Johns River Valley 131
RICHARD FRANZ

Acknowledgments 193

Notes 195
Bibliography 209
Index 215

# Illustrations

## Figures

1. William Bartram, limpkin (*Aramus guarauna*)  7
2. "Two Beautifull Species Annona"  68
3. Mount Royal Site, engraving by E. G. Squier based upon William Bartram's sketch in his 1789 *Observations on the Creek and Cherokee Indians*  71
4. "Alegator of St. Johns"  83
5. "Great Yellow Bream calld Old Wife"  104
6. *Ixia coelestina*  122
7. Memorial Bridge over the St. Johns River at Palatka, Florida  134
8. Swamps along the east side of the St. Johns River  140
9. River marsh on the back side of Tick Island, showing tussocks of sand cordgrass  143
10. Banded mystery shells washing out from an extensive shell midden along the banks of the St. Johns River  146
11. High pine landscape with large longleaf pines and a grassy understory  148
12. Pine flatwoods with shallow flatwoods pond  151

## Maps

1. General map of the St. Johns River, 1765–1774  ii
2. Amelia Island and the Lower St. Johns River, 1765–1774  15
3. Middle St. Johns River, 1765–1774  17
4. Upper St. Johns River, 1765–1774  23

# Foreword

No other continental state can match our Florida peninsula when it comes to the biological diversity of plants and animals that exist here.

When botanist John Bartram and his son William explored this new territory on behalf of the British government in 1765, they were entering a landscape that was virtually unknown, one that was closer to the subtropics in many ways. Earlier correspondents had reported on Florida, including Jean Ribault (1562) and Hernando de Escalante Fontaneda (held captive by the Calusas from 1549 to 1566). But their explorations were not driven by the sensibilities that motivated the Bartrams.

Both Bartrams wrote about their exploration here and, in doing so, helped provide the world with the first intimate look at La Florida of the late 1700s. Those observations generally were woven into broader stories of the American southeast. Certainly their descriptions also benefited from the fact that instead of using the far more convoluted Latin descriptions, the Bartrams were among the first to use the efficient taxonomy newly introduced by Linnaeus (via *Systema Naturae*) that categorized natural organisms as "genus" and "species."

The artist and naturalist son, "Billy," traveled with his father as far as they could up the St. Johns River as it was the most readily available "avenue" into the soggy terrain of this predredged peninsula. They were effectively exploring a subtropical appendage to an otherwise temperate land mass. In a biogeographical sense, La Florida was really more of an island than the rest of what was soon to become "America."

John recorded his observations in his diary while Billy did the same in the more extensive *Travels* (1791), which covered North and South Carolina and Georgia in addition to East and West Florida. Naturalist Helen G. Cruickshank excerpted Billy's narratives describing this region with *Bartram in Florida* in

1986. And personal letters—most previously unpublished—continued to define this strange foreign place. But the larger role the "Grand and Noble San Juan" specifically played in the Bartrams' experiences has—until now—gone virtually unexamined inside of one cover.

When researching a book about the St. Johns (*River of Lakes*) in 1999, I became intimately aware of the river's history and diversity. I also marveled at the extent of natural lands and wildlife that still remained in the basin and made every attempt I could to experience this for myself. The great irony is that—despite the tremendous loss of natural lands in Florida—almost one-third of our land and water is protected in public ownership (compared with an average of 16–17 percent in other states.)

While I benefited from the knowledge of very savvy scientists and escorts in my own travels, my true "guide"—spiritually and ecologically—was Billy Bartram. Indeed, there are few times that I still visit the springs, swamps, and shores of that river today without feeling Bartram's presence. This is an explorer, an artist, and an adventurer who described himself as a "philosophical pilgrim." He was also the first American to devote his entire life to experiencing and communicating—in art and words—our environment. And long before more modern naturalists began to understand the deeper spiritual manifestations of nature, Bartram's own Quaker spirituality served him well in that regard some 250 years ago.

The benefit the editors have provided with this insightful book about the St. Johns can be considered a gift they have hand-delivered from the Bartrams. It's a gift enhanced with the inclusion of some of the archival drawings of the plants and animals the Bartrams saw, as well as an indexed explanation of the specifics of many of their observations. In a sublime way, *Travels on the St. Johns River* also balances the ravages of our modern era with the transcendence that can still be experienced in the historic landscape that remains in the river basin.

Certainly this title could not be made available to us at a more appropriate time. Florida's natural areas are under siege as never before. In a recent report, even the Florida realtors state that property values are now being suppressed by almost $1 billion a year due to the decline in surface water quality. Our springs—once described by William as the "enchanting and amazing crystal" fountains holding the "blue ether of another world"—are losing flow and smothering with an increase of algae-stimulating nutrients. Springs specialist Dr. Bob Knight reported that Silver Springs—once the largest spring in the entire world—will stop flowing in 15 years if current trends continue.

Despite our bounty of publicly owned lands, it is clear that shortsighted politics—designed to exploit natural landscapes to earn short-term paybacks from timbering and agribusiness—are treating publicly owned land as they might any privately owned landscape they have exploited for soils and water. Essential conservation needs—such as protecting the "springsheds" where our magical (and economically beneficial) fresh water springs are recharged—are being blatantly ignored.

Placing land in public ownership is no longer enough to ensure its protection. We need to more fully acknowledge the activities that take place outside those parks, forests, and preserves that affect the health of the singular landscapes and the wondrous diversity of species that occupy them.

The spiritual losses of our natural landscapes exceed anything as utilitarian as economics. As William wrote in *Travels*:

> This world, as a glorious apartment of the boundless palace of the sovereign Creator, is furnished with an infinite variety of animated scenes, inexpressibly beautiful and pleasing, equally free to the inspection and enjoyment of all His creatures.

Indeed, the animals alone "excite our admiration and equally manifest the almighty power, wisdom, and beneficence of the Supreme Creator . . . of the Universe."

For the contemplative observer, a hike, a paddle, or just about any kind of thoughtful excursion into the healthiest portions of the St. Johns, its tributaries, its swamps, marshes, and springs today will still reveal wondrous doses of this "boundless palace of the sovereign Creator." When you go, take along a compass, a good map, and a copy of *Travels on the St. Johns River*.

Bill Belleville

# Introduction

THOMAS HALLOCK

After the Seven Years' or French and Indian War, the European empires in America shuffled their paper claims. The 1763 Peace of Paris stripped France of Canada and Louisiana but left the French Martinique, Guadeloupe, and Santa Lucia. Havana, which had fallen to England late in the war, was returned to Spain, and to compensate for the loss of Cuba, England gained rights to *la Florida*, which the Seminoles had occupied since the early eighteenth century. The British viewed their new subtropical territory—divided into two colonies, East and West Florida—with an eye toward the interior Indian trade and staple crop plantations. Speculation boomed. Exploration followed. John and William Bartram, the pioneering father-son naturalists, traveled south.

Their 1765–66 trip marked a turning point for the younger Bartram, a culmination for the elder. John, the father, embodied the practical intelligence and hard work of Benjamin Franklin's Philadelphia. Born in 1699, this humble Pennsylvania farmer had taught himself the Latin "characters," or parts of a plant, and leveraged his services as a horticulturalist to establish his place in a heady network of scientific exchange. The search for "nondescript," or undescribed, specimens took him through New Jersey and Pennsylvania, across New York to Niagara Falls, and as far as New England, making his garden on the west banks of the Schuylkill River in Kingsessing (now West Philadelphia) a required stop for luminaries and leaders of state. In 1743 John Bartram co-founded the American Philosophical Society with Franklin, and through the mediation of his longtime London correspondent Peter Collinson, he earned the praise of the venerable Hans Sloane, keeper of London's Kew Gardens, and the great systematizer Carl von Linné, or Linnaeus. When claims to Florida fell to England in 1763, George III awarded John Bartram the title of King's Botanist, with the expectation that he travel.

John, then in his mid-sixties, needed a companion, so he drafted his talented son "Billy" to join him. At this point in life, the twenty-six-year-old William Bartram was adrift. Despite connections and an outstanding, if abridged, education at the Philadelphia Academy (what would become the University of Pennsylvania), William had little yet to show for his tremendous potential. A decade earlier, watercolors of Pennsylvania birds had caught the eye of patrons in England, and Billy had already accompanied his father on other expeditions. Botany and drawing were his "darling delights," but even in a bustling provincial capital like Philadelphia, those talents would not translate into a profitable career. In 1765 William Bartram was living with his uncle on the Cape Fear River in North Carolina, hoping to establish himself as a trader. A letter came from his father, instructing him to sell his merchandise at "publick vandue" and prepare for a journey. "Son William" had little choice but to comply.[1]

Their journey lasted roughly eight months, from July 1765 to spring 1766. The two Bartrams reunited in North Carolina, then rode horseback to Charleston, Savannah, and Augusta, where they reestablished connections and sought out new plants, including their most impressive joint discovery, the *Franklinia altamaha*. In November 1765 they started up the north-flowing St. Johns, where they witnessed a Creek-British conference at Fort Picolata, crucial for maintaining peace in the territory they were set to explore.[2] At Beauclerc Bluff, an indigo plantation owned by Robert Davis on the St. Johns, the Bartrams formed a small expedition party, which included John Davis (Robert's son), Dr. David Yeats, and an enslaved black man from Davis's plantation. The five travelers then journeyed by flat-bottomed bateau up the river's wide main stem, passed the lower store owned by James Spalding near present-day Palatka, and followed the chain of sheet-flow lakes to the St. Johns's upper reaches, Lake Loughman, where in John's words, the "weeds and reeds finally stopped our battoe."[3]

By mid-February the two naturalists were back in St. Augustine. John stayed in Florida until March, then stopped in Charleston to recover from his long trip. William purchased a 500-acre tract near Fort Picolata, where he hoped to establish himself as a planter. Drawing from his son's inheritance, John sent "6 likely negroes" and supplies down from South Carolina. Land speculation was booming in Florida, although family and friends held out little faith in this latest, ill-advised venture; their concerns proved well founded. Within a year, William Bartram would pull up stakes on the St. Johns, presumably sell his slaves, and bounce from city to town, trying his hand at various occupations, settling at none, while continuing to grow as a naturalist and artist. Some scholars speculate that he worked as a surveyor for William Gerard de Brahm, who was then charting the coastal South. A 1767 letter to Benjamin Rush, one of the finest examples of Bartram's prose, describes the rare *Calydorea coelestina*, an Ixia endemic to northeast Florida that was not described again scientifically until the twentieth century. The American Philosophical Society elected him a member in 1768. During this period, even family members lost track of the peripatetic son. Letters would find him in Philadelphia, North Carolina, and back in East Florida for reasons unknown. A cryptic 1772 missive from John railed at William's "wild notion of going to Augustine."[4]

The child possessed of "darling delights" needed a job. Opportunity came his way in late 1772, unsurprisingly, through family connections. The London physician and gardener John Fothergill proposed a tour of the southern colonies, with the promise of fifty pounds annually, plus further compensation for sketches and presumably new plants.[5] William Bartram embarked upon a four-year journey that took him into eight current-day states: from the St. Johns River to western North Carolina, and from the Georgia sea islands, across the territories of the Creek and Choctaw Indians, to the Mississippi River. Bartram detailed the first two years of his journey in a *Report* for Fothergill, which he sent to London (along with drawings and a *hortus siccus*, or collection of dried plants) in 1773 and 1774. But the complete story of his tour would emerge in 1791 with the book for which he is now famous: *Travels through North & South Carolina, Georgia, East & West Florida, the Cherokee Country, the Extensive Territories of the Muscogulges, or Creek Confederacy, and the Country of the Chactaws: Containing An Account of the Soil and Natural Productions of those Regions; together with Observations on the Manners of the Indians*.[6]

Most people simply call the book *Travels*. It is a big book, 500+ pages, not one "that requires reading from front to back," as the novelist Charles Frazier quipped.[7] Readers often have their favorite passages, typically reflecting some geographic loyalty, although scholarly consensus regards the St. Johns section as the work's liquid heart. The chapters featured in the pages that follow cover a complicated sequence of events. Bartram journeyed up the St. Johns in spring and fall 1774, latching onto trading expeditions and breaking up his river travels with overland treks to the fabled Alachua Savannah (Paynes Prairie State Preserve, south of Gainesville) and the Suwannee (or Little St. Johns, San Juanito) River. Although *Travels* is sometimes approached as a straightforward itinerary, Bartram the writer folded content from the river tours into one single narrative, shuffling content to avoid repetition and build dramatic coherence.

To complicate matters further, *Travels* was a retrospective book, one that evolved through a long composition process. (The most reliable day-to-day record of the route through Florida is the *Report to Fothergill*.) Bartram's return to Philadelphia coincided with the British blockade of the city, and John Fothergill died in 1780; both events severed the provincial naturalist's patronage ties to England. We find mention of a manuscript in 1783, but by that point the work had taken a much more philosophical turn than the quotidian *Report*. Somewhere in the publication process, taxonomic descriptions were also folded in, either by Bartram or by an unknown hand, and so the resulting volume would present the "temperate flowery Regions" of the American South as both a subject of scientific description and literary pilgrimage, as natural history and meditation on the "Divine Monitor." Additional political and religious developments help explain the book's radical edge. Early reviewers scoffed at Bartram's "rhapsodical effusions," questioned his dramatic battles with "crocodiles," and took umbrage at his sympathetic portrayal of Native Americans.[8]

But the book was also too important to ignore. *Travels*, despite its perceived eccentricities, established a template for natural history in the new nation and a route of discovery for others to follow. In the decades following publication, colleagues wrote to Bartram for clarification about the specimens he described, they tapped into his store of knowledge, and they sought to claim, or take credit for, his principal discoveries. In 1817–18, fellow Philadelphians Thomas Say, Titian Peale, William Maclure, and George Ord voyaged "up the river St. Johns" with the familiar book close at hand. A letter by Say (regarded as the founder of American entomology) vividly describes preparations that included a perusal of *Travels*: "Mr. Ord is purchasing stores at this moment, Mr. Maclure is looking for a pilot, Mr. Peale is sitting by our cabin fire (though it is not so cold as to need one), reading Bartram's travels."[9]

John James Audubon, who toured Florida in 1831, also used Bartram as a blueprint. Since these early readings, *Travels* has served as a vehicle for transporting us across space and time. Poets and artists continue to tap into his works for inspiration, while naturalists mine him as a sourcebook. Bartram's impassioned Quaker sensibility continues to script our explorations of the natural world, providing the necessary terms for connecting natural beauty and ecology, science and spirit.

This fusion of sensibilities, what we now might regard as a holistic education, was actually a hallmark of eighteenth-century intellectual life. *Travels* coalesced around several strains of enlightenment and early romantic letters. Bartram's observations on American birds bookend the celebrated Audubon, the lesser-known Mark Catesby (with whom Bartram was compared), and protégé Alexander Wilson (whose *American Ornithology* is sadly out of print). *Travels* belongs on the same shelf as Hector St. John de Crèvecoeur's *Letters from an American Farmer* (1782) and Thomas Jefferson's *Notes on the State of Virginia* (1785)—these three books qualifying 1782–91 as the most productive decade for environmental writing in all of U.S. literature. Bartram's southern tour preceded the more famous expedition of Meriwether Lewis and William Clark (1804–6), Alexander von Humboldt's explorations of the Andes, or the South Sea voyages of James Cook. *Travels* also falls within a line of spiritualized nature observation that runs from Gilbert White's *Natural History of Selborne* (1789), through Henry David Thoreau's *Walden* (1854), to the tweedy and earnest tradition that thrives to this day. Bartram's lyrical rhapsodies hail from a time when botanists wrote poetry and poets botanized. Erasmus Darwin (Charles's grandfather) explained the Linnaean system in verse couplets with *Loves of the Plants* (1798), while Samuel Taylor Coleridge borrowed from Bartram's description of Salt Springs to render the "mighty fountain" of Kubla Khan:

> . . . Huge fragments vaulted like rebounding hail,
> Or chaffy grain beneath the thresher's flail:
> And amid these dancing rocks at once and ever
> It flung up momently the sacred river.[10]

The reading of Bartram by Coleridge (which has been described, with some hyperbole, as influence) testifies to the confluence of science and dreamscape, taxonomy and wonder.

Popular myth holds that William Bartram accomplished little else after *Travels*, that he published his one book and then puttered idly in his garden until his death in 1823. The more interesting truth is that he remained active in intellectual circles, often invisibly as a collaborator, into his final decades. The family business fell to the younger John Bartram, William's brother, but it was William who prepared orders and catalogues. And while William Bartram never married or had children (he claimed the title of "dishonourable bachelor"), he was a favorite uncle who tutored nieces and nephews and who from his "Seminary of American Vegetables" mentored a generation of naturalists.[11] His illustrations would grace *The Elements of Botany* (1803–4) by longtime collaborator Benjamin Smith Barton, and provide the frontispiece for a still-undetermined number of pamphlets, proceedings and essays. Although he has been cast as a lone eccentric or solitary wilderness adventurer, Bartram's deep engagement in American intellectual life spanned a remarkable six decades.

In 1818, five years before the octogenarian William Bartram collapsed outside his Kingsessing home (by a favorite pear tree planted by his father), Benjamin Smith Barton published a short pamphlet describing a favorite Florida bird, the limpkin: *Some Account of the Tantalous ephouskyca*. Barton, who was never anywhere near the limpkin's limited range, relied upon the observations of his friend. *Travels* described the limpkin (now *Aramus guarauna*) as a "very curious bird . . . about the size of a large domestic hen," the native name "ephouskyca" signifying "the crying bird."[12] The image fronting Barton's pamphlet in no way ranks among Bartram's best work. The abstract background allows for little sense of the native habitat, the anatomy feels disjointed, and the crude engraving fails to capture the limpkin's gangly, doe-like grace. But the illustration does connect us. The same bird, even if not so much recently, is still found on the St. Johns. Readers of *Travels* who see a limpkin in the wild hold a special kinship to William Bartram. His presence cuts across centuries.

This book, *Travels on the St. Johns River*, seeks to foster connection and kinship: it is about a river and two of its early explorers. Part 1 presents selections from the vast array of materials that followed the Bartrams' wanderings through "East Florida." Part 2 situates their discoveries in a scientific and historical context, updating the taxa (or names and classification of the flora and fauna) for the first time in a generation. Thomas Hallock and Matthew Jackson edited part 1, Richard Franz (with his "brother gardeners") prepared the materials in part 2, and Dean Campbell created the map. Read together, these texts bring us closer to the river; at the same time, the words and images take us to an earlier, lost milieu. All too often the name Bartram serves as an easy shorthand, as a "sound bite" for stewardship and natural beauty, with little consideration for the authors in their own time. Our goal is to build upon the remarkable body of Bartram scholarship from the past few decades and present core texts in reliable form to as many readers as possible—to students and river rats, backpackers, birders, conservative politicians and left-wing activists, native plant nuts and armchair explorers alike. This book allows for many paths of discovery.

Chapter 1, part 1, presents the Florida section of John Bartram's *Diary*. (William left no record of this trip.) John's manuscript journal is now preserved at the Historical Society of Pennsylvania, although the Florida section (19 December 1765 to 12 February 1766) remains missing. The elder Bartram most likely sent this portion to England, where it appeared as an appendix to Wil-

William Bartram's drawing of a limpkin (*Aramus guarauna*). Frontispiece to Benjamin Smith Barton, *Some Account of the Tantalous ephouskyca* (1818). Courtesy of George A. Smathers Libraries, University of Florida.

liam Stork's promotional pamphlet/natural history, *An Account of East-Florida* (1767), and serially in the popular *Gentleman's Magazine*. Scholars have made great use of the *Diary*: Francis Harper prepared a definitive edition in 1942, and John Bartram anchors historian Daniel Schafer's online survey of East Florida plantations.[13] The version reprinted here, from the 1767 *Account of East-Florida*, reproduces the original text, including the previously ignored footnotes. Probably penned by Collinson, the secondhand notes make comparisons to Linnaeus's *Species plantarum* (the standard source for classification) and weigh out Florida's potential economic impact. John's vivid but terse descriptions teach us who lived where, the flora and fauna encountered, how vegetation overtook the river's slow current, and what the spring waters tasted like.

Chapter 2 reprints five core chapters from William's *Travels*. In this celebrated portion of the book, we follow the naturalist from his base off coastal Georgia, up the St. Johns River to Blue Springs—retracing, but not venturing as far as his intrepid father. (Trade paths shaped the younger Bartram's journey, and he had no interest in returning to the pistia-choked upper reaches alone.) The St. Johns section, as noted, condensed multiple trips into one narrative and evolved over long delays and editorial tinkering. Careful readers will observe lapses and inconsistencies. A spring "tempest" more closely resembles an August or September storm. And Bartram falls silent at key points, failing to mention, for instance, the site of his former plantation. The voice (or style) jumps abruptly, shifting from science to poetry, from travel to static description in ways that can be explained through the book's evolution. Like the river he described, Bartram's account is beautiful, complex, full of cross-currents and unmarked springs, and it rewards those who explore its hidden corners. The text here reprints the 1791 Philadelphia edition. Breaking from precedent, the editors retain idiosyncrasies in the original (the use of "sat" in the past tense of "set out," or "spirted" for "spirited"), making silent changes only to obvious printers' errors (missing or reversed letters, punctuation, etc.) and end-line hyphens. The bracketed numbers refer to original pages, left for comparison with other editions. Readers of this volume experience *Travels* as it originally appeared in print.

Chapter 3 presents a brief portfolio of letters, telling the backstory of *Travels* and showcasing Bartram's abilities as a naturalist and artist, while providing important details about his complicated past. The correspondence can be used to fill in puzzling gaps. When the botanic pilgrim passes the site of his former plantation in *Travels*, for example, he waxes poetic over the larval mayfly's "resurrection from the deep."[14] A letter from his father, with the follow-up from

Henry Laurens, discloses the personal depths that would precede this "resurrection" and why William would gloss over this ignoble chapter of his own life. A lyrical description of the *Ixia Coelistina* (a plant barely mentioned in *Travels*) captures Bartram at his finest as an artist—but personally at a low. Against the correspondence, we may read *Travels* as the portrait of an author who was talented but inconsistent, who took pride in but was also stymied by his strong-willed father, who changed over time (as people do), and who recognized the moral contradictions of the early American republic, a point that becomes even more poignant because Bartram was himself such a gentle, if sometimes flawed soul.

*Travels on the St. Johns River* invites readers to wander through this archival maze so they may better understand the St. Johns River and two of its early explorers. Readers may then come to see "East Florida" as an "apartment" in this "boundless palace of the sovereign Creator," one defined (with a touch of radicalism) as "furnished with an infinite variety of animated scenes, inexpressibly beautiful and pleasing, equally free to the inspection and enjoyment of all his creatures."[15] The St. Johns, as nature writer Bill Belleville observes in his preface, awaits our discovery. Despite the mounds removed for road fill, the hum of outboard engines and traffic from the two interstates that cross it, the river is still gloriously well preserved. Trips there have a way of leading one to a different plane of time, *river time*, and those patient enough to surrender to its currents and tides, to its complex ebbs and flow, will find themselves sliding across centuries. As we follow the Bartrams, sipping spring water that tastes like a gun barrel, hooking bream at the edge of an algae mat, netting crabs in fresh water, or marking the narrows where alligators battled, we enter into a space of shared engagement with the natural world.

The eighteenth century had a word for this engagement: curious. Our closest equivalent is the scientific "cool," the wonder that precedes analysis. But it also implied community. For the curious, the process of discovery was ongoing; curiosity involved not just travel and the observation of physical properties but also the evolving effort to find meaning, to bring our own moral bearing to a place. In curiosity, we find kinship with earlier sensibilities. If this book moves the curious from a library onto a river, or from the river back to words and images, then we as editors have done our job. As books go, this volume came together quickly; it was an easier task than most, however, because it grew organically from already thriving community initiatives. *Travels on the St. Johns River* builds from decades of research and outreach by the Bartram Trail Conference (or BTC) and from hard work by preservationists in Putnam County, Florida, especially. In superficial readings of *Travels*, some see William Bartram as the lone explorer of an empty wilderness. As we study the record more closely, however, we actually find the opposite: people joined by a shared love for, or curiosity about, nature, finding fellowship in the continuing regard for a place. *Travels on the St. Johns River* marks just one more pass in this beautiful, ongoing journey. All royalties for this book will be donated to the BTC's Fothergill Fund, which supports research on William Bartram and his world. We hope you will purchase a copy of the book for yourself—and maybe another for a friend. Then we hope, together, you go explore the river.

# Part I

# 1

## Diary

JOHN BARTRAM

In late 1765 King George III rewarded John Bartram for a lifetime of botanic work with a fifty pound annual stipend and the illustrious title of Botanist to the King. John, then sixty-six, responded with a tour of the southern British colonies, including the newly designated territory of East Florida (ceded in exchange for Cuba following the Seven Years' War). Needing an assistant, the elder Bartram instructed his son William to liquidate his stock in North Carolina, where he was running a store. The two met near the home of John's brother and journeyed south. John kept a detailed diary of the tour, which passed through the Carolinas, Georgia, and of course, East Florida. The two Bartrams toured the St. Johns from 19 December to 12 February 1766. They left chilly St. Augustine that December; near present-day Mandarin, they met John Davis, Dr. David Yeats, and an unnamed enslaved black man; and they traveled until their flat-bottomed boat reached the river's swampy headwaters near Lake Loughman, roughly between today's Orlando and Cape Canaveral.

The manuscript to John's diary survives in the collections of the Historical Society of Pennsylvania, and Bartram scholar Francis Harper prepared an edition in 1942, working from a copy prepared by nineteenth-century Bartram scholar William Darlington. (Those seeking to retrace the 1765–66 tour should consult Harper's exhaustive footnotes.) After the East Florida exploration, John apparently sent this portion of the diary to England. No manuscript record of the tour survives from the St. Johns portion, but John's account found its way into London publications. William Stork appended his second edition of the *Account of East-Florida* (1767) with a version of the *Journal,* and a slightly different text with some modifications appeared in the widely read *Gentleman's Magazine.* The text reprinted here is from William Stork's 1767 edition, with the footnotes by an unknown hand retained. Stork's pamphlet also includes "Remarks on the River St. John's," plus a map and brief description of the Bay of the Espiritu Santo, or Tampa Bay.

DECEMBER the 19th, 1765, set out from St. Augustine early in the morning, which was frosty, the ground being covered with a white hoar frost. We travelled to Greenwood's house, where we lodged;[1] the roads were very wet, by reason of much rain that lately fell; here I observed very large oaks, magnolias,[2] liquid-amber,[3] near 100 foot high, and guilandina[4] 30; these grew on a high bluff 8 or 10 foot above the surface of the river, which rises here 18 inches at high water, and in dry seasons is sometimes brackish, but in wet is drinkable to Cow-ford, which is 12 miles below this, and about 24 from its mouth.

20th. Set out for Robert Davis's,[5] whose son the Governor had ordered to take us up to search for the head of the river St. John's; and having necessaries provided, I, my son William, Mr. Yates, and Mr. Davis embarked in a battoe; Mr. Davis was not only to conduct us, but also to hunt venison for us, being a good hunter, and his Negro was to row and cook for us all, the Governor bearing our expences.

21st. Thermometer 74. P.M. The wind blew from the south right against us, so strong that we could not advance; so staid at Mr. Davis's, who walked with us about his land, on which grew very large evergreen and water oaks, magnolia, liquid amber, red bay[6] 2 foot in diameter and 100 high, and some curious shrubs and plants we never observed before, with orange-trees amongst them, large zanthoxylum,[7] and purple-berried bay.[8]

22d. Thermometer 70, wind S.W. Cleared up, and we set out from Mr. Davis's; but the wind turning south again and blowing hard against us, we rowed but a few miles, then landed and walked on shore, found a pretty evergreen,[9]

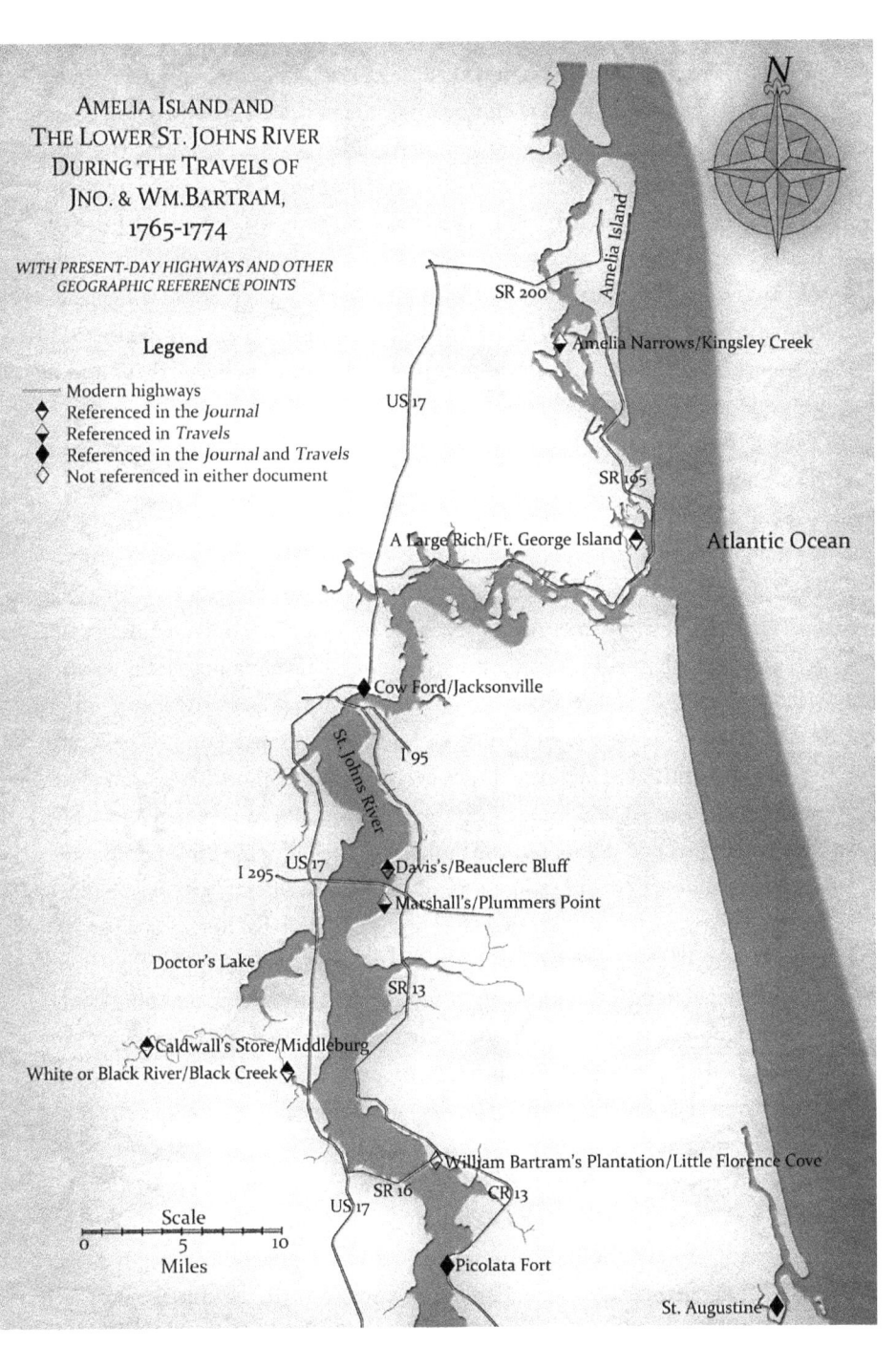

which produces nuts or stones as big as acorns, and good to eat, and perhaps may be improved by culture to be near as good as almonds; it bears plentifully, grows 8 or 10 foot high, the people call them wild limes, for this shrub much resembles that tree; here grew chinquapins, the middling ground being generally 300 yards broad to the higher land, some little swamps bordering the small rivulets; we encamped, saw a large allegator. The shores of the river are generally very shoal for above 100 miles, at 50 yards distance more or less from the banks, the lowish or middle ground between the swamp and pine land is generally sand mixed with black mould, formed from the rotting of the fallen leaves from the thick brush and tall trees, which generally grow plentifully in this kind of ground; the palmettos likewise grow pretty plentifully between these middle grounds and pine lands.

23d. Cold morning, thermometer 42, wind N.W. Arrived and lodged at Picolata.

24. Cold morning, thermometer 50, wind N.W. [10] Blowed pretty fresh, but ceased towards night; landed, and Mr. Davis shot a deer, and his Negro a turkey. I and my son walked in the woods to observe the soil and plants, with a man that went to fell some trees for honey: he felled one that contained only some yellow wasps, that had taken up their winter-quarters in a pine tree; we then walked to another hollow tree, wherein was a swarm of bees and some honey; but both the white people and Indians often meet with such good success, as to find great quantities of honey and wax, even ten gallons, more or less, out of one tree; the Indians eat much of it with their venison and sour oranges, of which they cut off one end, then pour the honey into the pulp, and scoup both out as a relishing morsel. We then soon crossed the river to a point, where we lodged, and saw many rocks of congealed snail and muscle-shells; here was a patch of good swamp, but the pine-lands approached near the river, and generally a perch or more of palmetto-ground, gently rising between the swamp and pine-land.

25th. Cool hazy morning, thermometer 46 in the open air, (in which all my thermometrical observations up the river are taken). After several miles, by choice swamps near the river, we landed at a point of high ground, which has been an ancient plantation of Indians or Spaniards; many live oak-trees grew upon it near two foot diameter, and plenty of oranges; the soil was sandy but pretty good; we walked back from the river, the ground rising gradually from the swamp on the right-hand, where grow small evergreen-oaks, hiccory, chinquapins, and great magnolia, and in the swamp grows the swamp[11] or northern kind 18 inches diameter, and 60 foot high, liquid-amber and red-maple 3 foot diameter, elm, ash, and bays; the plants were most sorts of the northern ferns,

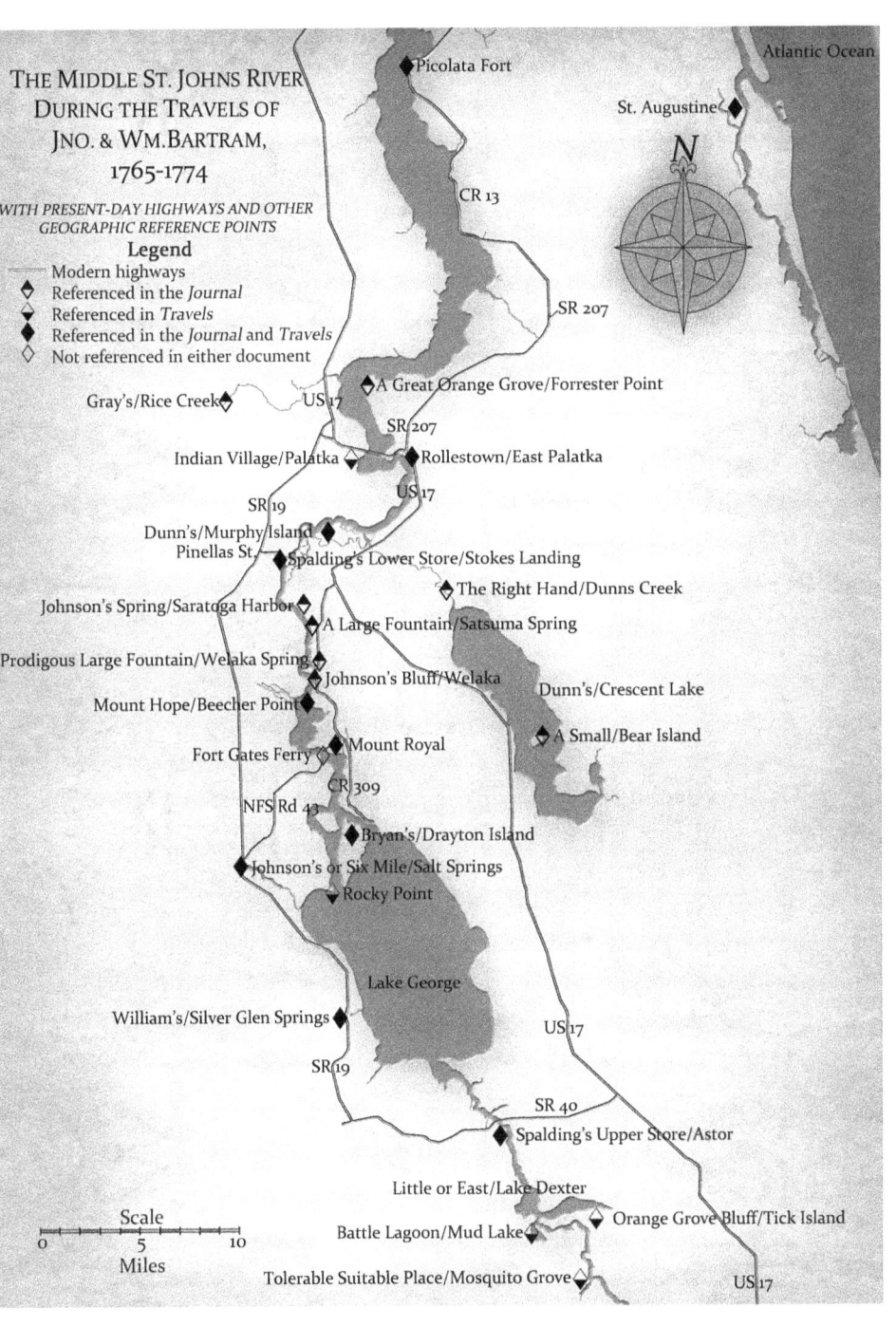

saururus,[12] iris,[13] pancratium,[14] large long flowering convolvulus[15] running 20 foot high, chenopodium[16] as high, and 4 inches diameter, pontedereia[17] and dracontium. Cloudy cool day, arrived at squire Roll's, a bluff point 17 foot high, more or less, of which 5 foot is composed of snail and muscle-shells, mixed with black mould or rotten vegetables, intermixed with sand, 20 paces distant from the shore, and diminishing all the way to the yellow soil, on which grows large evergreen-oaks, evergreen shrub-oaks, where the pine-lands begin at 50 yards from the river: This shell-bluff is 300 yards more or less along the river's bank, gradually descending each way to a little swamp, round the head of which the pine-lands continue down the river a good way, and a little way up it; the bluff seems all soil and shells, but back near the Savanna's is found some clay; there is a small Spanish intrenchment on the bluff about 20 paces square, and pieces of Indian pots; the river is very deep near the bluff, though there is a great barr opposite to the town, and a very rich extensive swamp.

26th. Thermometer temperate, fine day, wind south. Excellent swamps on both sides of the river, some 2 or 3 miles deep; landed on Dunn's Island on a large snail shell ridge,[18] the adjacent swamp excellent, and the middle ground rich for corn, turkeys and alligators plenty, saw a middling sized Indian tumulus, 20 yards diameter and 6 or 8 foot high; arrived soon at Spalding's Lower-store, on the west-side of the river, 37 miles from Picolata and 50 from Latchaway,[19] an inland Indian town, near half the way pine-land and palmetto-ground. It is generally affirmed, that the soil at Latchaway is excellent, and produceth good corn and rich pasture; we encamped on a bluff in the pine-land, over-against a rich little island.

27th. Thermometer 50, fine morning. Set out from the Store, and about 5 miles above, landed on a high bluff, on the east-side of the river, at Johnson's Spring, a run of clear and sweet water, then travelled on foot along thick woody but loamy ground, looking rich on the surface by reason of the continual falling leaves, and by the constant evergreen shade rotting to soil, as the sun never shines on the ground strong enough to exhale their virtue before their dissolution, as under deciduous trees: We crossed several small rivulets of clear sweet water, and as many narrow moist swamps. 'Tis diverting to observe the monstrous grape-vines, 8 inches in diameter, running up the oaks 6 foot in diameter, swamp-magnolia 70 foot high strait, and a foot diameter, the great magnolia very large, liquid-amber, white swamp and live oaks, chinquapines[20] and cluster-cherry[21] all of an uncommon size, mixed with orange-trees, either full of fruit or scattered on the ground, where the sun can hardly shine for the green leaves at Christmas, and all in a mass of white or yellow soil 16 foot more or less above the surface of the river. We came down a steep hill 20 foot high and about 4 or 500 yards from the river, under the foot of which issued out a large fountain (big enough to turn a mill) of warm clear water of a very offensive taste, and smelt like bilge-water, or the washings of a gun-barrel; the sediment that adhered to the trees fallen therein, looked of a pale white or bluish cast, like milk and water mixed: We then crossed the swamp, and ascended and descended two hills and narrow swamps more; at the foot of the last issued out another warm spring of clear water like the other, but not so large. Then travelling alternately over hills and swamps, in all about 3 or 4 miles, came to a great cove, near a quarter of a mile from the river, out of the head of which arose a prodigious large fountain of clear water of loathsome taste, like the other two before-mentioned;[22] it directly formed a large deep creek 40 or 50 yards wide to the river, and deep enough for a large boat to swim loaded to its head, which boils up near 8 foot deep from under the shelly rocks; 'tis full of large fish, as cats, garr, mullets, and several other kinds, and plenty of alligators:—Lodged at Johnson's Bluff, where for a mile the sandy pine-barren comes close or near the shore, and here grew plenty of what is called wild limes, which shows that they will grow in poor soil though chiefly in rich.

28th. Set out from Johnson's Bluff; foggy morning, wind N.E. thermometer 56. Came in a few miles to Mount Hope,[23] at the entrance of a little lake, the east and south-side of which is pine-land, reaching to Johnson's Bluff, except a point of good swamp: Mount Hope is 50 yards long and 30 wide; near 20 foot high, composed all of fresh water snail and muscle-shells of various dimensions, the small ones drove into the large, and the broken and powdered ones into the interstices of both; these are very fertile soils as far as the shells reach, and if not the only, yet the common planting grounds of the former Florida Indians, as is proved by the numerous pieces of broken Indian pots scattered all over all these shelly bluffs, and the vestiges of the corn hills still remaining, although many pretty large live oaks, red-cedars, and palms, now grow upon them: the west wind hath a long and full stroke against this mount, which perhaps raised it to that height: Saw many alligators, and killed one; 'tis certain that both jaws open by a joint nearly alike to both: Here and near the river's bank grows the short-poded gleditsia,[24] elm and black-ash, with most of the South-Carolina plants: Landed at Mount-Royal,[25] where there are 50 acres of cleared old fields, fine oranges in the woods, and a fine spring issuing out above a mile from the river, making a stream big enough to turn a mill, on the back of which the pine-lands begin: the bank and for 50 yards back is composed of sandy soil mixed with snail-shells, which for a foot or more thick is indurated to a soft rock, from which a fine south prospect opens to the great lake (the river here is above half a mile wide) near the entrance of which is a large island: we encamped on the east-side of the river opposite to the island, from whence we heard a bear roaring in the night; we lay on a low bluff of snail-shells, amongst plenty of bitter-sweet oranges, next in goodness to the China, and here the woods are full of them; we walked back over a dry kind of rich swamp full of shells mixed with black tenacious mud, under which is a white tenacious clay or marl, and in about 400 yards came to rising ground, pretty rich, and good corn-land, then to palmetto yet blackish soil, then to whitish, in which grew pines, then savannahs and ponds, which are interspersed generally in the pine-lands in most part of the southern provinces, together with the cypress[26] and bay-swamps, and have for the most part good feeding round their borders. This rich swamp terminated at the bend of the river where the pine-land reaches close to its banks; so that the banks of this fine river are a continual alternate change of pine-land, bluffs, cypress, swamps, marshes, and rich ash, and maple-swamps: the hammocks of live-oaks and palmettos[27] are generally surrounded either with swamp or marsh: sometimes the deep rich swamps are 2 or 3 miles deep from the river to the pines, and reach along the river from one mile to 4, 5 or 6 at uncertain depths. These swamps are supposed to be the best rice-grounds, as neither the dry weather nor wet can hurt them so much as where there is no water in dry times, and in wet there is too much, for this is rarely overflowed but in spring-tides, and these will always keep them wet enough in the dryest seasons, especially below the great lake.[28]

29th. Foggy morning; thermometer 52. Landed opposite to the mouth of the lake, which hath a full stroke with a south wind; the rock is all composed of snail and muscle-shells, hard enough to build with about 4 foot thick, and will split horizontally; some parts look like limestone, but whether for want of salt that abounds in sea-shells they will make such strong lime, I cannot say. Thermometer 72. P.M. Fish jumping continually; we encamped on a rocky point near a fine swamp of 25 acres, then a marsh of 20, near the end of an island on which some pines grew, then a great rich swamp round the cove; a very rainy night welcomed us.

30th. Rainy warm morning; thermometer 64. Set out and came to a point of piney land, but between it and the common fast ground is a great swamp, which continues a great part of the cove to the mouth of the river, except a few piney points: We landed at the neck, which is about 8 foot above the water, the upper strata was 2 or 3 foot of white sand covered with a thin coat of black-coloured with dissolved rotten leaves of the kalmia,[29] vaccinium,[30] dwarf-myrtle,[31] Andromeda,[32] palmetto, pines, and other evergreens, which though always green, yet are mostly shedding their former year's leaves; but next the water was a hard blackish sand like a soft stone, which though it will crumble betwixt the thumb and fingers, yet is almost impenetrable to water. Thermometer 72, P.M. Arrived at the head of the great lake 20 or more miles long, one and a half fathom deep, and 12 miles wide, as it is commonly reckoned: We landed on a fine shelly bluff 10 foot above the water; here grows red-cedar, live-oak, great palmetto, and good oranges, behind which is a high rich clear marsh producing grass as high as one's head, reaching to the pine-lands, and the cove of the great lake, which is supposed to be the extent of the real tides flowing; but a strong north-wind will force the water of the lake many miles up the river, and the floods above coming down after great rains swell the river so as to overflow its banks and cover a vast body of reedy marsh.

31st. Cool morning; thermometer 56. wind N. Set out, and in half a mile came to a middling creek 2 fathom deep, and from 50 to 100 yards wide, a rich island on the south-side hard enough for a horse to walk upon, and pretty full of wood, as maple and ash; on the north side is a great extent of clear marsh, producing tall grass towards the head of the creek-branches on both sides in the marsh, many of which branches head in a great cypress swamp, in the pine barrens and in the adjacent marshes: We rowed or set the battoe as far as she could swim, then came back to the river, which is lined on both sides with very rich hard swamps, 2 or 3 miles long, and near one broad more or less, producing good grass: It is remarkable that at the entrance of the river into the great lake there floats prodigious quantities of the pistia,[33] which grows in great plenty most of the way from hence to the head of the river, and is continually driving down with the current, and great quantities lodged all along the extensive shores of this river and its islands, where it is entangled with a large species of water-numularia, persicaria, water-grass, and saxifrage, all which send down very long fibrous roots deep into the water by which they are nourished, growing all matted together in such a manner as to stop up the mouth of a large creek, so that a boat can hardly be pushed through them, though in 4 foot water; these by storms are broke from their natural beds and float down the river in great patches, the roots striking deep, often touch the muddy bottom, and there anchor and fasten, and are ready to catch and entangle those that drive down upon them, and all together gather mud, by the daily accumulation of which they are formed into islands which are very numerous in this river, and are much enlarged by these plants fixing on their shores. We now came to plenty of the tree palmetto, which the inhabitants call cabbage-tree,[34] and is much eaten both raw and boiled.

January the 1st, 1766. Hazy morning; thermometer 52. Set out from Spalding's Upper store, about 50 miles above the Lower;[35] the river here is 200 yards broad, and 9 foot deep in the channel; in long continued rains it hath been known to rise here 3 foot perpendicular; no tides from the sea reach here. Thermometer 72. P.M. Landed at a high shelly bluff, where thousands of orange-trees surrounded us, with red cedars and live-oaks, beyond which is a rich swamp and marsh, then pine-land; landed again at a point on the north-side of a great cove on the east lake where we lodged.

2d. White frost on the boat; thermometer 35. Set out to view the cove, which was surrounded with extensive marshes on the south-side, on the east and west with marshes, several hundred yards wide, then a narrow cypress-swamp joined to the common pine-land; we came again into the river 80 yards broad, which ran at first a south course, then bended east for several miles: We saw very extensive marshes on each side (with several short cypress-trees and maple-hammocks interspersed) until we came to a pond on the south, soon after which we landed and climbed up a tree, from which we had a prospect of the lake lying N.W. with an extensive marsh between: We observed many short willows, but the woody swamps are chiefly black and white ash, with red maple next the river, and generally a cypress-swamp interposed between the pine-lands and swamps of ash; we rowed several courses in sight of extensive marshes and swamps, 2, 3 or 4 miles wide more or less; the river was pretty high, 2 foot above the driest times, by reason of the great rains, yet it barely covered the swamps even in pretty low places, but indeed there is little difference in their height for scores of miles, unless near the palmetto and pine-lands: We landed on a shelly bluff of 2 or three acres of sour orange-trees full of fruit; then rowing along the cypress-trees, which grew here next the river, a deep swamp interposed between the cypress and pine-lands; we came to Clement's Bluff, where we encamped on a shelly bank 12 foot perpendicular; the lower part next the water was an indurated shelly rock, the bluff is 300 yards long and one broad, more or less, beyond which it gradually declines back to a fine savannah, then to the pine lands, palmetto and shrubby oaks; this is on the west-side of the river, as is the orange-grove; thermometer 48. P.M.

3d. Clear cold morning; thermometer 26. Wind N.W. The ground was froze an inch thick on the banks: this was the fatal night that destroyed the lime, citron, and banana trees in Augustine, many curious evergreens up the river, that were near 20 years old, and in a flourishing state; the young green shoots of the maple, elm, and pavia, with many flowering plants and shrubs never before hurt: Set out from Clement's Bluff, rowed by much rich swamp and marsh;

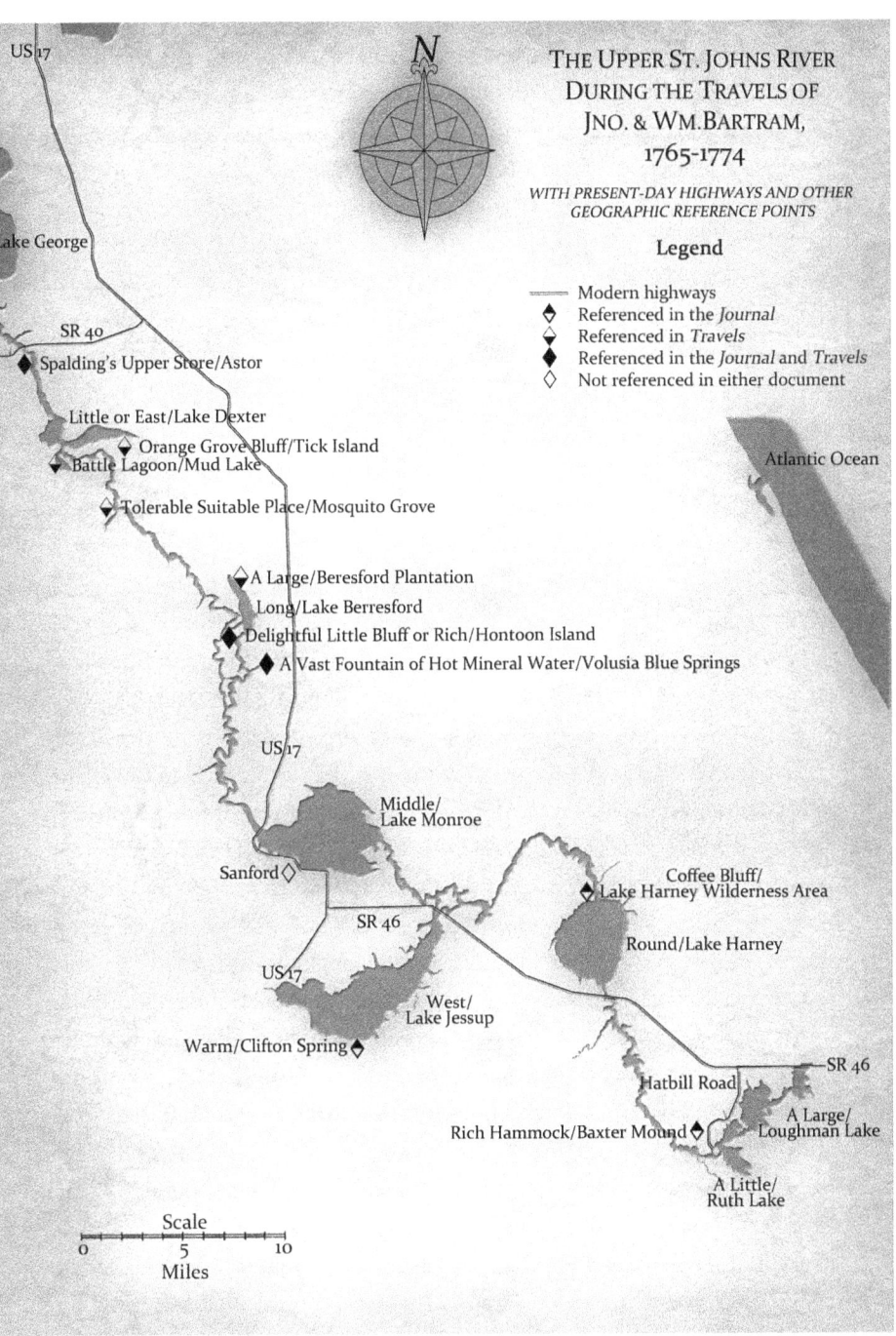

saw many elder-trees in flower (which grow in plenty close to the river next the water reeds) and many alligators, though so very cold that it had froze the great convolvolus and coreopsis, yet the great shrub after held out: The banks were in several places 2 or 3 foot high, shelly, and two rood broad; then fell back to a fine rich grassy swamp, chiefly ash, elm, and cypress, but much more open than down the river below the great lake, with more frequent patches of marsh and high grass and small maples, willows, and cephalanthus thinly scattered upon them; the higher banks with live and water-oaks. Landed about noon on the east-side on a bluff, 6 or 8 foot high, and 150 yards broad, but soon falls back to a cypress-swamp, at the upper end of which oaks and palmettos join the river, and a little back the pines begin.

4th. Pleasant morning; thermometer 50. Set out from Whitlow's Bluff; the river makes a great easy bend, and sends out a branch, then the course is from east to south, then S. E. the east banks being sandy 8 or 10 foot perpendicular, full of live and swamp-oaks, great magnolia, bay and liquidamber, but none of them very large; then pine-land to the south bend, then lower ground, but on the west side very good swamp; it then takes a contrary bend to the south, then east, where there is a fine orange grove on each side of the river: at the corner of the south bend, the mouth of a lake appears, one mile wide and 2 or 3 long, which we entered;[36] the course is near south and north, the east side is lined with a narrow cypress-swamp, and live-oaks alternately; the west-side with pines, but above the marshes are very rich, full of water-reeds and elders on both sides the river, which is about 30 yards broad, and near three fathom deep. We landed where a sandy bluff joined the river; it produced live and water-oak, palms and bay; coasting the east-side, we soon came to a creek, up which we rowed a mile, in 4 and 6 foot water and 30 yards broad, of the colour of the sea, smelled like bilge water, tasting sweetish and loathsome, warm and very clear, but a whitish matter adhered to the fallen trees near the bottom; the spring-head is about 30 yards broad, and boils up from the bottom like a pot; plummed it, and found about five fathom water; multitudes of fish resort to its head, as very large garr, cats, and several other sorts; the alligators very numerous either on the shore or swimming on the surface of the water, and some on the bottom, so tame, or rather bold, as to allow us to row very near to them.[37] What a surprizing fountain must it be, to furnish such a stream, and what a great space of ground must be taken up in the pine-lands, ponds, savannahs, and swamps, to support and maintain so constant a fountain, continually boiling right up from under the deep rocks, which undoubtedly continue under most part of the country at uncertain depths?

5th. Rainy morning; thermometer 54. Staid at Mount-joy. This mount is formed of snail and muscle-shells, and is 8 or 10 foot perpendicular, about 150 yards long and 20 broad, on the south-east side of the river, declining gradually at each end to an extensive stiff moistish marsh, producing a great quantity of tall grass, as thick as it can grow, of several hundred acres; a pine ridge appears at half a mile distance on the south side. The mount and its declining sides and ends are full of live-oaks and large palm-trees; there are also some hammocks of live-oaks and myrtles interspersed in the adjacent marsh: opposite to the mount, on the other side of the river, is a large swamp or reedy marsh, and beyond it a cypress-swamp of great extent farther than the eye can reach.

6th. Clear morning; thermometer 38. Strong wind at N. W. Set out and soon saw a great body of very different swamp and marsh joining it, some dry, others middling moist, and some very wet, some reedy soil, some myrtle, oak, cypress, and lastly pine; then we came a little farther to tall water-reeds on both sides, and much elder grew next the river and close to the reeds, which last grew very thick close to the bank, and from 14 to 16 foot high; sometimes a narrow ridge, about a rood[38] wide and a foot or two high, would run close to the river, on which grew oaks, hiccory, maple, and ash, the ground back being scarcely above the common flow of the river; but as we rowed higher up, the soil was in many places of an unknown depth, of tenacious rich mud, especially on the Indian side, which is generally higher than ours, and so stiff that cattle may walk upon it very safe, and bears choice grass, though full of tall trees, as hiccory, maple, water-oak, and ash: We rowed by a very large island on the east side and another on the west, the best I have seen in Florida; the river, for these two days, has run very crooked. Landed on a high rich shelly bluff, some good flat soil, but full of palms, and a little back the pine-lands begin: The last frost killed the young shoots of ash, hiccory, eupatorium, peanines,[39] sun-flowers, and the tops of two lovely evergreen shrubs, one of which would have grown all winter, if the frost had not killed it; the bark was burst from the wood, but the lower part was not hurt, the other was full of flowers, green and ripe berries, yet the tender tops for half a foot were killed: 'Tis very common in this country for vegetables to produce at the same time flowers, green and ripe fruit; and if the tender shoots are by chance killed, they soon send out fresh ones; here is a native gourd or squash, which runs 20 foot up the trees, close to the river; the people eat them when young, but they are bitter when old, and about the size of a man's fist.

7th. Clear morning; thermometer 36. Set out from Cabbage-bluff, so called from the great number of palm or cabbage-trees growing there; after some miles rowing round several points of the compass, it being generally good reed-marsh and some cypress-swamps, we came to the middle lake, 1, 2, or 3 miles broad, and 8 long;[40] its general course is S. E. at the N. E. end is high ground, producing oak, palm, myrtle, bay, and a fine new evergreen, something like the purple-berried bay, but the leaves grow alternately, and the berries close to the stem, like myrtle; here is a pretty stream of sweet water, small enough to run through the bung-hole of a barrel, and at about 200 yards distance from it runs out a large stream of water, so warm as to support the thermometer at 71 in it, feels warm to a coolish hand, tastes more loathsome than the others beforementioned of the same kind, and may be smelt at some roods distant; hereabout is drove on shore, the most delicate crystalline sand I ever saw, except what is got on an island near our capes, though this is still finer: A few hundred yards from the last spring is another much like it in taste, but much larger, and near 30 yards broad, having three heads within 30 yards; the water is very loathsome and warm, but not so hot as one's blood: This differs from the other in having most of its surface covered with duck-meat;[41] its banks full of shelly stone of the snail-shell kind, and running level with the river; the last had some fall; they are not above 200 yards from the lake. Set out and arrived at a rocky bluff, at the entrance of the head of the river, which was two or more miles wide, but gradually narrowed; this bluff is composed of snail and muscle-shells, indurated into hard rocks, which would break or split for building or burning into lime; but a bluff we landed at in the forenoon was more remarkable; for as the bank was perpendicular, we had a better opportunity of searching deeper; we saw about 3 foot above the water a mass of clustered sea-shells, as periwinkles, cockles, and clams, the very productions of the sea, and to what depth they went is unknown; but this I believe, that they reach all under this whole low country at uncertain depths, and support the superior soil, under which the prodigious sulphureous and saline fountains run, which are continually fed by the slow settling of rain-water.

8th. Clear fine morning; thermometer 44. Wind west by north. Rowed by much reedy ground, which is generally very wet, being often covered a foot more or less deep, after great rains; but the banks in many places are raised, a foot or more, by the trash floating down the river, which being drove on shore by the wind, there rots and is converted into stiff soil, on which the alligators love to bask in the sun-shine; every 20, 50, or 100 yards distance they are to be found: We encamped on a pleasant dry bank, but middling soil, in a grove of live-oaks; beyond which is a plain, and behind that a great inland pond or lake;[42] below where we lodged several inlets appeared to the northward, and above the river forked, and we rowed up the N. E. branch.

9th. Clear fine morning; thermometer 44. We rowed along several long beaches [reaches?] generally east and N. E. then came to a high bluff of sand on the east-side, under which was a strata four foot thick, of a brownish soft sand stone, easily rubbed to sand between the thumb and fingers; this was a point of pine-land, and on it grew great magnolia, sweet-bay, live-oak, palms, tall andromeda, vaccinium, red-cedar,[43] and an odd zanthoxylum; here we found an Indian hunting cabin covered with palmetto-leaves; we then rowed by a large marsh on the east side with a row of trees on the bank of hiccory, ash, and live-oak; then pine-land on our side for a long reach, and high banks and trees on the Indian side, after rowing several long reaches, generally poorish land, either near the river or at a distance from it, we came against a creek bearing northward, up which we rowed about a mile, where we saw some good swamps, and much long thick grass, some on pretty dry ground, but generally wet; this creek led us up to a great cypress-swamp, in which it divided invisibly as the other branches did in several parts of the marsh; we came back again to the river, up which we rowed 'till we came to a high bluff, where we encamped, and found 2 or 3 curious shrubs; opposite to this bluff is a very extensive marsh, part of which is reed, and some very good rich dry soil; here are some very large muscle-shells, of which this bluff is composed and enriched; this has been a fine piece of planting-ground.

10th. Pleasant morning; thermometer 50. The wolves howled, the first time I heard them in Florida; here we found a great nest of a wood-rat, built of long pieces of dry sticks, near 4 foot high and 5 in diameter, all laid confusedly together; on stirring the sticks to observe their structure, a large rat ran out, and up a very high saplin with a young one hanging to its tail.[44] Set out, and in half a mile came to a lake, and taking the north-east side, stretched eastward by a very extensive marsh, pretty low next the lake, but farther back good marsh, beyond which is a large cypress-swamp; then the pine-lands begin; we rowed to the east-side of the lake, near which is the mouth of a fine lagoon, a mile long and half as wide, bordered with a very large marsh extending to a large cypress-swamp; we then coasted southward along a sandy beach, back of which is a dryish marsh, then came to a ridge of oaks about 20 roods wide more or less, behind which is a marsh reaching to the cypress-swamp, but more south the pine-lands appear; at the south end of the oak-hammock runs eastward a large branch, which spreads into many branches in this large marsh, draining it and the adjacent cypress-swamps; this marsh is large and looks rich, and I believe reacheth from the lake to the cypress-swamp and pine-land: We then turned round a point, and landed at another sandy beech and hammock, beyond which is a large plain or savannah, half a mile wide more or less to the pines, producing pretty good grass, low shrubs, oaks, and myrtles, the soil black on the surface and moist, though stiff enough to ride upon; there is a small pond within the beech at the south-end, where ducks frequent; this upper lake may be 4 or 5 miles in diameter, and perhaps more in length, and one fathom deep more or less; but the river between this and the last is in many places two and a half fathoms, and in most places near 150 wide; we lodged at a sandy beech, and it rained towards morning, but soon cleared up.

11th. Clear morning; thermometer temperate. Set out and soon came into the river, which sends out numerous branches, that terminate in the east marsh, which is wonderfully intersected and divided with ponds and branches, and the river is also divided with numerous small and great islands of low marsh; so that it is difficult to find the main river, but by the strong current: We came at last to a fine lake[45] or rather three, the lowest of which is the biggest, being a mile diameter; on the east-side the pine-lands appear about two miles distant most of the way more or less from the lake we lodged at; but on the west side we could hardly see them, such a great body of marsh being between; after noon we came to where the river was more entire, and some of its banks 3 foot high and 7 or 8 foot broad to the west marsh, the river being 200 yards broad more or less, and one and a half fathom deep; here several more large branches or lagoons branched eastward, and spread their numerous branches in the marshes; we rowed several long beaches [reaches?] up the rivers, and at last to our great joy came to a bluff where we could set our feet on dry ground; this being a very rich hammock of 6 acres of light black shelly soil (thermometer 58. P.M.) producing red-cedar, celtis,[46] a curious zanthoxylium, and several others we never observed before, a few large orange-trees, and some young ones.

12th. Fine clear morning; thermometer 44. Set out, and rowing S. E. soon came to a little lake which we headed, it seemed to be surrounded with marsh, some few pines appeared at a distance; we turned back, and within a mile came into the main river, which turned various courses S. E. and north, but generally east by north; it sends out on each side lagoons and branches that drain those extensive marshes. We came now to a large lake 5 or 6 miles long and near one wide, a long tongue of low marsh comes from the N. E. end, where a long hammock of oaks runs a south course;[47] we then rowed out of the lake, and between several islands, and came again into the main river, which runs in general an east and west course on a sandy bottom, shoaling gradually until the weeds and reeds stopped our battoe in such a manner, that it was impossible to push her any farther, though the water was 3 foot deep, and a small current against us, which we suppose was the draining of the extensive marshes which opened towards the south-east, how far beyond our view we could not determine; the water-reeds grew here in the current as thick and close together as on the marsh, that is, as close as hemp; yet the current forceth its way through, and also under the great patches of the pistia, the water persicaria, and other water-plants, which are all entangled together, covering many thousands of acres on St. John's and its branches, which heads in numerous rich swamps and marshes. We returned to the rich hammock where we lodged last night.

13th. Fine pleasant morning; thermometer 54. Set out homeward from the rich hammock, the highest up the river we could land at. Thermometer 79. P.M. about one o'clock we came to Round-lake, so we called it, it being one of the roundest I ever saw, almost surrounded with palmetto, pine, and scrub-oak; the lake is 6 miles more or less in diameter, and generally all over the lake about 9 or 10 foot deep.

14th. Clear morning; wind north. Set out from Coffee bluff,[48] thermometer 52; a very long reach on the west side of the river, of piney, palmetto-ground, with scrub-oaks; about noon we entered the west lake steering S.W. a ridge of pine-land runs on the east side and a marsh a quarter of a mile more or less between it and the lake, which I think is 8 or 10 miles from north to south, and 5 or 6 miles broad, the marsh is in many places a mile or two wide, and then comes to hammocks of oaks; saw a mullet jump three times in a minute or two, which they generally do before they rest, so are called jumping-mullets; on the south side of this lake is a great low cypress-swamp; here to my great disappointment my thermometer was broke accidentally in striving to take a swarm of bees for their honey, which is practised both by the whites and Indians, who take great quantities in the cypress-swamps and pine-lands. We landed on the west side, which was low and rich for 100 yards back, rising gradually from the water to 4 or 5 foot perpendicular, then comes to a level, looking rich and black on the surface for an inch or two, then under it a fine sand to a great depth; this level produceth red-bay, great magnolia, water and live-oaks, liquid amber, hiccory, and some oranges, but no large trees; the lower rich ground produceth gledistia, pishamins, cephalanthus, ash, cypress, and cornu femina: Our hunter killed a large he-bear supposed to weigh 400 pounds, was 7 foot long, cut 4 inches thick of fat on the side, its fore-paw 5 inches broad, his skin when stretched measured five foot and a half long, and 4 foot 10 inches in breadth, and yielded 15 or 16 gallons of clear oil; two of us had never eat an ounce of bears meat before, but we found it to our surprize to be very mild and sweet, above all four-footed creatures, except venison; although it was an old he-bear, his fat, though I loathed the sight of it at first, was incomparably milder than hogs-lard, and near as sweet as oil of olives; it was not hunger that engaged us in its favour; for we had a fat young buck and three turkeys fresh shot at the same time, and some boiled with the bear, but we chose the last for its sweetness and good relish.

15. This morning was very warm and a little showery; the muskatoes were troublesome last night, and this morning the flies blowed our meat before 10 o'clock; the ticks creeping and lizards running about our tent; we staid here all day to barbacue our meat to serve us down the river, which would soon spoil if not preserved either by fire or salt, and of which last we had only enough to season our victuals with it; rained fast, yet we walked to see several warm springs on the west-end of the lake, one of which was about 40 or 50 yards broad at the head, and held the same width for 300 yards down to the lake, without much current, the head being near even with the lake; the water had a greenish cast, was very loathsome, and full of great gar-fish; the other rises near half a mile from the lake, and hath a middling fall, very convenient to turn a mill, with a little dam having high banks on each side, and no floods can hurt it, as the mill may be near half a mile from the spring-head; the worst is, the stream is full small; there is a fine large cypress-swamp on each side close to the lake, the farthest of which is about half a mile; this fine stream hath five heads, the banks are 10 or 15 foot perpendicular; three of the heads boil up like a pot in a pure white sand, every minute it boils up above the surface of the common pond or bason, then the surrounding sand slips into the cavity, which presses down the spring until the water below is collected from the back under-ground stream so strong as to force the sand and water above the common surface, so that there is a continual periodical motion; one of these springs was so warm, that although I was in a sweat, yet it seemed warm to my hand; they are all of them warm, and of a loathsome taste, their sediment is white, and one may smell them at many yards distance.[49]

16th. Very cold windy day, the lake being so rough that we could not stir; so our hunters rendered the bear's oil, and stretched and dried the skin.

17. Fine still morning, and moderate. Set out and rowed up the lake; past by a long point of marsh with a hammock of palms projecting out from near the west side of the lake, it being supposed to be an island from which is extended numerous little turfs of grass a great way farther into the lake, and in time may unite into a long point; the depth is generally 7 foot, one place 8: About 12 o'clock we came to the middle lake,[50] and having in our going up the river viewed the north side and stinking springs, we now coasted the south-west or

Indian side, which is surrounded with pine-barrens, interspersed with some cypress, but generally poor sandy palmetto-ground, its length may be near 8 miles, and breadth 3 or 4; some small marsh points project a little way into it, it is about 10 feet deep, generally so is the river, its course east and west: A few miles below the lake we came to a fine rich low dry bluff 4 foot above the water; it declined gradually to a fine marsh, near half a mile wide to the pine-lands, and a very extensive prospect to the Indian side over marshes and large swamps; this is the finest piece of rich dry ground I observed since we left the head of the river; it produced very good rich grass[,] palms and liveoaks, the dry ground may be 8 roods wide and 40 long; here we cut down three tall palm or cabbage-trees, and cut out the top bud, the white tender part, or the rudiments of the great leaves, which will be six or 7 foot long, when full grown, and the palmed part 4 in diameter; this tender part will be three or 4 inches in diameter tapering near a foot, and cuts as white and tender as a turnip; this they slice into a pot and stew with water, then, when almost tender, they pour some bears oil into it, and stew it a little longer, when it eats pleasant and much more mild than a cabbage: I never eat half so much cabbage at a time, and it agreed the best with me of any sauce I ever eat, either alone or with meat: Our hunters frequently eat it raw, and will live upon it several days; the small palmetto or chamærops yields a small white bud no bigger than one's finger, which is eaten by men, bears, and horses, in case of great need; this situation pleased me so much we called it Bartram's Bluff, and for an industrious planter with a few hands may be a pretty estate.

18th. Set out from Bartram's Bluff, a lovely fine morning and warm, stopped at Mount-joy for a little, and after several miles rowing came to a rich island,[51] and took the left hand branch, down which we rowed several very crooked courses by some oak and pine-bluffs 5 or 6 foot high, excellent swamps, some cypress-trees, and much maple and ash being on both sides the river, which is two fathom deep, and, where we entered it, not above 20 yards wide, but at the lower end twice as much; it opened into the main river, a little below a high bluff of sour oranges, and on the opposite side grow great quantities of what is called bitter sweets, which are next in goodness to the china; we ate abundance of them, and found them very wholesome; they last much longer than the sweet, which continue only to March.

The common current of the river here is not above two miles an hour, the uncommon rains last summer and part of the fall had raised it 2 foot or more higher than at present, and then the current no doubt ran swifter, and our pilot said he had known it to be 3 foot lower than now; but suppose it only two, then there must be very little current.—This night was very warm, and the muskitoes troublesome, so that we smoaked our tent twice.

19th. Fine warm morning, birds singing, fish jumping, and turkies gobling. Set out, and presently came to a rich island, and ran between it and the Indian land, which is high and shelly, then lower, and very good on each side: We soon came into the river again, and rowed down it, till we came to a small branch on the east side, down which we rowed near half a mile, where we were entirely stopped by the pistia and persicaria growing all in a matt; we then turned back, concluding it to run on the east side of an island, and to join the river below in some of its eastern lagoons to the river, down which we proceeded, and crossed the mouth of the east lake,[52] and in an hour or two arrived at Spalding's Upper-store, where we staid all night, which was very warm, and the muskitoes very troublesome, as much so as any time since I left Charles-Town.

20th. Fine warm morning, but the south-west wind soon blew so hard, that we durst not venture to sail on the great lake, and our pilot wanted to dry his skins, so we staid here all day: but in the afternoon our host went over the river to shoot geese in the pine-land ponds, where they generally feed on the grass growing there; for they don't frequent the river, as we did not see one all the way, but multitudes of ducks: We landed on a bank of the river, a little above the place where the Indians swim their horses over, about 4 foot above the water; the bank was composed of snail and muscle-shells, a strata of which, that was even or under the surface of the river, was converted into a concrete as hard as a soft stone, as are most of the banks of the upper part of the river, which will burn to lime; we walked from the landing directly towards the pine-lands, at first over a rich level, then ascended a hill 6 feet perpendicular, formed all of shells mixed with a little black sandy mould, scarce enough to fill up the vacuities betwixt one shell and the other, although the small ones and broken pieces are drove as close together as possible; this composition lasted for near 200 yards, the shells diminishing gradually, and the fine sand appearing more and more, until no more shells were seen mixed with it; we still came to rising ground producing hiccory, magnolia, bay and water-oak, then ground-oak, chamærops, then pine-land, dwarf-myrtle, kalmia, vaccinium, andromeda, small pines and long grass in the ponds, where the water was about knee-deep more or less, some of which contain from 1 to 10 acres; but some ponds are a mile or two big, more or less, some surrounded close with the adjacent pine-lands, and others with large savannahs at one or both sides, with a rivulet running out, and sometimes with a bay or cypress-swamp at the head. I was talking to our host that I could not find any good clay up the river;

he said there was good white clay to be got on the west side of the river near his house; we went to look at it, and taking a hoe, I cut a piece of it up, which was a close compact mass of ground sea-shells a little above the surface of the water, the lower the more it looked and felt like clay. Quere, whether or not some sorts of clay are not formed out of sea-shells ground minutely to powder in a long series of time?

21st. Warm morning; set out from Spalding's Upper-store, wind south; it soon fell a raining, so that we encamped near the head of the great lake, at an orange grove on a bluff, where we gathered good bitter-sweets, the sour ones lay scattered all about on the ground; there are two large and some small islands near the head of the great lake.

22d. Cold morning, and the wind so high, durst not venture on the lake it being very rough; so we staid here all night, and fired the marsh.

23d. Very cool, clear morning, wind N. W. Set out early, and coasted the west side of the lake, which was part sandy-beech, part marsh, some cypress-swamp, and much oak banks, until we came to William's Spring,[53] a creek of very clear warm water, 30 yards broad and 2 foot deep, the spring heads even with the river; we landed near its mouth on a shelly-bluff amongst thousands of orange-trees, growing so thick that we could hardly pass between them for a quarter of a mile; we walked near a mile up to two or three of its heads, and left one on the right hand which we did not search, because we could not get at it without a boat; the land near the creek was a rich but narrow swamp 100 yards wide more or less, adjacent to which was a high shelly-bluff, on which the Indians had planted; it is remarkable that the Florida Indians planted on all these shelly-bluffs, as being the most fertile parts, except the swamps and marshes, which are only proper for rice, and which the Indians never planted, as they would never take the pains of raising and shelling of it; and the pine-lands not being suitable for corn by their method of cultivation; but whether they planted the intermediate declining grounds I can't say, as large trees of cedar, celtes, and palms, with many other kinds, grow on most of them: About noon we set out from this place, and coasted still on the west side, being very warm, and we still observed either oak-hammocks, or high pines; about half way down the lake is a high bluff, the upper part white soil, the lower yellow, it produced spruce-pine and scrub-oaks; we could not bring our boat near the shore, for this west side is very shoal most of the way, and the land mostly palmetto-ground, and some few cypress-swamps; we encamped on a descending bank, on the back of which was scrub-oaks and dwarf-palmetto or chamærops; here we cooked a fine mess of palm-cabbage.

24th. Moderate clear morning; rowed early by a bank of pine-land for several miles and some cypress-swamps, then came to a large creek called Johnson's Spring,[54] the west end of the lake about 80 yards near broad, but after it widens to about 200; the pine-land comes pretty close to its banks, then a narrow low marsh interposes, and after we rowed higher up we saw narrow cypress-swamps, loblolly-bays, and some few oak hammocks; the creek abounds with fish, many stengrays near its mouth; it is supposed to run 7 miles from its head to the lake, where the bar is about 18 inches deep, but the creek is 3, 4, and 5 foot up to the spring, which is nearly level with the lake, and full of grass and weeds at the bottom, many of which reach to the top of the water, and are a great obstruction to boats in going up, without they keep directly in the channel; on the north side towards its head a large marsh brancheth out; we came at last to where the cat-tails and bull-rushes grew so thick, that we could not force the battoe through them, though it was 100 yards broad, and 3 or 4 foot deep, so clear that we could see the muscle-shells on its shelly bottom in patches 3 or 4 foot diameter between the great patches of grass and weeds; we landed to search the head springs, and passed through an orange-grove and an old field of the Florida Indians, then came to the main springs, where a prodigious quantity of very clear warm brackish water boiled up between vast rocks of unknown depth, we could not reach the bottom by a very long pole; this was on the north bank, about 12 foot high above the water, which spreads immediately 50 or 60 yards broad: We walked round the west end towards the south bank, where the bare flat rocks appeared above water, and a great stream boiled up of a salt and sourish taste, but not near so loathsome as several before-described, nor had it any bad smell, or whitish sediment as they; we examined the composition of the rocks, and found some of them to be a concrete redish sand, some whitish mixed with clay, others a ferruginous irregular concrete, and many a combination of all these materials with sea-shells, clams, and cockles; we found in the bank an ash-coloured tenacious earth, and a strata of yellow sand beneath; near here my son found a lovely sweet tree,[55] with leaves like the sweet bay, which smelled like sassafras, and produce a very strange kind of seed-pod, but the seed was all shed, the severe frost had not hurt it; some of them grew near 20 foot high, a charming bright evergreen aromatic: We saw near the spring numbers of large garr, cats, mullets, trouts, and several other kinds unknown to us, some in chace of others, which run into the grass to hide them from their enemies; in going down to the lake the fish were continually jumping; we observed on the north end of the lake a hammock of oak. We then steered our course to Bryan's Island,[56] on which there is some good land and rich swamp, with pretty much pine-land, it is supposed to contain about 1500 acres; here we encamped on a rocky rising ground, and found numbers of great and small oyster-shells, clams, perriwinkles, sea-muscles, and cockles, all cemented together with broken fragments, some ground as fine as coarse sand; they were all confusedly mixed and jumbled together as upon our sea-coast; first a strata of shells, then a strata of shells and fragments fill up the least cavity; it is remarkable that we never found any scallops to the south of Carolina, either on the coast or up in the country.

25th. Fine pleasant morning, although a little frost in the pine-lands; saw several flocks of pigeons flying about both yesterday and to-day: About noon we landed at Mount-Royal,[57] and went to an Indian tumulus, which was about 100 yards in diameter, nearly round, and near 20 foot high, found some bones scattered on it, it must be very ancient, as live-oaks are growing upon it three foot in diameter; what a prodigious multitude of Indians must have laboured to raise it? to what height we can't say, as it must have settled much in such a number of years, and it is surprizing where they brought the sand from, and how, as they had nothing but baskets or bowls to carry it in; there seems to be a little hollow near the adjacent level on one side, though not likely to raise such a tumulus the 50th part of what it is, but directly north from the tumulus is a fine straight avenue about 60 yards broad, all the surface of which has been taken off, and thrown on each side, which makes a bank of about a rood wide and a foot high more or less, as the unevenness of the ground required, for the avenue is as level as a floor from bank to bank, and continues so for about three quarters of a mile to a pond of about 100 yards broad and 150 long N. and S. seemed to be an oblong square, and its banks 4 foot perpendicular, gradually sloping every way to the water, the depth of which we could not say, but do not imagine it deep, as the grass grows all over it; by its regularity it seems to be artificial; if so, perhaps the sand was carried from hence to raise the tumulus, as the one directly faces the other at each end of the avenue; on the south side of the tumulus I found a very large rattle-snake sunning himself, I suppose this to be his winter-quarters; here had formerly been a large Indian town; I suppose there is 50 acres of planting ground cleared and of a middling soil, a good part of which is mixed with small shells; no doubt this large tumulus was their burying-place or sepulchre: Whether the Florida Indians buried the bones after the flesh was rotted off them, as the present southern Indians do, I can't say: We then rowed down the river, and encamped at Spalding's Lower-store, opposite to a small rich island on the west side of the river.

26th. Fine morning, warm and pleasant; observed a plum-tree in full blossom; here I saw many pine-trees, that had lately been cut down, and though 18 inches in diameter, they were the greatest part sap; I counted their years growth, and found some to be about 50, some 40, and others 30, but one large tree two foot in diameter, had only four inches of sap, and I counted 130 years growth or red circles; here was a well dug on declining ground, the water, which was sweet, rose to within 5 or 6 foot of the surface of the ground, at the distance of 100 yards from the river, and perhaps eight foot above it.

We rowed four miles down the river to Dunn's Island,[58] which Lord Adam Gordon has petitioned for; it contains about 1500 acres more or less of good swamp, and some hammock. We then took the right-hand creek up to Dunn's lake, observing much good swamp on both sides, the creek being generally 150 yards broad, and two fathom deep; on the west side there is two points of low land, which comes close to the creek: About noon we entered the lake, whose general course is N. W. and S. E. and about 15 miles long, the upper end turns towards the east: We encamped on the north side in a cypress-swamp, part of it marshy, its bank next the lake was a foot above the water, but back was lower until the pine-lands began within half a mile; this north side is generally a narrow cypress-swamp to the pines, widening a little in some branches.

27th. Fine pleasant morning. Set out early, and landed on a small island of near 100 acres, part cypress-swamp, part marsh, and piney palmetto, a very rotten black soil, mixed with white sand: We landed on a low bluff of muscle and snail-shells, generally broken and powdered by the surges of the lake; here, as well as in most other places on any high dry bank on the river or its branches where the soil is good, are found fragments of old Indian pots and orange-trees, which clearly demonstrates, that the Florida Indians inhabited every fertile spot on St. John's river, lakes, and branches; now the ash, maple, elm, and pavia, are all green, and shot out several inches, the cypress is in full bloom, the water-oak begins to look yellow, and the sweet-gum just casting its leaves: the north end of this island is pine and palmetto, then high swamp; the east end low. Leaving the island, we encamped where we did the night before, on a bed of long tree-moss, to preserve us from the very low damp ground, which is very unpleasant and dangerous.

28th. Fine morning; set down Dunn's lake, the west side of which is generally pine-land, but at the head westward are some very good swamps, which hold generally down the river; squire Roll claims all the north or north-east side from his town to the head of the lake; from the lower end of which 'tis reckoned 13 miles to the river, thence down to Roll's 4;[59] on the west side of the river is a very rich extensive marsh, which colonel Middleton claims; about one o'clock we arrived at Charlottenburgh, Roll's town, and staid all night.

29th. Fine clear morning and warm day, like the first of our May; walked all about the town and adjacent woods: near the banks of the river are the remains of an old Spanish entrenchment, 12 yards one way and 14 the other, about 5 foot high; on three sides being open to the river; the town is half a mile long, with half a score of scattered houses in it, built of round loggs; the streets are laid out at right angles, one of them is 100 foot broad, the other 60; the land back is all pine and scrub-oaks; the bluff continues half a mile down the river, which is 7 fathom deep near the town, but towards the opposite shore there is a sand-bar, it is not above half a mile wide here, but soon widens above.

30th. Fine morning; set out from Roll's, whose steward, Mr. Banks, was very kind to us, and seems to be a sober, careful, and agreeable man; we rowed 8 miles, crossing the river to Gray's creek,[60] which is 60 yards wide, and two fathom and a half deep; we went about 7 miles up it; its general course is west by south, and generally pretty straight, good high swamps on each side, though on the north side the pines come near, especially near the upper part, where the ground is poor; we could not pass near so far, as we had depth of water, by reason of many old trees fallen across the creek at 7 foot deep and 10 or 12 yards broad; great floods certainly come down it, for there were great banks of sand 4 foot, more or less high, drove on its banks; here is very good grass growing in the pine-woods knee high. We rowed down again, crossed the river, and encamped at a great orange-grove, where thousands of orange trees grow as thick as possible, and full of sour and bitter-sweet fruits; this is about four miles by land from Mr. Roll's, though near 8 by water; he claims it in his 20,000 acres; some of it is good swamp, but mostly pine-land.

31st. Fine morning: rowed for several miles on the west side of the river, having crossed it, and observed several good cypress-swamps, and oak-hammocks alternately mixed with pine-land, which comes close to the river's bank, in other places they come close to the swamps, which are here from 50 yards deep to 500 or more; we then crossed the river to the east side, along which we rowed, the pine-lands still approaching near the banks most of the way, some few cypress and maple-trees grow near the shore; we rowed into a great cove, on the north side of which is a fine rich high swamp; we encamped at a point on the east side on middling high ground sloping towards the river, back of which is palmetto-ground and black soil well timbered with live-oaks.

February the first. Walked in a fine rich open marsh, then palmetto and myrtles join the pine-lands, in which a little spring heads the swamp, which may be a quarter of a mile deep: We got to Picolata by noon, the north wind being against us as the day before; we then rowed to a low bluff of middling land, well timbered with live and water-oak, great magnolia and sweet-gum; here was also a rich swamp of ash and maple; but generally below Roll's town there is no such large bodies of swamps as above, especially on the east side, though at the mouth of Picolata creek, about 6 miles below the fort, there is a pretty large swamp.

2d. Walked this morning to observe the soil, the wind north, and cool, landed at Popa fort,[61] a small shallow entrenchment almost filled up with length of time; 'tis 20 yards square; and as many from the river; a few yards back of it there is another about twice as big; here is a grove of orange-trees, and many acres of large live-oaks, 2 or 3 foot in diameter, adjacent to which is a shallow but good swamp with some cypress-trees; nearly opposite to this on the west side branches out a creek running 3 or 4 miles, on which grow large red cedars; and about two miles below it, branches out White or Black River, it bears both names, the last by the English; 'tis navigable above 20 miles, some say 30, 'tis reckoned 20 to Caldwall's store, our present boundary with the Creek Indians; this river or creek is about 100 yards wide and 3 fathom deep, more or less, its general course is west; we landed at a pine-bluff, 300 yards long and 10 foot perpendicular, more or less, the upper surface of which, for a foot or more deep, is white sand, then 2 foot of an ash-coloured clay mixed with red and yellow sand, then 5 foot of a fine yellow sand, (no coarse sand is to be found in any of the southern provinces) then a tenacious ash-coloured clay to an unknown depth, reaching below the surface of the creek; there is a pretty spring runs into the creek just above the bluff; we lodged near its mouth.

3d. Set out early, cool morning, with white frost, wind N. W. Saw many high bluffs, near 20 foot high, but poor and sandy; some have a cypress-swamp behind them, others are level with the adjacent pine-land, in which is plenty of rank grass knee-high; on one or both sides of these bluffs frequently runs out a small spring: We called at the Store, (this was a fine warm day) above which, the land is still higher, and produces live-oak, red and purple-berried bay, alder, maple, chinquapins, elm, linden, water-oak, myrtle, dogwood, vaccinium, palmetto, hamamelis,[62] and cedar; here the creek divides into two branches nearly equal; we took the left-hand one, which had generally high banks on each side, raised by the floods 12 or more feet with white sand; in many places the level pine-lands come close to its banks; in others again, there is a pond or cypress-swamp just behind the bank, in which very large trees grow in the pine-lands; there are a number of shallow ponds, on the borders of which there is much green grass all the winter: We rowed up this branch, until the great trees, that had fallen across the creek, stopped our passage, and there the creeks were 4 or 5 foot deep and 10 yards broad, on a sandy bottom; we returned to the Store, where we lodged, and before day it began to rain.

4th. Warm rainy morning; it cleared up, and we set out up the north-branch, the banks of which were 12 or 13 foot high most of the way, more or less, in many places rocks under the surface 3 or 4 foot, reaching below the surface of the water to an unknown depth in some places; the first strata is sandy, then a gritty rock for a foot, then a softish rock full of sea-shells, of the cockle and perriwinkle kind, mixed close with broken or ground shells to a solid mass for two foot, more or less, then a deep mass of soft, in some places, hard rocks: We rowed up this branch until we were stopped by trees, as in the other, and here the creek was 10 yards broad and a fathom deep; we walked up it a good way farther, but found little alteration, except in its being fuller of old trees; the traders say, it heads in a great lake 5 miles long and 3 broad; there are some middling good cypress-swamps near its banks, the floods had been so high up this branch, as to flow over its banks, and the first rising of the pine-lands; they had not been quite so high in the other branch; near the Store was a deep gut [cut?] with a middling stream of water, which headed about a quarter of a mile up in the pine-lands, and gushed out over the rocks, where it had worn a deep narrow gully 8 or 10 foot deep, the rocks reached to within 4 foot, more or less of the surface, and to an unknown depth, all of ground or broken sea-shells; in some places there is a strata of tenacious clay, either above, under, or without this shelly strata.

5th. Set out from the Store down the river, near the mouth of which are some good cypress-swamps, and up it generally very large ones; about 4 miles up, there is a very extensive one, reaching a mile and a half north-eastward, to a place called the Doctor's lake, narrowing gradually to the mouth of the creek and upwards, till a pine-bluff interposes; opposite to this is another extensive swamp, upwards of 1000 acres; pretty near the mouth of the creek there are two small islands; a large point of land projects out from the main on the east side of the river opposite to the mouth of Doctor's lake, which runs near south partly parallel with the river: We arrived this evening at Mr. Davis's.

6th. Set out for the Doctor's lake, which is half a mile or more broad, and 6 or 7 long; at the head of which is a large creek, about 100 or more yards broad, and near a mile and a half long, heading in a rich swamp with 3 or 4 branches, which drain it: On the west side there is a hammock of oak, hiccory, magnolia, and hornbeam, and a fine spring of clear water almost big enough to turn a mill, boiling up from under the main body of the country rocks, as all the great fountains do; the soil looks rich.

7th. Cloudy morning; we crossed a branch, landed, and walked over a rich swamp 2 or 300 yards wide, then came to cutting-grass, then palmetto for 100 yards, then to a pine-savannah of a vast extent, moist, and producing a great burthen of pretty good grass, knee-deep; we returned and rowed down the lake and river about 14 miles to Davis's, against a strong wind, rain, and thunder, all wet and cold.

8th. Fine clear morning, wind west. Set out after noon, having dried our cloaths and blankets, rowed to Greenwood's, and encamped by a grove of orange-trees; from hence to the Cow-ford; the banks are generally high, with very large oak, bay, and great magnolia, the soil, though sandy, is pretty good.

9th. A fine morning; rowed down to the Cattle-ford, below which is a marsh on both sides, then pines, then another pretty large marsh, and so on alternately high oak-banks, open marshes, and flat pine-woods and savannahs; back there is pretty high sand-hills, and some ponds; came to William's point and creek, the water is pretty deep at the point, out of which issue several little springs: We then soon came to Forbes's bluff, where grows a good sort of rush to bottom chairs with, or make matts, much better than the common bull-rush or the three-square ones; it rained in the evening, but cleared up about midnight; this bluff is very productive, being covered with shells of oysters, which the Florida Indians fed much upon near the sea-coast.

10th. Pleasant morning, wind blowing strong at N. W. Breakfasted on a mess of tanniers, a species of eddo,[63] which being boiled with meat is good food; the roots are 4 inches in diameter, and 5 long, wholesome, and of great increase, when planted in moistish rich ground, but will do in middling soil. Set out, and sailed through the narrow passage, not being much above a quarter of a mile wide, running between two large marshes a little above a high bluff, called Oglethorpe's or Hesler's bluff, (an exceeding convenient situation for the building of a fort to secure the inhabitants up the river in time of war, 'tis about 8 miles from the bar and sea) in this narrow passage 'tis very reasonable to suppose, that the flood-tide must run very rapid, as it has 200 miles up this broad river to flow, in many places 2 miles wide, and many branches and large lakes to fill; we landed about 2 miles above the bar, and walked along a fine sandy beech of regular descent, quite to the sea low-water-mark, to an inlet, up which we walked to one Hazard's, a good kind of a man, and one of the best planters in Florida; he is settled on a large rich island, great part of which is surrounded with marsh, which on one side is very extensive.[64]

11th. North-west wind very high; could not venture on the river, so walked all over the island; observing his [Hazard's] improvements; and the curiosities, both natural and artificial, of the Indians and Spaniards; of the former, were several middling tumulus's or sepulchres of the Florida Indians, with numerous heaps of oyster-shells, which one may reasonably suppose were many hundred years in collecting by as many thousands of Indians, also variety of old broken Indian pots. 'Tis very demonstrable that the Spaniards had a fine settlement here, as there still remain their cedar posts on each side their fine straight avenues, pieces of hewn live-oaks, and great trees girdled round to kill them, which are now very sound, though above 60 years since they were cut. This rich island, though it appears sandy on the surface, yet hath a clay bottom, above which in some places there is a dark-coloured strata of indurated sand-rock.

12th. Cool morning, with a little white frost, yet a pleasant day. Set out early, rowing up the river again; on the south side, near the bar, there are some very high sand-hills, a little above which is the mouth of Don Pablo's creek, which runs towards the head of the north river, that empties itself near St. Augustine; 'tis reckoned about 5 or 6 miles between them, where, if a good passage was cut, and could be kept open, there would be a fine communication from St. John's river to the town, without the hazard of going to sea, and crossing two troublesome bars: Four miles from the mouth of the river, on the north side, branches out a creek, called the Sisters, from two hammocks that are much alike; between them is a passage to Charles-Town for schooners; the large ships can come within 15 miles of St. John's: a little above this, there is another little creek and passage to Charles-Town; below which is an island of marsh. Past by Trout-creek, 300 yards broad, salt to its head, up which there is good pine-woods, and fine range for cattle, with some cypress-swamps; opposite to it, on the south side of the river, is Sandy-point, full of high pines, and back very large ponds. We arrived at Mr. Davis's near night, and next morning set out for Augustine.

As the lower part of the river and its branches are known, 'tis needless to be more particular in describing them.

## Remarks on the River St. Johns

The pine-lands, as they are here called, contain a variety of soil, according to their different situations; some very large shallow ponds, quite dry in dry seasons, but generally abounding with tall grass; some very extensive savannahs; producing rank good grass, as thick as it can grow, where great numbers of cattle may be raised; very lofty pines, and in many places cypress-swamps, the last of which are allowed to be excellent rice-grounds, if clay-bottoms are within a few feet, and a good lasting stream of water runs through them, to drain and flow them at pleasure; the bay-swamps are frequently found in the pine-lands, being the general heads of the cypress-branches: This pine-land, by the help of dung and cultivation, will produce good corn, potatoes and cotton; the large palmetto declining ground, between the pines and swamps, are most and seem rich, and perhaps will suit both corn and indigo; but the shelly bluffs seem to be the most fertile spots of high ground, and the Indians chief plantations for corn and pumkins: That which is called hammocky ground is generally full of large evergreen and water-oaks, mixed with red-bay and magnolia, and in many places the great palmetto or cabbage-tree; this is generally reckoned proper both for corn, cotton, and indigo: but the marshes and swamps (so very extensive upon the river St. John's) are exceedingly rich, the last of which are full of large ash, maple, and elm, being of an unknown depth of rich mud; so are the marshes on the upper part of the river, which are covered with water-canes and reeds, as the lower marshes are with rank grass and weeds; all of which when they are drained dry, will produce, in all probability, great crops of corn and indigo, and without much or any draining, a fine increase of rice; so would the vast cypress-swamps; and of the large cypress-trees may be made great quantities of choice shingles, pales, and boards, of long duration; the prodigious large live-oaks will make excellent strong and durable timbers for shipping, as the tall straight long-leaved pine for masts and yards, and the others for turpentine, tar, and pitch, as also for plank and scantlings.

St. Johns river, by its near affinity to the sea, is well replenished with variety of excellent fish, as bass, sea-trout, sheep-head, drums, mullets, cats, garr, sturgeon, stingrays; and near its mouth, oysters, crabs, and shrimps, sharks and porpoises, which doubtless will continue, as there is such a great extent of its waters in so many great lakes, ponds, and branches, continuing both deep and broad so near its head; its shores, being generally shoal, are full of grass and weeds, and afford a fine asylum to the young fry against their devouring enemies.

# 2

# Travels

WILLIAM BARTRAM

In March 1773 William Bartram boarded a packet ship from Philadelphia to Charleston, South Carolina, and embarked upon the first leg of his four-year tour that took him into eight present-day states. From a base in coastal Georgia, Bartram strengthened personal ties with local traders, including James Spalding, who had expanded commercial routes into what was then called East Florida. Spalding ran two trading posts on the St. Johns River, in present-day Palatka and Astor, and the ties to these trading networks, along with plantation stops, gave shape to Bartram's itinerary.

Starting from Georgia in spring 1774, Bartram crossed onto Amelia Island, then traveled up the St. Johns as far as Spalding's lower store. Along the way he passed several sites of historic and personal importance—Fort Picolata, Rollestown, and his own abandoned plantation, about which the author remains conspicuously silent. An overland trek took Bartram to the Seminole towns of Cuscowilla and the Alachua Savannah, or Paynes Prairie, near present-day Gainesville. (These sections, forming chapters 6 and 7 of *Travels*, are not included here.) In early summer 1774 he again journeyed upriver to explore Mount Royal, Lake George, and Lake Dexter, and where he found himself famously besieged by alligators. By June 1774 Bartram returned to the lower store, and after a second trip across peninsular Florida, he again journeyed up the St. Johns. He reached Beresford Plantation, and during hurricane season he was nearly flooded in the adjacent lake. Blue Springs marked the southernmost point of his tour. Bartram left East Florida in November 1774, never to return, and spent the following winter recuperating in Charleston, where he sent his drawings, plants, specimens, and journals to his patron, John Fothergill in London.

The record of William Bartram's journey in *Travels* unfolded through an equally complicated process of composition, and those seeking to follow the text literally will note occasional lapses and contradictions. Several accounts predated the 1791 book—letters, drawings, and a two-part *Report to Fothergill* (which actually provides the more reliable day-by-day account). Bartram composed the first draft of *Travels* well after his return to Philadelphia, most likely in the early 1780s. In its earliest form, which survives in manuscript notebooks, the St. Johns River tour reads like a spiritual autobiography, more like a literary *Pilgrim's Progress* than an exploration diary. Bartram collated multiple trips up the St. Johns into one narrative and shuffled scenes for coherence and dramatic effect. Scientific information was tipped in later, either by Bartram or by another hand, and this layering explains changes in subject and voice. *Travels* underwent still another round of editing before publication, altered again to suit the more conservative tastes and politics of 1791 readers (the bracketed numbers in the text below indicate the pages in the original 1791 *Travels*). To journey with Bartram on the St. Johns today is to enter into literary deep time, where one feels the same connection and admiration for a place that William Bartram experienced two hundred years ago.

## [57] PART II. CHAP. I.

WE are, all of us, subject to crosses and disappointments, but more especially the traveller; and when they surprise us, we frequently become restless and impatient under them: but let us rely on Providence, and by studying and contemplating the works and power of the Creator, learn wisdom and understanding in the economy of nature, and be seriously attentive to the divine monitor within. Let us be obedient to the ruling powers in such things as regard human affairs, our duties to each other, and all creatures and concerns that are submitted to our care and controul.

In the month of March, 1774, I sat off from Savanna, for Florida, proceeding by land to the Alatamaha, where I diverted my time agreeably in short excursions, picking up curiosities, until the arrival of a small vessel at Frederica, from Savanna, which was destined to an Indian trading house high up St. John's, in East Florida. Upon information of this vessel's arrival, I immediately took boat and descended the Alatamaha, calling by the way of Broughton Island, where I was kindly received by Mr. James Bailey, Mr. Laurens's agent. Leaving Broughton Island in the evening, I continued descending the south channel nine or ten miles, when, after crossing the sound, I arrived at Frederica, on the island of St. Simon, where I was well received and entertained by James Spalding, Esq; This gen[58]tleman carrying on a very considerable trade, and having extensive connections with the Indian tribes of East Florida, furnished me with letters to his agents residing at his trading houses, ordering them to furnish me with horses, guides, and every other convenient assistance.[1]

Before the vessel was ready to sail again for St. John's, I had time to explore the island. In the cool of the morning early, I rode out of the town, directing my course to the south end of the island. After penetrating a thick grove of oaks, which almost surrounded the town on the land side, suddenly a very extensive and beautiful green savanna opened to view, in length nearly two miles, and in breadth near a mile, well stocked with horned cattle, horses, sheep, and deer. Following an old highway, now out of repair, across the Savanna, I ascended the sloping green bank, and entered a noble forest of lofty pines, and then a venerable grove of Live Oaks, under whose shady spreading boughs opened a spacious avenue, leading to the former seat of General Oglethorp, but now the property of Capt. Raimond Demere. After leaving this town, I was led into a high pine forest; the trees were tall, and generally of the species called Broompine (P. palustris Linn.) the surface of the ground covered with grass, herbage, and some shrubbery: I continued through this forest nearly in a direct line towards the sea coast, five or six miles, when the land became uneven, with ridges of sand-hills, mixed with sea shells, and covered by almost impenetrable thickets, consisting of Live Oaks, Sweet-bay (L. Borbonia) Myrica, Ilex aquifolium, Rhamnus frangula, Cassine, Sideroxylon, Ptelea, Halesia, Callicarpa, Carpinus, entangled with Smilax, pseudo China, and other [59] species, Bignonia sempervirens, B. crucigera, Rhamnus volubllis, &c. This dark labyrinth is succeeded by a great extent of salt plains, beyond which the boundless ocean is seen. Betwixt the dark forest and the salt plains, I crossed a rivulet of fresh water, where I sat down a while to rest myself, under the shadow of sweet Bays and Oaks; the lively breezes were perfumed by the fragrant breath of the superb Crinum, called, by the inhabitants, White Lilly. This admirable beauty of the sea-coast-islands dwells in the humid shady groves, where the soil is made fertile and mellow by the admixture of sea shells. The delicate structure of its spadix, its green broad leaves, and the texture and whiteness of its flowers, at once charmed me. The Euphorbia picta, Salvia coccinea, and Ipomea erecta, were also seated in front of my resting place, as well as the Lycium salsum (perhaps L. Afrum Linn.) a very beautiful ever green shrub, its cerulean flowers, and coral red berries, always on its branches, forming not the least of its beauties.

Time now admonishing me to rise and be going, I, with reluctance, broke away from this assembly of maritime beauties.

CONTINUING on, southward, the salt plains on my left hand insensibly became narrower, and I at length reached the strand, which was level, firm and paved with shells, and afforded me a grand view of the boundless ocean.

O thou Creator supreme, almighty! how infinite and incomprehensible thy works! most perfect, and every way astonishing!

I CONTINUED nearly a mile along this firm sandy beach, the waves of the sea sometimes washing my [60] horse's feet. I observed a great variety of shell-fish, as Echinitis, Corallinus, Patella, Medusa, Buccina, Concha venerea, Auris marina, Cancer, Squilla, &c. some alive, and others dead, having been cast upon the beach by the seas, in times of tempest, where they became a prey to sea fowl, and other maritime animals, or perished by the heat of the sun and burning sands. At length I doubled the utmost south point of St. Simon's, which forms the north cape of the south channel of the great river Alatamaha. The sound, just within this cape, forms an excellent bay, or cove, on the south end of the island, on the opposite side of which I beheld a house and farm, where I soon arrived. This delightful habitation was situated in the midst of a spacious grove of Live Oaks and Palms, near the strand of the bay, commanding a view of the inlet. A cool area surrounded the low but convenient buildings, from whence, through the groves, was a spacious avenue into the island, terminated by a large savanna; each side of the avenue was lined with bee-hives, to the number of fifty or sixty; they seemed to be well peopled, and exhibited a lively image of a colony that has attained to a state of power and affluence, by the practice of virtue and industry.

WHEN I approached the house, the good man, who was reclining on a bearskin, spread under the shade of a Live Oak, smoking his pipe, rose and saluted me: "Welcome, stranger, I am indulging the rational dictates of nature, taking a little rest, having just come in from the chace and fishing." After some conversation and rest, his servant brought a bowl of honey and water, a very refreshing and agreeable liquor, of which I drank. On rising to take my departure, he objected, and [61] requested me to stay and dine with him; and on my pleading, for excuse, the necessity of my being at Frederica, "Yet, I pray you, stay a little, I will soon have some refreshment for you." Presently was laid before us a plentiful repast of venison, &c. our drink being honey and water, strengthened by the addition of brandy. Our rural table was spread under the shadow of Oaks, Palms, and Sweet Bays, fanned by the lively salubrious breezes wafted from the spicy groves. Our music was the responsive love-lays of the painted nonpareil, and the alert and gay mockbird; whilst the brilliant humming-bird darted through the flowery groves, suspended in air, and drank nectar from the flowers of the yellow Jasmine, Lonicera, Andromeda, and sweet Azalea.

BUT yet, how awfully great and sublime is the majestic scene east-ward! the solemn sound of the beating surf strikes our ears; the dashing of yon liquid mountains, like mighty giants, in vain assail the skies; they are beaten back, and fall prostrate upon the shores of the trembling island.

TAKING leave of my sylvan friend, I sat off on my return to the town, where I arrived before night, having observed, on the way, many curious vegetable productions, particularly Corypha Palma (or great Cabbage Palm) Corypha pumila, Corypha repens, frondibus expansis, flabelliformibus, plicatis, stipit. spinosis (Dwarf Saw Palmetto) Corypha obliqua,[2] caudex arboreus adscendens, frondibus expansis, flabelliformibus, plicatis, stipit. serratis, Cyrilla, Tillandsia monostachya, Till. lingulata, or Wild Pine; both these curious vegetables are parasites, living on the substance of others, particularly on the limbs of the Live Oak; the latter spe[62]cies is a very large flourishing plant, greatly resembling, at some distance, a well grown plant of the Bromelia Ananas: the large deep green leaves are placed in a imbricated order, and ascendant; but their extremities are reflex, their bases gibbous and hollowed, like a ladle, and capable of containing near a pint of water: heavy tempests of wind and rain tear these plants from the trees; yet they live and flourish on the earth, under the shadow of these great Live Oaks. A very large part of this island had formerly been cleared and planted by the English, as appeared evidently to me, by vestiges of plantations, ruins of costly buildings, highways, &c. but it is now overgrown with forests. Frederica was the first town built by the English in Georgia, and was founded by General Oglethorp, who began and established the colony. The fortress was regular and beautiful, constructed chiefly with brick, and was the largest, most regular, and perhaps most costly, of any in North America, of British construction: it is now in ruins, yet occupied by a small garrison; the ruins also of the town only remain; peach trees, figs, pomegranates, and other shrubs, grow out of the ruinous walls of former spacious and expensive buildings, not only in the town, but at a distance in various parts of the island; yet there are a few neat houses in good repair, and inhabited: it seems now recovering again, owing to the public and liberal spirit and exertions of J. Spalding, Esq; who is president of the island, and engaged in very extensive mercantile concerns.

## [63] CHAP. II.

THE vessel, in which I was to embark for East Florida, being now ready to pursue her voyage, we sat sail with a fair wind and tide. Our course was south, through the sound, betwixt a chain of sea-coast-islands, and the main. In the evening we came to, at the south end of St. Simons, having been hindered by the flood tide making against us. The Captain and myself, with one of our crew, went on shore, with a view of getting some venison and sea fowl. We had not the good fortune to see any deer, yet we were not altogether unsuccessful, having taken three young racoons (Ursus cauda elongata) which are excellent meat: we had them for supper, served up in a pillo. Next morning early, we again got under way, running by Jekyl and Cumberland Islands, large, beautiful and fertile, yet thinly inhabited, and consequently excellent haunts for deer, bears and other game.

As we ran by Cumberland Isle, keeping the channel through the sound, we saw a sail a-head coming up towards us. Our Captain knew it to be the trading schooner from the stores on St. John's, and immediately predicted bad news, as she was not to sail, until our arrival there. As she approached us, his apprehensions were more and more confirmed, from the appearance of a number of passengers on deck. We laid to, until she came up, when we hailed her, "What news?" "Bad; the Indians have plundered the upper store, and the traders have escaped, only with their lives." Upon this both vessels came to anchor very near each other, when, [64] learning the particulars, it appeared, that a large party of Indians, had surprised and plundered two trading houses, in the istmus, beyond the river St. Johns, and a third being timely apprised of their hostile intentions, by a faithful runner, had time to carry off part of the effects, which they secreted in a swamp at some distance from it, covering them with skins. The upper store had saved their goods in like manner, and the lower store, to which we were bound, had removed the chief of theirs, and deposited them on a small island, in the river, about five miles below the store. With these effects was my chest, which I had forwarded in this vessel, from Savanna, not being at that time determined, whether to make this journey by land, or water. The Captain of our vessel, resolved to put about and return to Frederica, for fresh instructions how to proceed; but for my part, I was determined to proceed for the island up St. John's, where my chest was lodged, there being some valuable books and papers in it, which I could not do well without. I accordingly desired our Captain to put me on shore, on Little St. Simon's,[3] which was not far distant, intending to walk a few miles to a fort, at the south end of that island, where some fishermen resided, who, as I expected, would set me over on Amelia Island, where was a large plantation, the property of Lord Egmont, a British nobleman, whose agent, while I was at Frederica, gave me an invitation to call on him, as I passed toward East Florida; and here I had expectations of getting a boat to carry me to St. John's. Agreeably to my desire, the Captain put me on shore, with a young man, a passenger, for East Florida, who promised to continue with me, and share my adventures. We landed safely, the Captain wishing us a prosperous journey, returned on [65] board his vessel, and we proceeded for the fort, encountering some harsh treatment from thorny thickets, and prickly vines. However we reached the fort in the evening. The commander was out in the forest, hunting. My companion being tired, or indolent, betook himself to rest, while I made a tour round the south point of the island, walking the shelly paved sea beach, and picking up novelties. I had not gone above a mile, before I came up to a roebuck, lying slain on the sands, and hearing the report of a gun, not far off, and supposing it to be from the Captain of the fort, whom I expected soon to return to take up his game, I retired to a little distance, mounted the sand hills, and sat down, enjoying a fine prospect of the rolling billows and foaming breakers, beating on the bar, and north promontory of Amelia Isle, opposite to me. The Captain of the fort soon came up, with a slain buck on his shoulders. We hailed each other, and returned together to the fort, where we were well treated, and next morning, at my request, the Captain obligingly sat us over, landing us safely on Amelia. After walking through a spacious forest of Live Oaks and Palms, and crossing a creek, that ran through a narrow salt marsh, I and my fellow traveller arrived safe at the plantation, where the agent, Mr. Egan, received us very politely and hospitably.[4] This gentleman is a very intelligent and able planter, having already greatly improved the estate, particularly in the cultivation of indigo. Great part of this island consists of excellent hommocky land, which is the soil this plant delights in, as well as cotton, corn, batatas, and almost every other esculent vegetable. Mr. Egan politely rode with me, over great part of the island. On [66] Egmont estate, are several very large Indian tumuli, which are called Ogeeche mounts, so named from that nation of Indians, who took shelter here, after being driven from their native settlements on the main near Ogeeche river. Here they were constantly harrassed by the Carolinians and Creeks, and at length slain by their conquerors, and their bones intombed in these heaps of earth and shells. I observed here the ravages of the common grey catterpillar, so destructive to forest and fruit trees, in Pennsylvania, and through the northern states, by stripping them of their leaves, in the spring, while young and tender (Phalena periodica.)

MR. Egan having business of importance to transact in St. Augustine, pressed me to continue with him, a few days, when he would accompany me to that place, and if I chose, I should have a passage, as far as the Cow-ford, on St. Johns, where he would procure me a boat to prosecute my voyage.

IT may be a subject worthy of some inquiry, why those fine islands, on the coast of Georgia, are so thinly inhabited; though perhaps Amelia may in some degree plead an exemption, as it is a very fertile island, on the north border of East Florida, and at the Capes of St. Mary, the finest harbour in this new colony. If I should give my opinion, the following seem to be the most probable reasons: the greatest part of these are as yet the property of a few wealthy planters, who having their residence on the continent, where lands on the large rivers, as Savanna, Ogeeche, Altamaha, St. Ille and others, are of a nature and quality adapted to the growth of rice, which the planters chiefly rely upon, for obtaining ready cash, and purchasing family articles; they settle a few poor families on their in[67]sular estates, who rear stocks of horned cattle, horses, swine and poultry, and protect the game for their proprietors. The inhabitants of these islands also lay open to the invasion and ravages of pirates, and in case of a war, to incursions from their enemies armed vessels, in which case they must either remove with their families and effects to the main, or be stripped of all their movables, and their houses laid in ruins.

THE soil of these islands appears to be particularly favourable to the culture of indigo and cotton, and there are on them some few large plantations for the cultivation and manufacture of those valuable articles. The cotton is planted only by the poorer class of people, just enough for their family consumption: they plant two species of it, the annual and West-Indian; the former is low, and planted every year; the balls of this are very large, and the phlox long, strong, and perfectly white; the West-Indian is a tall perennial plant, the stalk somewhat shrubby, several of which rise up from the root for several years successively, the stems of the former year being killed by the winter frosts. The balls of this latter species are not quite so large as those of the herbaceous cotton; but the phlox, or wool, is long, extremely fine, silky, and white. A plantation of this kind will last several years, with moderate labour and care, whereas the annual sort is planted every year.

THE coasts, sounds, and inlets, environing these islands, abound with a variety of excellent fish, particularly Rock, Bass, Drum, Mullet, Sheepshead, Whiting, Grooper, Flounder, Sea-Trout, (this last seems to be a species of Cod) Skate, Skipjack, Stingray, the Shark, and great Black Sting[68]ray, are insatiable cannibals, and very troublesome to the fishermen. The bays and lagoons are stored with oysters and varieties of other shell-fish, crabs, shrimp, &c. The clams, in particular, are large, their meat white, tender, and delicate.

THERE is a large space betwixt this chain of sea-coast-islands and the main land, perhaps generally near three leagues in breadth; but all this space is not covered with water: I estimate nearly two thirds of it to consist of low salt plains, which produce Barilla, Sedge, Rushes, &c. and which border on the main land, and the western coasts of the islands. The east side of these islands are, for the most part, clean, hard, sandy beaches, exposed to the wash of the ocean. Between these islands are the mouths or entrances of some rivers, which run down from the continent, winding about through these low salt marshes, and delivering their waters into the sounds, which are very extensive capacious harbours, from three to five and six to eight miles over, and communicate with each other by parallel salt rivers, or passes, that flow into the sound: they afford an extensive and secure inland navigation for most craft, such as large schooners, sloops, pettiaugers, boats, and canoes; and this inland communication of waters extends along the sea coast with but few and short interruptions, from the bay of Chesapeak, in Virginia, to the Missisippi, and how much farther I know not, perhaps as far as Vera Cruz. Whether this chain of sea-coast-islands is a step, or advance which this part of our continent is now making on the Atlantic ocean, we must leave to future ages to determine. But it seems evident, even to demonstration, that those salt marshes adjoining the coast of the main, and the reedy and grassy islands and marshes in the rivers, which are now overflowed at [69] every tide, were formerly high swamps of firm land, affording forests of Cypress, Tupilo, Magnolia grandiflora, Oak, Ash, Sweet Bay, and other timber trees, the same as are now growing on the river swamps, whose surface is two feet or more above the spring tides that flow at this day; and it is plainly to be seen, by every planter along the coast of Carolina, Georgia, and Florida, to the Missisippi, when they bank in these grassy tide marshes for cultivation, that they cannot sink their drains above three or four feet below the surface, before they come to strata of Cypress stumps and other trees, as close together as they now grow in the swamps.

## CHAP. III.

[70]   BEING now in readiness to prosecute our voyage to St. John's, we sat sail in a handsome pleasure-boat, manned with four stout negro slaves, to row in case of necessity. After passing Amelia Narrows,[5] we had a pleasant run, across Fort George's sound, where, observing the pelicans fishing, Mr. Egan shot one of them, which we took into the boat. I was greatly surprised on observing the pouch or sack, which hangs under the bill: it is capable of being expanded to a prodigious size. One of the people on board, said, that he had seen more than half a bushel of bran, crammed into one of their pouches. The body is larger than that of a tame goose, the legs extremely short, the feet webbed, the bill of a great length, bent inwards like a scythe, the wings extend near seven feet from tip to tip, the tail is very short, the head, neck and breast, nearly white, the body of a light bluish grey, except the quill feathers of the wings, which are black. They seem to be of the gull kind, both in form and structure, as well as manner of fishing. The evening following, we landed on the main. It was a promontory of high land, covered with orange-trees, and projecting into the sound, forming a convenient port. We pitched our tent under the shelter of a forest of Live Oaks, Palms and Sweet Bays; and having in the course of the day, procured plenty of sea fowl, such as curlews, willets, snipes, sand birds and others; we had them dressed for supper, and seasoned with excellent oysters, which lay in heaps in the water, close to our landing place. [71] The shrub Capsicum growing here in abundance, afforded us a very good pepper: we drank of a well of fresh water just at hand, amidst a grove of Myrtles (Myrica carefera.) Our repose however was incompleat, from the stings of musquetoes, the roaring of crocadiles, and the continual noise and restlessness of the sea fowl, thousands of them having their roosting-places very near us, particularly loons of various species, herons, pelicans, Spanish curlews, &c. all promiscuously lodging together, and in such

incredible numbers, that the trees were entirely covered. They roost in inaccessible islets in the salt marshes, surrounded by lagoons, and shallow water. Just without the trees, betwixt them, the water and marshes, is a barricade of Palmetto royal (Yucca gloriosa) or Adam's needle, which grows so thick together, that a rat, or bird, can scarcely pass thro' them; and the stiff leaves of this Sword plant, standing nearly horizontally, are as impenetrable to man, or any other animal, as if they were a regiment of grenadiers with their bayonets pointed at you. The Palmetto royal is, however, a very singular and beautiful production. It may be termed a tree, from its durability and magnitude, as likewise from the ligneous quality of its stem, or trunk, when old; yet from its form and texture, I should be inclined to rank it amongst the herbaceous plants, for even the glorious Palm, although it rises to the altitude of a tree, and even transcends most of them, yet it bears the characters of the herbaceous ones: and this, like the Palm tree, rises with a strait, erect stem, about ten or twelve feet high, crowned with a beautiful chaplet of sword or dagger-like leaves, of a perfect green colour, each terminated with a stiff, sharp spur, and their edges finely crenated. This thorny crown is crested with a pyramid of sil[72]ver white flowers, each resembling a tulip or lilly. These flowers are succeeded by a large fruit, nearly of the form and size of a slender cucumber, and when ripe, is of a deep purple colour, the skin smooth and shining, its pulp soft, very juicy, and of an agreeable aromatic flavour but rather bitter to the taste; it is, however, frequently eaten, but if eaten to excess, proves violently purgative. The seeds are numerous, flat and lunated.

The plant, or tree, when grown old, sometimes divides into two or three stems, which seem of equal height and thickness, and indeed nearly of the same thickness with the main stem; but generally, when they arrive to this age and magnitude, their own weight brings them to the ground, where they soon decay, the heart or pith first, leaving a hollow fibrous reticulated trunk or sleeve, which likewise soon after decays, and in fine, all is again reduced to its original earth, and replaces the vegetative mould. But the deceased are soon replaced by others, as there are younger ones of all ages and stature, ready to succeed their predecessors, and flourish for a time, with the same regal pomp and splendor. These plants are so multitudinous, where-ever they get a footing, that the earth is completely occupied with them, and scarcely any other vegetable is to be seen, where they are; yet they are sometimes scattered amongst other trees and vegetables.

IN three days after leaving Amelia, we arrived at the Cow-ford, a public ferry, over St. Johns, about thirty miles above the bar or capes, the river here being above a mile wide.[6]

MR. Egan, after procuring a neat little sail-boat [73] for me, at a large Indigo plantation near the ferry, and for which I paid three guineas, departed for St. Augustine, which is on the sea-coast about forty-five miles over land.

IT was now about the middle of April, vegetation appearing every where in high progress, I was anxious to be advancing southerly; and having at this plantation, stored myself with necessaries for my voyage, I sailed in the morning, with a fair wind. I was now again alone, for the young man my fellow traveller, though stouter and heartier than myself, having repented of his promise to accompany me, to the Indian trading houses, I suppose not relishing the hardship and dangers, which might perhaps befall us, chose rather to stay behind, amongst the settlements. His leaving me, however, I did not greatly regret, as I could not consider it a disappointment much to my disadvantage at the moment. Our views were probably totally opposite; he, a young mechanic on his adventures, seemed to be actuated by no other motives, than either to establish himself, in some well inhabited part of the country, where, by following his occupation, he might be enabled to procure without much toil and danger, the necessaries and conveniences of life; or by industry and frugality, perhaps establish his fortune. Whilst I, continually impelled by a restless spirit of curiosity, in pursuit of new productions of nature, my chief happiness consisted in tracing and admiring the infinite power, majesty and perfection of the great Almighty Creator, and in the contemplation, that through divine aid and permission, I might be instrumental in discovering, and introducing into my native country, some original [74] productions of nature, which might become useful to society. Each of our pursuits, were perhaps equally laudable; and upon this supposition, I was quite willing to part with him upon amicable terms.

My little vessel being furnished with a good sail, and having fishing tackle, a neat light fusee, powder and ball, I found myself well equipped, for my voyage, about one hundred miles to the trading house.

I CROSSED the river to a high promontory of wood-land, on the west shore, and being struck with the magnificence of a venerable grove of Live Oak, Palms and Laurel (Magnolia grandiflora) I stepped on shore to take a view of the place. Orange trees were in full bloom, and filled the air with fragrance.

It was now past noon, and this place being about eight miles above the Cowford, and the river near three miles in breadth, I wanted to reach a plantation in sight, on the opposite shore, in order to get some repairs, my vessel having sustained some damage from the violence of the wind, in crossing over. I arrived late in the evening, and finding a convenient landing place and harbour,

I concluded to remain here till morning, and then coast it, close along shore to the plantation.

IT beginning to thunder, I was sufficiently warned to prepare against a wet night, and observing a very large Oak tree, which had been thrown down, by a hurricane and offered me a convenient shelter, as its enormous limbs bore up the trunk, a sufficient height from the earth, to admit me to sit or lie down under it, I spread my sail, slanting from the trunk of the tree, to the ground, on the [75] windward side; and having collected a quantity of wood, sufficient to keep up a fire, during the night, I struck one up in front, and spreading skins on the ground, and upon these placing a blanket, one half I laid down upon, turning the other over me for a covering.

THE storm came up, with a furious wind and tremendous thunder and lightning, from the opposite N. W. coast, but luckily for me, little rain fell, and I rested very well. But as the wind next morning blew very fresh, right in upon the shore, there was no possibility of moving, with safety, from my present situation. I however arose to reconnoitre the ground, round about my habitation, being roused by the report of a musquet not far off. I had not left sight of my encampment, following a winding path through a grove of Live Oak, Laurel (Magn. grandiflora) and Sapindus, before an Indian stepped out of a thicket and crossed the path just before me, having a large turkey cock, slung across his shoulders, he saw me and stepping up and smiling, spoke to me in English, bidding me good-morning. I saluted him with "Its well brother," led him to my camp, and treated him with a dram. This friendly Indian informed me that he lived at the next plantation, employed as a hunter, I asked him how far it was to the house; he answered about half a mile by land, and invited me to go there, telling me that his master was a very good, kind man, and would be glad to see me. I replied, that I would, if my boat and effects in the mean time could be safe, he said that he would immediately return to the house, and acquaint his master of it, who would send trusty Negroes to bring my vessel [76] round the point, to the landing, I thanked him for his civility, and not willing to be troublesome, I told him I would leave my boat, and follow after him; so taking my fusee on my shoulder, and after dragging my bark as high up on shore as I could, I followed the Indian, and soon reached the house.[7]

THE gentleman received me, in the most polite manner, and after hearing my situation, he requested me to make my abode with him, a few days, to rest and refresh myself. I thanked him and told him I would stay a day. He immediately sent slaves who brought my boat round, and having carpenters at work, on a new building, he sat them about repairing my vessel, which by night was completely refitted.

I SPENT the day in the most agreeable manner, in the society of this man of singular worth, he led me over his extensive improvements, and we returned in company with several of his neighbours. In the afternoon the most sultry time of the day, we retired to the fragrant shades of an Orange grove. The house was situated on an eminence, about one hundred and fifty yards, from the river. On the right hand was the Orangery, consisting of many hundred trees, natives of the place, and left standing, when the ground about it was cleared. These trees where [were] large, flourishing and in perfect bloom, and loaded with their ripe golden fruit. On the other side was a spacious garden, occupying a regular slope of ground, down to the water; and a pleasant lawn lay between. Here were large plantations of the Indigo plant, which appeared in a very thriving condition: it was then about five or six inches high, growing in streight parallel rows, about eighteen inches apart. The [77] Corn (Zea) and Potatoes (Convolv. Batata) were greatly advanced in growth, and promised a plentiful crop. The Indigo made in East Florida is esteemed almost equal to the best Spanish, especially that sort, which they call Flora. Mr. Marshall presented me, with a specimen of his own manufacture, at this plantation: it was very little, if any inferior; to the best Prussian blue.

IN the morning following, intimating my intentions of proceeding on my voyage, Mr. Marshall, again importuned me to stay, but I obtained his consent to depart, on my promising to visit him, at my return to Georgia. After breakfast I therefore took my leave, attended to the shore, by several slaves, loaded with ammunition and provisions, which my friend had provided for me. On my expressing some difficulty in receiving so large a share of his bounty, he civilly replied, that it was too little to mention, and that, if I had continued with him a day or two longer, he should have had time to have served me in a much better manner.

TAKING my leave of Mr. Marshall, I again embarked alone on board my little vessel, and blessed with a favourable steady gale, I set sail. The day was extremely pleasant, the late thunder storm had purified the air, by disuniting and dissipating the noxious vapours. The falling of heavy showers, with thunder and brisk winds, from the cool regions of the N. W. contributes greatly towards restoring the salubrity of the air, and purity of the waters, by precipitating the putrescent scum,[8] that rises from the bottom, and floats upon the surface, near the shores of the rivers, in these southern climates, during the hot seasons. The [78] shores of this great river St. Juan, are very level and shoal, extending in some places, a mile or two, into the river, betwixt the high land, and the clear waters of the river, which is so level, as to be covered not above a foot or two deep, with water, and at a little distance appears as a green meadow having water-grass and other amphibious vegetables, growing in the oozy bottom, and floating upon the water.

HAVING a lively leading breeze, I kept as near the East shore, as possible, often surprised by the plunging of alligators, and greatly delighted with the pleasing prospect of cultivation, and the encrease of human industry, which frequently struck my view from the elevated, distant shores.

AT night I ran in shore, at a convenient harbour, where I was received and welcomed by the gentleman, who was agent for the plantation, and at whose pleasant habitation, near the harbour, I took up my quarters for the night.

THIS very civil man, happened to be a person with whom I had formerly been acquainted in St. Augustine; and as he lived about twenty miles distant from it, I had good reason to expect that he would be a proper person, to obtain intelligence from, concerning the disturbances, which were thought still to subsist, between the Lower Creeks and the white inhabitants of East Florida. Upon enquiry, and conversation with him, I found my conjectures on that head, to have been well founded. My friend informed me, that there had, but a few days since, been a counsel held at St. Augustine, between the governor of East Florida, and the chiefs of the Lower Creeks.[9] They had been delegated by their [79] towns, to make enquiry, concerning the late alarm and depredations, committed by the Indians upon the traders, which the nation being apprised of, recommended these deputies to be chosen and sent, as soon as possible, in order to make reasonable concessions, before the flame, already kindled, should spread into a general war. The parties accordingly met in St. Augustine, and the affair was amicably adjusted, to the satisfaction of both parties. The chiefs of the delinquent bands, whose young warriors had committed the mischief, promised to indemnify the traders for the loss of their goods, and requested that they might return to their store-houses, with goods as usual, and that they should be safe in their persons and property. The traders at this time, were actually preparing to return. It appeared upon a strict investigation of facts, that the affair had taken its rise from the licentious conduct of a few vagrant young hunters of the Siminole nation, who, imagining themselves to have been ill treated, in their dealings, with the traders (which by the bye was likely enough to be true) took this violent method of doing themselves justice. The culprits however endeavoured to exculpate themselves, by asserting, that they had no design or intention of robbing the traders of their effects, but meant it only as a threat, and that the traders, from a conciousness of their dishonesty, had been terrified and fled, leaving their stores, which they took possession of, to prevent their being totally lost. This troublesome affair being adjusted, was very agreeable news to me, as I could now, without apprehensions, ascend this grand river, and visit its delightful shores, where, and when I pleased.

BIDDING adieu to my obliging friend, I spread my sail to the favourable breeze, and by noon, came to [80] a-breast of fort Picolata, where, being desirous of gaining yet farther intelligence, I landed, but to my disappointment, found the fort dismantled and deserted.[10] This fortress is very ancient, and was built by the Spaniards. It is a square tower, thirty feet high, invested with a high wall, without bastions, about breast high, pierced with loop holes and surrounded with a deep ditch. The upper story is open on each side, with battlements, supporting a cupola or roof: these battlements were formerly mounted with eight four pounders, two on each side.

THE works are constructed with hewn stone, cemented with lime. The stone was cut out of quarries, on St. Anastatius Island, opposite St. Augustine: it is of a pale reddish brick colour, and a testacious composition, consisting of small fragments of sea-shells and fine sand. It is well adapted to the constructing of fortifications. It lies in horizontal masses in the quarry, and constitutes the foundation of that island. The castle at St. Augustine, and most of the buildings of the town, are of this stone.

LEAVING Picolata, I continued to ascend the river. I observed this day, during my progress up the river, incredible numbers of small flying insects, of the genus, termed by naturalists, Ephemera, continually emerging from the shallow water, near shore, some of them immediately taking their flight to the land, whilst myriads, crept up the grass and herbage, where remaining, for a short time, as they acquired sufficient strength, they took their flight also, following their kindred, to the main land. This resurrection from the deep, if I may so express it, commences early in the morning, and ceases after the sun is up. At evening they are seen in [81] clouds of innumerable millions, swarming and wantoning in the still air, gradually drawing near the river, descend upon its surface, and there quickly end their day, after committing their eggs to the deep; which being for a little while tossed about, enveloped in a viscid scum, are hatched, and the little Larva descend into their secure and dark habitation, in the oozy bed beneath, where they remain, gradually increasing in size, until the returning spring; they then change to a Nymph, when the genial heat brings them, as it were, into existence, and they again arise into the world. This fly seems to be delicious food for birds, frogs and fish. In the morning, when they arise, and in the evening, when they return, the tumult is great indeed, and the surface of the water along shore broken into bubbles, or spirted into the air, by the contending aquatic tribes, and such is the avidity of the fish and frogs, that they spring into the air, after this delicious prey.

EARLY in the evening, after a pleasant days voyage, I made a convenient and safe harbour, in a little lagoon, under an elevated bank, on the West shore of the river, where I shall intreat the reader's patience, whilst we behold the closing scene of the short-lived Ephemera, and communicate to each other the reflections which so singular an exhibition might rationally suggest to an inquisitive mind. Our place of observation is happily situated, under the protecting shade of majestic Live Oaks, glorious Magnolias and the fragrant Orange, open to the view of the great river, and still waters of the lagoon just before us.

AT the cool eves approach, the sweet enchanting [82] melody of the feathered songsters gradually ceases, and they betake themselves to their leafy coverts for security and repose.

SOLEMNLY and slowly move onward, to the river's shore, the rustling clouds of the Ephemera. How awful the procession! innumerable millions of winged beings, voluntarily verging on to destruction, to the brink of the grave, where they behold bands of their enemies with wide open jaws, ready to receive them. But as if insensible of their danger, gay and tranquil each meets his beloved mate, in the still air, inimitably bedecked in their new nuptial robes. What eye can trace them, in their varied wanton amorous chaces, bounding and fluttering on the odoriferous air? with what peace, love and joy, do they end the last moments of their existence?

I THINK we may assert, without any fear of exaggeration, that there are annually of these beautiful winged beings, which rise into existence, and for a few moments take a transient view of the glory of the Creator's works, a number greater than the whole race of mankind that have ever existed since the creation; and that only, from the shore of this river. How many then must have been produced since the creation, when we consider the number of large rivers in America, in comparison with which, this river is but a brook or rivulet.

THE importance of the existence of these beautiful and delicately formed little creatures, in the creation, whose frame and organization is equally wonderful, more delicate, and perhaps as complicated as that of the most perfect human being, is well worth a few moments contemplation; I mean par[83]ticularly when they appear in the fly state. And if we consider the very short period, of that stage of existence, which we may reasonably suppose, to be the only space of their life that admits of pleasure and enjoyment, what a lesson doth it not afford us of the vanity of our own pursuits.

THEIR whole existence in this world, is but one compleat year, and at least three hundred and sixty days of that time, they are in the form of an ugly grub, buried in mud, eighteen inches under water, and in this condition scarcely locomotive, as each Larva or grub, has but its own narrow solitary cell, from which it never travels, or moves, but in a perpendicular progression, of a few inches, up and down, from the bottom to the surface of the mud, in order to intercept the passing atoms for its food, and get a momentary respiration of fresh air; and even here it must be perpetually on its guard, in order to escape the troops of fish and shrimps watching to catch it, and from whom it has no escape, but by instantly retreating back into its cell. One would be apt almost to imagine them created merely for the food of fish and other animals.

HAVING rested very well during the night, I was awakened in the morning early, by the cheering converse of the wild turkey-cock (Meleagris occidentalis) saluting each other, from the sun-brightened tops of the lofty Cupressus disticha and Magnolia grandiflora. They begin at early dawn, and continue till sun rise, from March to the last of April. The high forests ring with the noise, like the crowing of the domestic cock, of these social centinels, the watch-word being caught and repeated, from one to another, for hundreds of miles [84] around; insomuch that the whole country, is for an hour or more, in an universal shout. A little after sun-rise, their crowing gradually ceases, they quit their high lodging places, and alight on the earth, where, expanding their silver bordered train, they strut and dance round about the coy female, while the deep forests seem to tremble with their shrill noise.

THIS morning the winds on the great river, were high and against me, I was therefore obliged to keep in port, a great part of the day, which I employed in little excursions round about my encampment. The Live Oaks are of an astonishing magnitude, and one tree contains a prodigious quantity of timber, yet comparatively, they are not tall, even in these forests, where growing on strong land, in company with others of great altitude (such as Fagus sylvatica, Liquid-amber, Magnolia grandiflora, and the high Palm tree) they strive while young to be upon an equality with their neighbours, and to enjoy the influence of the sun-beams, and of the pure animating air; but the others at last prevail, and their proud heads are seen at a great distance, towering far above the rest of the forest, which consists chiefly of this species of oak, Fraxinus, Ulmus, Acer rubrum, Laurus Borbonia, Quercus dentata, Ilex aquifolium, Olea Americana, Morus, Gleditsia triacanthus, and I believe a species of Sapindus. But the latter spreads abroad his brawny arms, to a great distance. The trunk of the Live Oak is generally from twelve to eighteen feet in girt, and rises ten or twelve feet erect from the earth; some I have seen eighteen or twenty; then divides itself into three, four, or five great limbs, [85] which continue to grow in nearly an horizontal direction, each limb forming a gentle curve, or arch, from its base to its extremity. I have stepped above fifty paces, on a strait line, from the trunk of one of these trees, to the extremity of the limbs. They are ever green, and the wood almost incorruptible, even in the open air. It bears a prodigious quantity of fruit; the acorn is small, but sweet and agreeable to the taste when roasted, and is food for almost all animals. The Indians obtain from it a sweet oil, which they use in the cooking of hommony, rice, &c. and they also roast them in hot embers, eating them as we do chesnuts.

THE wind being fair in the evening, I sat sail again, and crossing the river, made a good harbour on the East shore, where I pitched my tent for the night. The bank of the river was about twelve or fifteen feet perpendicular, from its surface, but the ascent gentle. Although I arrived here early in the evening, I found sufficient attractions to choose it for my lodging-place, and an ample field for botanical employment. It was a high, airy situation, and commanded an extensive and varied prospect of the river and its shores, up and down.[11]

BEHOLD yon promontory, projecting far into the great river, beyond the still lagoon, half a mile distance from me, what a magnificent grove arises on its banks! how glorious the Palm! how majestically stands the Laurel, its head forming a perfect cone! its dark green foliage, seems silvered over with milk-white flowers. They are so large, as to be distinctly visible at the distance of a mile or more. The Laurel Magnolia, which grows on this river are the most beautiful and tall, that I have any where seen, unless we except those, which stand [86] on the banks of the Missisippi; yet even these must yield, to those of St. Juan, in neatness of form, beauty of foliage, and I think, in largeness and fragrance of flower. Their usual height is about one hundred feet, and some greatly exceed that. The trunk is perfectly erect, rising in the form of a beautiful column, and supporting a head like an obtuse cone. The flowers are on the extremities of the subdivisions of the branches, in the center of a coronet of dark green, shining, ovate pointed entire leaves: they are large, perfectly white, and expanded like a full blown Rose. They are polypetalous, consisting of fifteen, twenty, or twenty-five petals: these are of a thick coriaceous texture, and deeply concave, their edges being somewhat reflex, when mature. In the center stands the young cone, which is large, of a flesh colour, and elegantly studded with a gold coloured stigma; that by the end of summer, is greatly enlarged, and in the autumn ripens to a large crimson cone or strobile, disclosing multitudes of large coral red berries, which for a time hang down from them, suspended by a fine, white silky thread, four, six to nine inches in length. The flowers of this tree are the largest, and most compleat of any yet known: when fully expanded, they are of six, eight and nine inches diameter. The pericarpium and berries, possess an agreeable spicy scent, and an aromatic bitter taste. The wood when seasoned is of a straw colour, compact, and harder and firmer than that of the Poplar.

IT is really astonishing to behold the Grape-Vines in this place. From their bulk and strength, one would imagine, they were combined to pull down these mighty trees, to the earth, when in fact, a[87]mongst other good purposes, they serve to uphold them: they are frequently nine, ten, and twelve inches in diameter, and twine round the trunks of the trees, climb to their very tops, and then spread along their limbs, from tree to tree, throughout the forest; the fruit is but small and ill tasted. The Grape vines with the Rhamnus volubilis, Bignonia radicans, Bignonia crucigera, and another rambling shrubby vine, which seems allied to the Rhamnus, perhaps Zizyphus scandens, seem to tie the trees together, with garlands and festoons, and form enchanting shades. The long moss, so called, (Tillandsea usneascites) is a singular and surprising vegetable production: it grows from the limbs and twigs of all trees in these southern regions, from N. lat. 35 down as far as 28, and I believe every where within the tropics. Wherever it fixes itself, on a limb, or branch, it spreads into short and intricate divarications; these in time collect dust, wafted by the wind, and which, probably by the moisture it absorbs, softens the bark and sappy part of the tree, about the roots of the plant, and renders it more fit for it to establish itself; and from this small beginning, it encreases, by sending downwards and obliquely, on all sides, long pendant branches, which divide and subdivide themselves ad infinitum. It is common to find the spaces, betwixt the limbs of large trees, almost occupied by this plant; it also hangs waving in the wind, like streamers, from the lower limbs, to the length of fifteen or twenty feet, and of bulk and weight, more than several men together could carry; and in some places, cart loads of it are lying on the ground, torn off, by the violence of the wind. Any part of the living plant, torn off and caught, in the limbs of a tree, will presently take root, [88] grow and encrease, in the same degree of perfection, as if it had sprung up from the seed. When fresh, cattle and deer will eat it in the winter season. It seems particularly adapted to the purpose of stuffing mattrasses, chairs, saddles, collars, &c. and for these purposes, nothing yet known equals it. The Spaniards in South America, and the West-Indies, work it into cables that are said to be very strong and durable; but, in order to render it useful, it ought to be thrown into shallow ponds of water, and exposed to the sun, where it soon rots, and the outside furry substance is dissolved. It is then taken out of the water, and spread to dry; when, after a little beating and shaking, it is sufficiently clean, nothing remaining but the interior, hard, black, elastic filament, entangled together, and greatly resembling horse-hair.

THE Zanthoxilum clava Herculis also grows here. It is a beautiful spreading tree, and much like a well grown apple tree. Its aromatic berry is delicious food for the little turtle dove; and epicures say that it gives their flesh a fine flavor.

HAVING finished my observation, I betook myself to rest; and when the plunging and roaring of the crocodiles, and the croaking of the frogs, had ceased, I slept very well during the remainder of the night, as a breeze from the river had scattered the clouds of musquitoes that at first infested me.

IT being a fine cool morning, and fair wind, I sat sail early, and saw, this day, vast quantities of the Pistia stratiotes, a very singular aquatic plant. It associates in large communities, or floating islands, some of them a quarter of a mile in extent, and are impelled to and fro, as the wind and [89] current may direct. They are first produced on, or close to the shore, in eddy water, where they gradually spread themselves into the river, forming most delightful green plains, several miles in length, and in some places a quarter of a mile in breadth. These plants are nourished and kept in their proper horizontal situation, by means of long fibrous roots, which descend from the nether center, downwards, towards the muddy bottom. Each plant, when full grown, bears a general resemblance to a well grown plant of garden lettice, though the leaves are more nervous, of a firmer contexture, and of a full green colour, inclining to yellow. It vegetates on the surface of the still stagnant water, and in its natural situation, is propagated from seed only. In great storms of wind and rain, when the river is suddenly raised, large masses of these floating plains are broken loose, and driven from the shores, into the wide water, where they have the appearance of islets, and float about, until broken to pieces by the winds and waves; or driven again to shore, on some distant coast of the river, where they again find footing, and there, forming new colonies, spread and extend themselves again, until again broken up and dispersed as before. These floating islands present a very entertaining prospect; for although we behold an assemblage of the primary productions of nature only, yet the imagination seems to remain in suspence and doubt; as in order to enliven the delusion and form a most picturesque appearance, we see not only flowery plants, clumps of shrubs, old weather-beaten trees, hoary and barbed, with the long moss waving from their snags, but we also see them compleatly inhabited, and alive, with crocodiles, serpents, frogs, ot[90]ters, crows, herons, curlews, jackdaws, &c. there seems, in short, nothing wanted but the appearance of a wigwam and a canoe to complete the scene.

KEEPING along the West or Indian shore, I saw basking on the sedgy banks, numbers of alligators, some of them of an enormous size.[12]

THE high forests on this coast, now wore a grand and sublime appearance, the earth rising gradually, from the river Westward, by easy swelling ridges, behind one another, and lifted the distant groves up into the skies. The trees are of the lofty kind, as the grand Laurel Magnolia, Palm elata, Liquid-amber styraciflua, Fagus sylvatica, Querci, Juglans hiccory, Fraxinus, and others.

ON my doubling a long point of land, the river appeared surprisingly widened, forming a large bay, of an oval form, and several miles in extent. On the West side it was bordered round with low marshes, and invested with a swamp of Cypress, the trees so lofty, as to preclude the sight of the high-land forests, beyond them; and these trees, having flat tops, and all of equal height, seemed to be a green plain, lifted up and supported upon columns in the air, round the West side of the bay.

THE Cupressus disticha stands in the first order of North American trees. Its majestic stature is surprising, and on approaching them, we are struck with a kind of awe, at beholding the stateliness of the trunk, lifting its cumbrous top towards the skies, and casting a wide shade upon the ground, as a dark intervening cloud, which, for a time, precludes [91] the rays of the sun. The delicacy of its colour, and texture of its leaves, exceed every thing in vegetation. It generally grows in the water, or in low flat lands, near the banks of great rivers and lakes, that are covered, great part of the year, with two or three feet depth of water, and that part of the trunk, which is subject to be under water, and four or five feet higher up, is greatly enlarged, by prodigious buttresses, or pilasters, which, in full grown trees, project out on every side, to such a distance, that several men might easily hide themselves in the hollows between. Each pilaster terminates under ground, in a very large, strong, serpentine root, which strikes off, and branches every way, just under the surface of the earth; and from these roots grow woody cones, called cypress knees, four, five, and six feet high, and from six to eighteen inches and two feet in diameter at their bases. The large ones are hollow, and serve very well for bee-hives; a small space of the tree itself is hollow, nearly as high as the buttresses already mentioned. From this place the tree, as it were, takes another beginning, forming a grand strait column eighty or ninety feet high, when it divides every way around into an extensive flat horizontal top, like an umbrella, where eagles have their secure nests, and cranes and storks their temporary resting places; and what adds to the magnificence of their appearance, is the streamers of long moss that hang from the lofty limbs and float in the winds. This is their majestic appearance, when standing alone, in large rice plantations, or thinly planted on the banks of great rivers.

PAROQUETS are commonly seen hovering and fluttering on their tops: they delight to shell the [92] balls, its seed being their favourite food. The trunks of these trees when hollowed out, make large and durable pettiaugers and canoes, and afford excellent shingles, boards, and other timber, adapted to every purpose in frame buildings. When the planters fell these mighty trees, they raise a stage round them, as high as to reach above the buttresses; on this stage, eight or ten negroes ascend with their axes, and fall to work round its trunk. I have seen trunks of these trees that would measure eight, ten, and twelve feet in diameter, for forty and fifty feet strait shaft.

AS I continued coasting the Indian shore of this bay, on doubling a promontory, I suddenly saw before me an Indian settlement, or village.[13] It was a fine situation, the bank rising gradually from the water. There were eight or ten habitations, in a row, or street, fronting the water, and about fifty yards distance from it. Some of the youth were naked, up to their hips in the water, fishing with rods and lines, whilst others, younger, were diverting themselves in shooting frogs with bows and arrows. On my near approach, the little children took to their heels, and ran to some women, who were hoeing corn; but the stouter youth stood their ground, and, smiling, called to me. As I passed along, I observed some elderly people reclined on skins spread on the ground, under the cool shade of spreading Oaks and Palms, that were ranged in front of their houses; they arose, and eyed me as I passed, but perceiving that I kept on, without stopping, they resumed their former position. They were civil, and appeared happy in their situation.

THERE was a large Orange grove at the upper [93] end of their village; the trees were large, carefully pruned, and the ground under them clean, open, and airy. There seemed to be several hundred acres of cleared land, about the village; a considerable portion of which was planted, chiefly with corn (Zea) Batatas, Beans, Pompions, Squashes, (Cucurbita verrucosa) Melons (Cucurbita citrullus) Tobacco (Nicotiana) &c. abundantly sufficient for the inhabitants of the village.[14]

AFTER leaving this village, and coasting a considerable cove of the lake, I perceived the river before me much contracted within its late bounds, but still retaining the appearance of a wide and deep river, both coasts bordered, for several miles, with rich deep swamps, well timbered with Cypress, Ash, Elm, Oak, Hiccory, Scarlet Maple, Nyssa aquatica, Nyssa tupilo, Gordonia lasianthus, Corypha palma, Corypha pumila, Laurus Borbonia, &c. The river gradually narrowing, I came in sight of Charlotia, where it is not above half a mile wide, but deep; and as there was a considerable current against me, I came here to an anchor. This town was founded by Den. Rolle, Esq; and is situated on a high bluff, on the east coast, fifteen or twenty feet perpendicular from the river, and is in length half a mile, or more, upon its banks.[15] The upper stratum of the earth consists entirely of several species of fresh water Cochlae, as Cochelix, Coch. labyrinthus, and Coch. voluta; the second, of marine shells, as Concha mytulus, Concostrea, Conc. peeton, Haliotis auris marina, Hal. patella, &c. mixed with sea sand; and the third, or lower stratum, which was a little above the comman level of the river, was horizontal masses of a pretty hard rock, composed almost entirely of the above shell, generally whole, and lying in every direction, pe[94]trefied or cemented together, with fine white sand; and these rocks were bedded in a stratum of clay. I saw many fragments of the earthen ware of the ancient inhabitants, and bones of animals, amongst the shells, and mixed with the earth, to a great depth. This high shelly bank continues, by gentle parallel ridges, near a quarter of a mile back from the river, gradually diminishing to the level of the sandy plains, which widen before and on each side eastward, to a seemingly unlimited distance, and appear green and delightful, being covered with grass and the Corypha repens, and thinly planted with trees of the long leaved, or Broom Pine, and decorated with clumps, or coppices of floriferous, evergreen, and aromatic shrubs, and enamelled with patches of the beautiful little Kalmea ciliata. These shelly ridges have a vegetable surface of loose black mould, very fertile, and naturally produces Orange groves, Live Oak, Laurus Borbonia, Palma elata, Carica papaya, Sapindus, Liquid-amber, Fraxinus exelsior, Morus rubra, Ulmns, Tilia, Sambucus, Ptelea, Tallow-nut, or Wild Lime, and many others.

MR. Rolle obtained from the crown, a grant of forty thousand acres of land, in any part of East Florida, where the land was unlocated. It seems his views were to take up his grant near St. Marks, in the bay of Aplatchi; and sat sail from England, with about one hundred families, for that place; but by contrary winds, and stress of weather, he missed his aim, and being obliged to put into St. Juan's, he, with some of the principal of his adherents, ascended the river in a boat, and being struck with its majesty, the grand situations of its banks, and fertility of its lands, and at the same time, considering the extensive navigation of the [95] river, and its near vicinity to St. Augustine, the capital and seat of government, he altered his views on St. Marks, and suddenly determined on this place, where he landed his first little colony. But it seems from an ill concerted plan, in its infant establishment, negligence, or extreme parsimony, in sending proper recruits, and other necessaries, together with a bad choice of citizens, the settlement by degrees grew weeker, and at length totally fell to the ground. Those of them who escaped the constant contagious fevers, fled the dreaded place, betaking themselves for subsistence, to the more fruitful and populous regions of Georgia and Carolina.

THE remaining old habitations, are mouldering to earth, except the mansion house, which is a large frame building, of Cypress wood, yet in tolerable repair, and inhabited by an overseer and his family. There is also a black-smith with his shop and family, at a small distance from it. The most valuable district belonging to Mr. Rolle's grant, lies on Dunn's lake, and on a little river, which runs from it into St. Juan. This district consists of a vast body of rich swamp land, fit for the growth of Rice, and some very excellent high land surrounding it. Large swamps of excellent rice land are also situated on the West shore of the river, opposite to Charlotia.

THE aborigines of America, had a very great town in this place, as appears from the great tumuli, and conical mounts of earth and shells, and other traces of a settlement which yet remain. There grew in the old fields on these heights great quantities of Callicarpa and of the beautiful shrub Annona: the flowers of the latter are large, white and sweet scented.

[96] HAVING obtained from the people here, directions for discovering the little remote island, where the traders and their goods were secreted, which was about seven miles higher up, I sat sail again, with a fair wind, and in about one hour and an half, arrived at the desired place, having fortunately taken the right channel of the river, amongst a multitude of others, occasioned by a number of low swampy islands.[16] But I should have ran by the landing, if the centinels had not, by chance seen me drawing near them; and who perceiving that I was a whiteman, ventured to hail me; upon which I immediately struck sail, and came too. Upon my landing they conducted me to their encampment, forty or fifty yards from the river, in an almost impenetrable thicket. Upon my inquiry, they confirmed the accounts of the amicable treaty at St. Augustine, and in consequence thereof, they had already removed great part of the goods, to the trading-house, which was a few miles higher up, on the Indian shore.

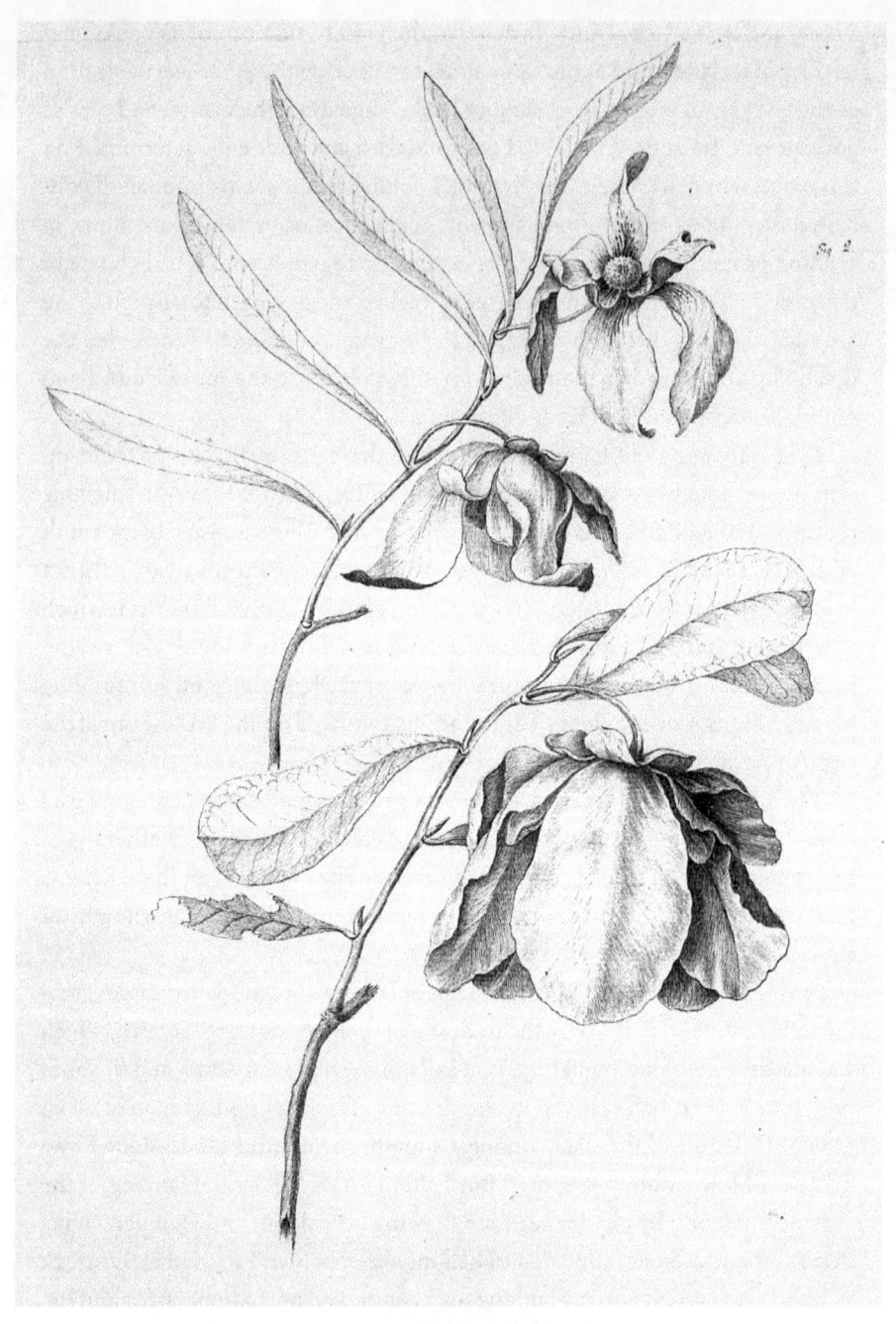

William Bartram, "Two Beautifull Species Annona," drawing sent to John Fothergill in 1774. By permission of the Natural History Museum, London.

They shewed me my chest, which had been carefully preserved, and upon inspection I found every thing in good order. Having learned from them, that all the effects would, in a few days time, be removed to the store-house, I bid adieu to them, and in a little time, arrived at the trading-house, where I was received with great politeness, and treated during a residence of several months, with the utmost civility and friendship, by Mr. C. M'Latche, Messrs. Spalding and Kelsall's agent.[17]

THE river almost from Charlotia, and for near twelve mile higher up is divided into many channels by a great number of islands.

[97] CHAP. IV.[18]

HAVING rested myself a few days, and by ranging about the neighbouring plains and groves, surrounding this pleasant place, pretty well recovered my strength and spirits, I began to think of planning my future excursions, at a distance round about this center. I found from frequent conferences with Mr. M'Latche, that I might with safety, extend my journeys every way, and with prudence, even into the towns and settlement of the Indians, as they were perfectly reconciled to us, and sincerely wished for the renewal of our trade.

THERE were three trading-houses to be established this summer, each of which had its supplier from the store on St. Juan, where I now had my residence, and in which the produce or returns were to center annually, in order to be shipped for Savanna or Sunbury, and from thence to Europe.

ONE of these trading-houses was to be fixed about sixty miles higher up the river, from this place, by the name of Spalding's upper store; a second at Alachua, about fifty miles West from the river St. Juan; and a third at Talahasochte, a considerable town of the Siminoles, on the river Little St. Juan, near the bay of Apalachi, about one hundred and twenty miles distance. Each of these places I designed to visit, before the return of the vessel to Frederica, in the autumn, that I might avail myself of an opportunity so favourable, for transporting my collections so far on their way towards Charleston.

[98] THE company for Alachua, were to set off in about a month. That to Little St. Juan, in July, which suited me exceedingly well, as I might make my tour to the upper store directly, that part of the country being at this season, enrobed in her richest and gayest apparel.

ABOUT the middle of May, every thing being in readiness, to proceed up the river, we sat sail. The traders with their goods in a large boat, went ahead, and myself in my little vessel followed them; and as their boat was large, and deeply laden, I found that I could easily keep up with them, and if I chose, outsail them; but I preferred keeping them company, as well for the sake of collecting what I could from conversation, as on account of my safety in crossing the great lake, expecting to return alone, and descend the river at my own leisure.

WE had a pleasant day, the wind fair and moderate, and ran by Mount Hope,[19] so named by my father John Bartram, when he ascended this river, about fifteen years ago. It is a very high shelly bluff, upon the little lake. It was at that time a fine Orange grove, but now cleared and converted into a large Indigo plantation, the property of an English gentleman, under the care of an agent. In the evening we arrived at Mount Royal,[20] where we came to, and stayed all night: we were treated with great civility, by a gentleman whose name was———Kean, and had been an Indian trader.

FROM this place we enjoyed a most enchanting prospect of the great Lake George, through a grand avenue, if I may so term this narrow reach of the river, which widens gradually for about two miles, [99] towards its entrance into the lake, so as to elude the exact rules of perspective and appears of an equal width.

AT about fifty yards distance from the landing place, stands a magnificent Indian mount. About fifteen years ago I visited this place, at which time there were no settlements of white people, but all appeared wild and savage; yet in that uncultivated state, it possessed an almost inexpressible air of grandeur, which was now entirely changed. At that time there was a very considerable extent of old fields, round about the mount; there was also a large Orange grove, together with Palms and Live Oaks, extending from near the mount, along the banks, downwards, all of which has since been cleared away to make room for planting ground. But what greatly contributed towards compleating the magnificence of the scene, was a noble Indian highway, which led from the great mount, on a strait line, three quarters of a mile, first through a point or wing of the Orange grove, and continuing thence through an awful forest, of Live Oaks, it was terminated by Palms and Laurel Magnolias, on the verge of an oblong artificial lake, which was on the edge of an extensive green level savanna. This grand highway was about fifty yards wide, sunk a little below the common level, and the earth thrown up on each side, making a bank of about two feet high. Neither nature nor art, could any where present a more striking contrast, as you approach this savanna. The glittering water pond, plays on the sight, through the dark grove, like a brilliant diamond, on the bosom of the illumined savanna, bordered with various flowery shrubs and plants; and as we advance into the plain, the [100] sight is agreeably relieved by a distant view of the forests, which partly environ the green expanse, on the left hand, whilst the imagination is

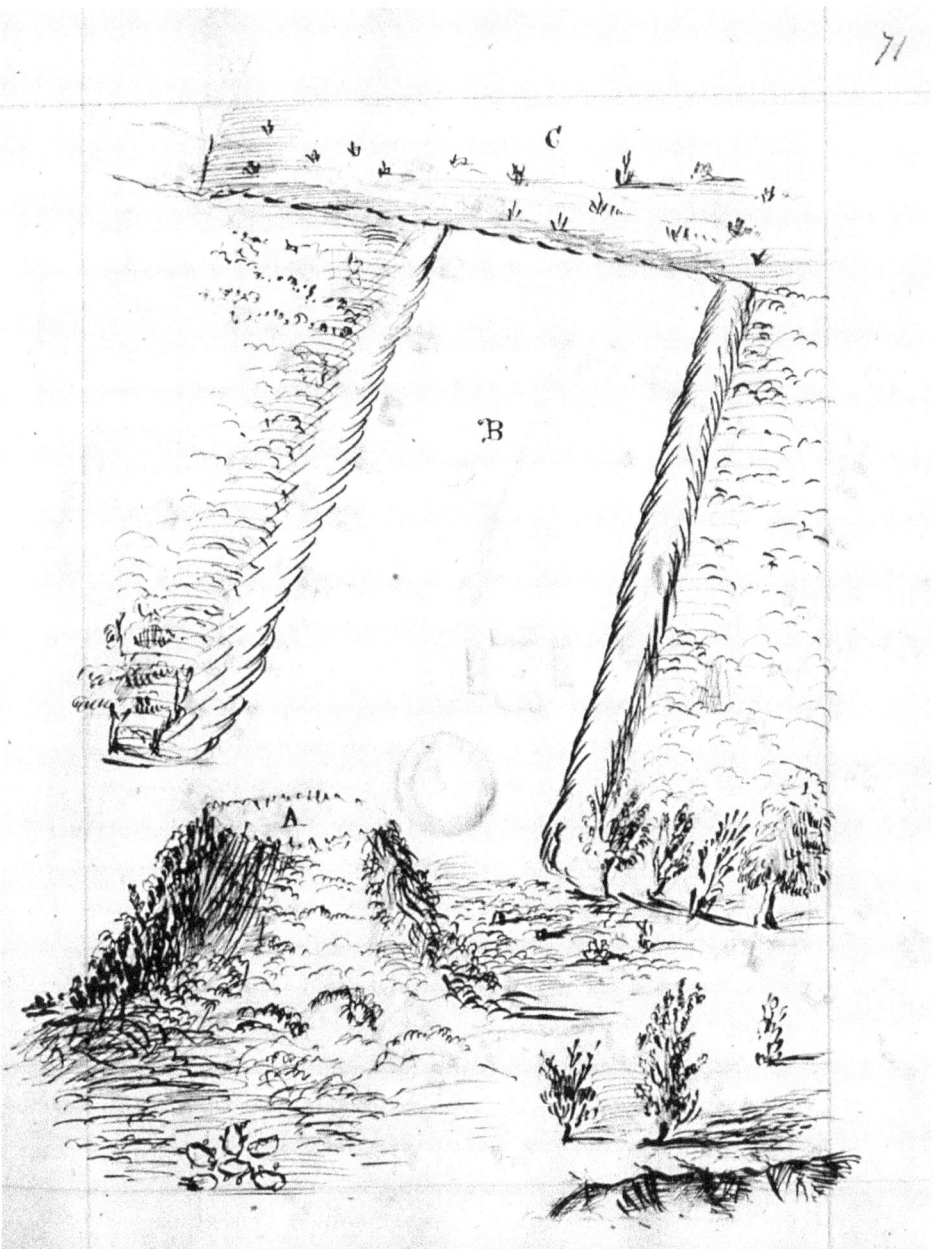

Mount Royal Site. Engraving by E. G. Squier based on William Bartram's sketch in his 1789 *Observations on the Creek and Cherokee Indians* (Historical Society of Pennsylvania). In his "Observations," Bartram describes "pyramidal mounts" with a "Great Highway or Avenue sunk below the common level of the ground, and terminating either in a vast Savana or Natural Plain, or Artificial Pond or Lake, and sometimes both together, as of that Remarkable One of [Mount] *Royal*, from whence opens a glorious view of *Lake George* and its invirons" (Waselkov and Braund 168).

still flattered and entertained by the far distant misty points of the surrounding forests, which project into the plain, alternately appearing and disappearing, making a grand sweep round on the right, to the distant banks of the great lake. But that venerable grove is now no more. All has been cleared away and planted with Indigo, Corn and Cotton, but since deserted: there was now scarcely five acres of ground under fence. It appeared like a desart, to a great extent, and terminated, on the land side, by frightful thickets, and open Pine forests.

IT appears however, that the late proprietor had some taste, as he has preserved the mount, and this little adjoining grove inviolate. The prospect from this station is so happily situated by nature, as to comprise at one view, the whole of the sublime and pleasing.

AT the reanimating appearance of the rising sun, nature again revives; and I obey the chearful summons of the gentle monitors of the meads and groves.[21]

YE vigilant and faithful servants of the Most High! ye who worship the Creator, morning, noon and eve, in simplicity of heart; I haste to join the universal anthem. My heart and voice unite with yours, in sincere homage to the great Creator, the universal sovereign.

O MAY I be permitted to approach the throne of mercy! may these my humble and penitent supplications, amidst the universal shouts of homage, from thy creatures, meet with thy acceptance.

[101] AND although, I am sensible, that my service, cannot encrease, or diminish thy glory, yet it is pleasing to thy servant, to be permitted to sound thy praise; for O sovereign Lord! we know that thou alone art perfect, and worthy to be worshiped. O universal Father! look down upon us we beseech thee, with an eye of pity and compassion, and grant that universal peace and love, may prevail in the earth, even that divine harmony, which fills the heavens, thy glorious habitation.

AND O sovereign Lord! since it has pleased thee to endue man with power, and pre-eminence, here on earth, and establish his dominion over all creatures, may we look up to thee, that our understanding may be so illuminated with wisdom and our hearts warmed and animated, with a due sense of charity, that we may be enabled to do thy will, and perform our duty towards those submitted to our service, and protection, and be merciful to them even as we hope for mercy.

THUS may we be worthy of the dignity, and superiority of the high, and distinguished station, in which thou hast placed us here on earth.

THE morning being fair, and having a gentle favourable gale, we left our pleasant harbour, in pursuit of our desired port.

NOW as we approach the capes, behold the little ocean of Lake George, the distant circular coast gradually rising to view, from his misty fringed horizon. I cannot entirely suppress my apprehension of danger. My vessel at once diminished to a nut-shell, on the swelling seas, and at the distance of a few miles, must appear to the surprised [102] observer, as some aquatic animal, at intervals emerging from its surface. This lake is a large and beautiful piece of water; it is a dilatation of the river St. Juan, and is about fifteen miles wide, and generally about fifteen or twenty feet deep, excepting at the entrance of the river, where lies a bar, which carries eight or nine feet water. The lake is beautified with two or three fertile islands.[22] The first lies in the bay, as we ascend into the lake, near the West coast, about S. W. from Mount Royal, from whence it appears to form part of the West shore of the bay. The second island seems to ride on the lake before us as we enter, about a mile within it. This island is about two miles in breadth, and three quarters of a mile where broadest, mostly high land, well timbered, and fertile. The third and last, lies at the South end of the lake, and near the entrance of the river; it is nearly circular, and contains but a few acres of land, the earth high and fertile, and almost an entire Orange grove, with grand Magnolias and Palms.

SOON after entering the lake, the wind blew so briskly from the West, and thunder-clouds gathering upon the horizon, we were obliged to seek a shelter, from the approaching tempest, on the large beautiful island, before mentioned. Where, having gained the South promontory, we met with an excellent harbour, in which we continued the remaining part of the day and the night. This circumstance gave me an opportunity to explore the greatest part of it.

THIS island appears, from obvious vestiges, to have been once the chosen residence of an Indian prince, there being to this day, evident remains of [103] a large town of the Aborigines. It was situated on an eminence, near the banks of the lake, and commanded a comprehensive and charming prospect of the waters, islands, East and West shores of the lake, the capes, the bay and Mount Royal, and to the South the view is in a manner infinite, where the skies and waters seem to unite. On the site of this ancient town, stands a very pompous Indian mount, or conical pyramid of earth, from which runs in a strait line, a grand avenue or Indian highway, through a magnificent grove of Magnolias, Live Oaks, Palms and Orange trees, terminating at the verge of a large green level savanna. This island appears to have been well inhabited, as is very evident, from the quantities of fragments of Indian earthen-ware, bones of animals and other remains, particularly in the shelly heights and ridges, all over the island. There are no habitations at present on the island, but a great number of deer, turkeys, bears, wolves, wild cats, squirrels, racoons, and opossums. The bears are invited here to partake of the fruit of the Orange tree, which they are immoderately fond of, and both they and turkeys are made extremely fat and delicious, from their feeding on the sweet acorns of the Live Oak.

THERE grows on this island, many curious shrubs, particularly a beautiful species of Lantana (perhaps Lant. camerara. Lin. Syst. Veget. p. 473.) It grows in coppices in old fields, about five or six feet high, the branches adorned with rough serrated leaves, which sit opposite, and the twigs terminate with umbelliferous tufts of orange coloured blossoms, which are succeeded by a cluster of small blue berries: the flowers are of various colours, on the same plant, and even in the same cluster. As [104] crimson, scarlet, orange and golden yellow: the whole plant is of a most agreeable scent. The orange flowered shrub Hibiscus is also conspicuously beautiful (perhaps Hibisc. spinifex of Linn.) it grows five or six feet high, and subramous. The branches are divergent, and furnished with cordated leaves, which are crenated. The flowers are of a moderate size, and of a deep splendid yellow. The pericarpii are spiny. I also saw a new and beautiful palmated leaved convolvulus.[23] This Vine rambles over the shrubs, and strolls about on the ground, its leaves are elegantly sinuated, of a deep grass green, and sit on long petioles. The flowers are very large, infundibuliform, of a pale incarnate colour, having a deep crimson eye.

THERE are some rich swamps on the shores of the island, and these are verged on the outside with large marshes, covered entirely with tall grass, rushes, and herbacious plants: amongst these are several species of Hibiscus, particularly the Hibiscus coccineus. This most stately of all herbacious plants, grows ten or twelve feet high, branching regularly, so as to form a sharp cone. These branches also divide again, and are embellished with large expanded crimson flowers: I have seen this plant of the size and figure of a beautiful little tree, having at once several hundred of these splendid flowers, and which may be then seen at a great distance. They continue to flower in succession all summer and autumn, when the stems wither and decay; but the perennial root sends forth new stems the next spring, and so on for many years. Its leaves are large, deeply and elegantly sinuated, having six or seven very narrow dentated seg[105]ments; the surface of the leaves, and of the whole plant, are smooth and polished. Another species of Hibiscus, worthy of particular notice, is likewise a tall flourishing plant; several strong stems arise from a root, five, six, and seven feet high, embellished with ovate lanceolate leaves, covered with a fine down on their nether surfaces: the flowers are very large, and of a deep incarnate colour.

THE last we shall now mention seems nearly allied to the Alcea; the flowers are a size less than the Hibiscus, and of a fine damask rose colour, and are produced in great profusion on the tall pyramidal stems.

THE Lobelia cardinalis grows in great plenty here, and has a most splendid appearance amidst extensive meadows of the golden Corymbous Jacobea (Senecio Jacobea) and odorous Pancratium.

HAVING finished my tour, on this princely island, I prepared for repose. A calm evening had succeeded the stormy day. The late tumultuous winds had now ceased, the face of the lake had become placid, and the skies serene; the balmy winds breathed the animating odours of the groves around me; and as I reclined on the elevated banks of the lake, at the foot of a Live Oak, I enjoyed the prospect of its wide waters, its fringed coasts, and of the distant horizon.

THE squadrons of aquatic fowls, emerging out of the water, and hastening to their leafy coverts on shore, closed the varied scenes of the past day. I was lulled asleep by the mixed sounds of the wearied [106] surf, lapsing on the hard beaten shore, and the tender warblings of the painted nonpareil and other winged inhabitants of the groves.

AT the approach of day, the dreaded voice of the alligators shook the isle, and resounded along the neighbouring coasts, proclaiming the appearance of the glorious sun. I arose, and prepared to accomplish my daily task. A gentle favourable gale led us out of the harbour: we sailed across the lake, and, towards evening, entered the river, on the opposite South coast, where we made a pleasant and safe harbour, at a shelly promontory, the East cape of the river on that side of the lake. It is a most desirable situation, commanding a full view of the lake. The cape opposite to us was a vast cypress swamp, environed by a border of grassy marshes, which were projected farther into the lake, by floating fields of the bright green Pistia stratoites, which rose and fell alternately with the waters. Just to leeward of this point, and about half a mile in the lake, is the little round island already mentioned. But let us take notice of our harbour and its environs: it is a beautiful little cove, just within the sandy point, which defends it from the beating surf of the lake. From a shelly bank, ten or twelve feet perpendicular from the water, we entered a grove of Live Oaks, Palm, Magnolia, and Orange trees, which grow amongst shelly hills, and low ridges, occupying about three acres of ground, comprehending the isthmus, and a part of the peninsula, which joins it to the grassy plains. This enchanting little forest is partly encircled by a deep creek, a branch of the river, that has its source in the high forests of the main, South East from us, and winds through the extensive grassy plains which [107] surround this peninsula, to an almost infinite distance, and then unites its waters with those of the river, in this little bay which formed our harbour. This bay, about the mouth of the creek, is almost covered with the leaves of the Nymphaea nilumbo: its large sweet-scented yellow flowers are listed up two or three feet above the surface of the water, each upon a green standard, representing the cap of Liberty.

THE evening drawing on, and there being no convenient landing place, for several miles higher up the river, we concluded to remain here all night. Whilst my fellow travellers were employing themselves in collecting fire-wood, and fixing our camp, I improved the opportunity, in reconnoitering our ground; and taking my fusee with me, I penetrated the grove, and afterwards entered some almost unlimited savannas and plains, which were absolutely enchanting; they had been lately burnt by the Indian hunters, and had just now recovered their vernal verdure and gaiety.

HOW happily situated is this retired spot of earth! What an elisium it is! where the wandering Siminole, the naked red warrior, roams at large, and after the vigorous chase retires from the scorching heat of the meridian sun. Here he reclines, and reposes under the odoriferous shades of Zanthoxilon, his verdant couch guarded by the Deity; Liberty, and the Muses, inspiring him with wisdom and valour, whilst the balmy zephyrs fan him to sleep.

SEDUCED by these sublime enchanting scenes of primitive nature, and these visions of terrestrial happiness, I had roved far away from Cedar Point, [108] but awakening to my cares, I turned about, and in the evening regained our camp.

ON my return, I found some of my companions fishing for trout, round about the edges of the floating nymphaea, and not unsuccessfully, having then caught more than sufficient for us all. As the method of taking these fish is curious and singular, I shall just mention it.

THEY are taken with a hook and line, but without any bait. Two people are in a little canoe, one sitting in the stern to steer, and the other near the bow, having a rod ten or twelve feet in length, to one end of which is tied a strong line, about twenty inches in length, to which is fastened three large hooks, back to back. These are fixed very securely, and covered with the white hair of a deer's tail, shreds of a red garter, and some particoloured feathers, all which form a tuft, or tassel, nearly as large as one's fist, and entirely cover and conceal the hooks: this is called a bob. The steersman paddles softly, and proceeds slowly along shore, keeping the boat parallel to it, at a distance just sufficient to admit the fisherman to reach the edge of the floating weeds along shore: he now ingeniously swings the bob backwards and forwards, just above the surface, and sometimes tips the water with it; when the unfortunate cheated trout instantly springs from under the weeds, and seizes the supposed prey. Thus he is caught without a possibility of escape, unless he break the hooks, line, or rod, which he, however, sometime does by dint of strength; but, to prevent this, the fisherman used to the sport is careful not to raise the reed suddenly up, but jerks it instantly backwards, then steadily drags the sturdy reluctant fish to the side of the [109] canoe, and with a sudden upright jerk brings him into it.

THE head of this fish makes about one third of his length, and consequently the mouth is very large: birds, fish, frogs, and even serpents, are frequently found in its stomach.

THE trout is of lead colour, inclining to a deep blue, and marked with transverse waved lists, of a deep slate colour, and when fully grown, has a cast of red, or brick colour. The fins, with the tail, which is large, and beautifully formed, are of a light reddish purple, or flesh colour, the whole body is covered with large scales. But what is most singular, this fish is remarkably ravenous; nothing living, that he can seize upon, escapes his jaws, and the opening and extending of the branchiostega, at the moment he rises to the surface to seize his prey, discovering his bright red gills, through the transparent waters, give him a very terible appearance. Indeed it may be observed, that all fish of prey have this opening and covering of the gills very large, in order to discharge the great quantity of water, which they take in at their mouth, when they strike at their prey. This fish is nearly cuniform, the body tapering gradually from the breast to the tail, and lightly compressed on each side. They frequently weigh fifteen, twenty and thirty pounds, and are delicious food.

MY companion, the trader, being desirous of crossing the river to the opposite shore, in hopes of getting a turkey, I chose to accompany him, as it offered a good opportunity to observe the natural productions of those rich swamps and islands of the river. Having crossed the river, which is here [110] five or six hundred yards wide, we entered a narrow channel, which after a serpentine course, for some miles, rejoins the main river again, above; forming a large fertile island, of rich low land. We landed on this island, and soon saw a fine roebuck,[24] at some distance from us, who appeared leader of a company of deer, that were feeding near him, on the verge of a green meadow. My companion parting from me, in pursuit of the deer, one way, and I, observing a flock of turkeys at some distance, on the other, directed my steps towards them, and with great caution, got near them; when singling out a large cock, and being just on the point of firing, I observed that several young cocks were affrighted, and in their language, warned the rest to be on their guard, against an enemy, whom I plainly perceived was industriously making his subtile approaches towards them, behind the fallen trunk of a tree, about twenty yards from me. This cunning fellow hunter, was a large fat wild cat (lynx) he saw me, and at times seemed to watch my motions, as if determined to seize the delicious prey before me. Upon which I changed my object, and levelled my piece at him. At that instant, my companion, at a distance, also discharged his piece at the deer, the report of which alarmed the flock of turkeys, and my fellow hunter, the cat, sprang over the log and trotted off. The trader also missed his deer: thus we foiled each other. By this time it being near night, we returned to camp, where having a delicious meal, ready prepared for our hungry stomachs, we sat down in a circle round our wholesome repast.

HOW supremely blessed were our hours at this [111] time! plenty of delicious and healthful food, our stomachs keen, with contented minds; under no controul, but what reason and ordinate passions dictated, far removed from the seats of strife.

OUR situation was like that of the primitive state of man, peaceable, contented, and sociable. The simple and necessary calls of nature, being satisfied. We were altogether as brethren of one family, strangers to envy, malice and rapine.

THE night being over we arose, and pursued our course up the river, and in the evening reached the trading-house, Spalding's upper store, where I took up my quarters for several weeks.[25]

ON our arrival at the upper store, we found it occupied by a white trader, who had for a companion, a very handsome Siminole young woman. Her father, who was a prince, by the name of the White Captain, was an old chief of the Siminoles, and with part of his family, to the number of ten or twelve, were encamped in an Orange grove near the stores, having lately come in from a hunt.

THIS white trader, soon after our arrival, delivered up the goods and storehouses to my companion, and joined his father-in-law's camp, and soon after went away into the forests on hunting and trading amongst the flying camps of Siminoles.

HE is at this time, unhappy in his connections with his beautiful savage. It is but a few years since he came here, I think from North Carolina, a stout genteel well-bred man, active, and of a heroic and amiable disposition and by his industry, honesty, and engaging manners, had gained the affections of the Indians, and soon made a little for[112]tune by traffic with the Siminoles: when, unfortunately, meeting with this little charmer, they were married in the Indian manner. He loves her sincerely, as she possesses every perfection in her person to render a man happy. Her features are beautiful, and manners engaging. Innocence, modesty, and love, appear to a stranger in every action and movement; and these powerful graces she has so artfully played upon her beguiled and vanquished lover, and unhappy slave, as to have already drained him of all his possessions, which she dishonestly distributes amongst her savage relations. He is now poor, emaciated, and half distracted, often threatening to shoot her, and afterwards put an end to his own life; yet he has not resolution even to leave her; but now endeavours to drown and forget his sorrows, in deep draughts of brandy. Her father condemns her dishonest and cruel conduct.

THESE particulars were related to me by my old friend the trader, directly after a long conference which he had with the White Captain on the subject, his son in law being present. The scene was affecting; they both shed tears plentifully. My reasons for mentioning this affair, so foreign to my business, was to exhibit an instance of the power of beauty in a savage, and their art and finesse in improving it to their private ends. It is, however, but doing justice to the virtue and moral conduct of the Siminoles, and American Aborigines in general, to observe, that the character of this woman is condemned and detested by her own people, of both sexes; and if her husband should turn her away; according to the customs and usages of these people, she would not get a husband again, as a divorce seldom takes place but in consequence of a [113] deliberate impartial trial, and public condemnation, and then she would be looked upon as a harlot.

SUCH is the virtue of these untutored savages: but I am afraid this is a common phrase epithet, having no meaning, or at least improperly applied; for these people are both well tutored and civil; and it is apparent to an impartial observer, who resides but a little time amongst them, that it is from the most delicate sense of the honour and reputation of their tribes and families, that their laws and customs receive their force and energy. This is the divine principle which influences their moral conduct, and solely preserves their constitution and civil government in that purity in which they are found to prevail amongst them.

## [114] CHAP. V.

BEING desirous of continuing my travels and observations, higher up the river, and having an invitation from a gentleman who was agent for, and resident at a large plantation, the property of an English gentleman, about sixty miles higher up, I resolved to pursue my researches to that place; and having engaged in my service a young Indian, nephew to the White Captain, he agreed to assist me in working my vessel up as high as a certain bluff, where I was, by agreement, to land him, on the west or Indian shore, whence he designed to go in quest of the camp of the White Trader, his relation.[26]

PROVISIONS and all necessaries being procured, and the morning pleasant, we went on board and stood up the river. We passed for several miles on the left, by islands of high swamp land, exceedingly fertile, their banks for a good distance from the water, much higher than the interior part, and sufficiently so to build upon, and be out of the reach of inundations. They consist of a loose black mould, with a mixture of sand, shells and dissolved vegetables. The opposite Indian coast is a perpendicular bluff, ten or twelve feet high, consisting of a black sandy earth, mixed with a large proportion of shells, chiefly various species of fresh water Cochlea and Mytuli. Near the river, on this high shore, grew Corypha palma, Magnolia grandiflora, Live Oak, Callicarpa, Myrica cerifera, Hybiscus spinifex, and the beautiful evergreen shrub called Wild lime or Tallow nut. This last shrub grows six or eight feet high, many erect stems rising from a root; [115] the leaves are lanciolate and intire, two or three inches in length and one in breadth, of a deep green colour, and polished; at the foot of each leaf grows a stiff, sharp thorn; the flowers are small and in clusters, of a greenish yellow colour, and sweet scented; they are succeeded by a large oval fruit, of the shape and size of an ordinary plumb, of a fine yellow colour when ripe, a soft sweet pulp covers a nut which has a thin shell, enclosing a white kernel somewhat of the consistence and taste of the sweet Almond, but more oily and very much like hard tallow, which induced my father when he first observed it, to call it the Tallow nut.

AT the upper end of this bluff is a fine Orange grove. Here my Indian companion requested me set him on shore, being already tired of rowing under a fervid sun, and having for some time intimated a dislike to his situation, I readily complied with his desire, knowing the impossibility of compelling an Indian against his own inclinations, or even prevailing upon him by reasonable arguments, when labour is in the question; before my vessel reached the shore, he sprang out of her and landed, when uttering a shrill and terrible whoop, he bounded off like a roebuck, and I lost sight of him. I at first apprehended that as he took his gun with him, he intended to hunt for some game and return to me in the evening. The day being excessively hot and sultry, I concluded to take up my quarters here until next morning.

THE Indian not returning this morning, I sat sail alone. The coasts on each side had much the same appearance as already described. The Palm trees here seem to be of a different species from the Cabbage tree; their strait trunks are sixty, eighty or nine[116]ty feet high, with a beautiful taper of a bright ash colour, until within six or seven feet of the top, where it is a fine green colour, crowned with an orb of rich green plumed leaves: I have measured the stem of these plumes fifteen feet in length, besides the plume, which is nearly of the same length.

THE little lake, which is an expansion of the river, now appeared in view; on the East side are extensive marshes, and on the other high forests and Orange groves, and then a bay, lined with vast Cypress swamps, both coasts gradually approaching each other, to the opening of the river again, which is in this place about three hundred yards wide; evening now drawing on, I was anxious to reach some high bank of the river, where I intended to lodge, and agreeably to my wishes, I soon after discovered on the West shore, a little promontory, at the turning of the river, contracting it here to about one hundred and fifty yards in width.[27] This promontory is a peninsula, containing about three acres of high ground, and is one entire Orange grove, with a few Live Oaks, Magnolias and Palms. Upon doubling the point, I arrived at the landing, which is a circular harbour, at the foot of the bluff, the top of which is about twelve feet high; and back of it is a large Cypress swamp, that spreads each way, the right wing forming the West coast of the little lake, and the left stretching up the river many miles, and encompassing a vast space of low grassy marshes. From this promontory, looking Eastward across the river, we behold a landscape of low country, unparalleled as I think; on the left is the East coast of the little lake, which I had just passed, and from the Orange bluff at the lower end, the high forests begin, and increase in breadth from the shore of the lake, mak[117]ing a circular sweep to the right, and contain many hundred thousand acres of meadow, and this grand sweep of high forests encircles, as I apprehend, at least twenty miles of these green fields, interspersed with hommocks or islets of evergreen trees, where the sovereign Magnolia and lordly Palm stand conspicuous. The islets are high shelly knolls, on the sides of creeks or branches of the river, which wind about and drain off the super-abundant waters that cover these meadows, during the winter season.

THE evening was temperately cool and calm. The crocodiles began to roar and appear in uncommon numbers along the shores and in the river. I fixed my camp in an open plain, near the utmost projection of the promontory, under the shelter of a large Live Oak, which stood on the highest part of the ground and but a few yards from my boat. From this open, high situation, I had a free prospect of the river, which was a matter of no trivial consideration to me, having good reason to dread the subtle attacks of the allegators, who were crouding about my harbour. Having collected a good quantity of wood for the purpose of keeping up a light and smoke during the night, I began to think of preparing my supper, when, upon examining my stores, I found but a scanty provision, I thereupon determined, as the most expeditious way of supplying my necessities, to take my bob and try for some trout. About one hundred yards above my harbour, began a cove or bay of the river, out of which opened a large lagoon. The mouth or entrance from the river to it was narrow, but the waters soon after spread and formed a little lake, extending into the marshes, its entrance and shores with[118]in I observed to be verged with floating lawns of the Pistia and Nymphea and other aquatic plants; these I knew were excellent haunts for trout.

THE verges and islets of the lagoon were elegantly embellished with flowering plants and shrubs; the laughing coots with wings half spread were tripping over the little coves and hiding themselves in the tufts of grass; young broods of the painted summer teal, skimming the still surface of the waters, and following the watchful parent unconscious of danger, were frequently surprised by the voracious trout, and he in turn, as often by the subtle, greedy alligator. Behold him rushing forth from the flags and reeds. His enormous body swells. His plaited tail brandished high, floats upon the lake. The waters like a cataract descend from his opening jaws. Clouds of smoke issue from his dilated nostrils. The earth trembles with his thunder. When immediately from the opposite coast of the lagoon, emerges from the deep his rival champion. They suddenly dart upon each other. The boiling surface of the lake marks their rapid course, and a terrific conflict commences. They now sink to the bottom folded together in horrid wreaths. The water becomes thick and discoloured. Again they rise, their jaws clap together, re-echoing through the deep surrounding forests. Again they sink, when the contest ends at the muddy bottom of the lake, and the vanquished makes a hazardous escape, hiding himself in the muddy turbulent waters and sedge on a distant shore. The proud victor exulting returns to the place of action. The shores and forests resound his dreadful roar, together with the triumphing shouts of the plaited tribes around, witnesses of the horrid combat.

[119] MY apprehensions were highly alarmed after being a spectator of so dreadful a battle; it was obvious that every delay would but tend to encrease my dangers and difficulties, as the sun was near setting, and the alligators gathered around my harbour from all quarters; from these considerations I concluded to be expeditious in my trip to the lagoon, in order to take some fish. Not thinking it prudent to take my fusee with me, lest I might lose it overboard in

William Bartram, "Alegator of St. Johns," drawing sent to John Fothergill in 1775. Drawing 1 "Represents the actions of this terrible monster when they bellow in the Spring Season, they force the water out of their throat which falls from their mouth like a Cataract & a steam or vapour from their Nostrals like smoke." Drawing 2 "Represents them rising out of the water when they devour the fish &c." By permission of the Natural History Museum, London.

case of a battle, which I had every reason to dread before my return, I therefore furnished myself with a club for my defence, went on board, and penetrating the first line of those which surrounded my harbour, they gave way; but being pursued by several very large ones, I kept strictly on the watch, and paddled with all my might towards the entrance of the lagoon, hoping to be sheltered there from the multitude of my assailants; but ere I had half-way reached the place, I was attacked on all sides, several endeavouring to overset the canoe. My situation now became precarious to the last degree: two very large ones attacked me closely, at the same instant, rushing up with their heads and part of their bodies above the water, roaring terribly and belching floods of water over me. They struck their jaws together so close to my ears, as almost to stun me, and I expected every moment to be dragged out of the boat and instantly devoured, but I applied my weapons so effectually about me, though at random, that I was so successful as to beat them off a little; when, finding that they designed to renew the battle, I made for the shore, as the only means left me for my preservation, for, by keeping close to it, I should have my enemies on one side of me only, whereas I was before surrounded by them, and there was a probability, if pushed [120] to the last extremity, of saving myself, by jumping out of the canoe on shore, as it is easy to outwalk them on land, although comparatively as swift as lightning in the water. I found this last expedient alone could fully answer my expectations, for as soon as I gained the shore they drew off and kept aloof. This was a happy relief, as my confidence was, in some degree, recovered by it. On recollecting myself, I discovered that I had almost reached the entrance of the lagoon, and determined to venture in, if possible to take a few fish and then return to my harbour, while day-light continued; for I could now, with caution and resolution, make my way with safety along shore, and indeed there was no other way to regain my camp, without leaving my boat and making my retreat through the marshes and reeds, which, if I could even effect, would have been in a manner throwing myself away, for then there would have been no hopes of ever recovering my bark, and returning in safety to any settlements of men. I accordingly proceeded and made good my entrance into the lagoon, though not without opposition from the alligators, who formed a line across the entrance, but did not pursue me into it, nor was I molested by any there, though there were some very large ones in a cove at the upper end. I soon caught more trout than I had present occasion for, and the air was too hot and sultry to admit of their being kept for many hours, even though salted or barbecued. I now prepared for my return to camp, which I succeeded in with but little trouble, by keeping close to the shore, yet I was opposed upon re-entering the river out of the lagoon, and pursued near to my landing (though not closely attacked) particularly by an old daring one, about twelve feet in length, [121] who kept close after me, and when I stepped on shore and turned about, in order to draw up my canoe, he rushed up near my feet and lay there for some time, looking me in the face, his head and shoulders out of water; I resolved he should pay for his temerity, and having a heavy load in my fusee, I ran to my camp, and returning with my piece, found him with his foot on the gunwale of the boat, in search of fish, on my coming up he withdrew sullenly and slowly into the water, but soon returned and placed himself in his former position, looking at me and seeming neither fearful or any way disturbed. I soon dispatched him by lodging the contents of my gun in his head, and then proceeded to cleanse and prepare my fish for supper, and accordingly took them out of the boat, laid them down on the sand close to the water, and began to scale them, when, raising my head, I saw before me, through the clear water, the head and shoulders of a very large alligator, moving slowly towards me; I instantly stepped back, when, with a sweep of his tail, he brushed off several of my fish. It was certainly most providential that I looked up at that instant, as the monster would probably, in less than a minute, have seized and dragged me into the river. This incredible boldness of the animal disturbed me greatly, supposing there could now be no reasonable safety for me during the night, but by keeping continually on the watch; I therefore, as soon as I had prepared the fish, proceeded to secure myself and effects in the best manner I could: in the first place, I hauled my bark upon the shore, almost clear out of the water, to prevent their oversetting or sinking her, after this every moveable was taken out and carried to my camp, [122] which was but a few yards off; then ranging some dry wood in such order as was the most convenient, cleared the ground round about it, that there might be no impediment in my way, in case of an attack in the night, either from the water or the land; for I discovered by this time, that this small isthmus, from its remote situation and fruitfulness, was resorted to by bears and wolves. Having prepared myself in the best manner I could, I charged my gun and proceeded to reconnoitre my camp and the adjacent grounds; when I discovered that the peninsula and grove, at the distance of about two hundred yards from my encampment, on the land side, were invested by a Cypress swamp, covered with water, which below was joined to the shore of the little lake, and above to the marshes surrounding the lagoon, so that I was confined to an islet exceedingly circumscribed, and I found there was no other retreat for me, in case of an attack, but by either ascending one of the large Oaks, or pushing off with my boat.

IT was by this time dusk; and the alligators had nearly ceased their roar, when I was again alarmed by a tumultuous noise that seemed to be in my harbour, and therefore engaged my immediate attention. Returning to my camp I found it undisturbed, and then continued on to the extreme point of the promontory, where I saw a scene, new and surprising, which at first threw my senses into such a tumult, that it was some time before I could comprehend what was the matter; however, I soon accounted for the prodigious assemblage of crocodiles at this place, which exceeded every thing of the kind I had ever heard of.

HOW shall I express myself so as to convey an [123] adequate idea of it to the reader, and at the same time avoid raising suspicions of my want of veracity. Should I say, that the river (in this place) from shore to shore, and perhaps near half a mile above and below me, appeared to be one solid bank of fish, of various kinds, pushing through this narrow pass of St. Juans into the little lake, on their return down the river, and that the alligators were in such incredible numbers, and so close together from shore to shore, that it would have been easy to have walked across on their heads, had the animals been harmless. What expressions can sufficiently declare the shocking scene that for some minutes continued, whilst this mighty army of fish were forcing the pass? During this attempt, thousands, I may say hundreds of thousands of them were caught and swallowed by the devouring alligators. I have seen an alligator take up out of the water several great fish at a time, and just squeeze them betwixt his jaws, while the tails of the great trout flapped about his eyes and lips, ere he had swallowed them. The horrid noise of their closing jaws, their plunging amidst the broken banks of fish, and rising with their prey some feet upright above the water, the floods of water and blood rushing out of their mouths, and the clouds of vapour issuing from their wide nostrils, were truly frightful. This scene continued at intervals during the night, as the fish came to the pass. After this sight, shocking and tremendous as it was, I found myself somewhat easier and more reconciled to my situation, being convinced that their extraordinary assemblage here, was owing to this annual feast of fish, and that they were so well employed in their own element, that I had little occasion to fear their paying me a visit.

[124] IT being now almost night, I returned to my camp, where I had left my fish broiling, and my kettle of rice stewing, and having with me, oil, pepper and salt, and excellent oranges hanging in abundance over my head (a valuable substitute for vinegar) I sat down and regaled myself chearfully; having finished my repast, I re-kindled my fire for light, and whilst I was revising the notes of my past day's journey, I was suddenly roused with a noise behind me toward the main land; I sprang up on my feet, and listning, I distinctly heard some creature wading in the water of the isthmus; I seized my gun and went cautiously from my camp, directing my steps towards the noise; when I had advanced about thirty yards, I halted behind a coppice of Orange trees, and soon perceived two very large bears, which had made their way through the water, and had landed in the grove, about one hundred yards distance from me, and were advancing towards me. I waited until they were within thirty yards of me, they there began to snuff and look towards my camp, I snapped my piece, but it flashed, on which they both turned about and galloped off, plunging through the water and swamp, never halting as I suppose, until they reached fast land, as I could hear them leaping and plunging a long time; they did not presume to return again, nor was I molested by any other creature, except being occasion-

ally awakened by the whooping of owls, screaming of bitterns, or the wood-rats running amongst the leaves.

THE wood-rat is a very curious animal, they are not half the size of the domestic rat; of a dark brown or black colour; their tail slender and shorter in proportion, and covered thinly with short hair; they are [125] singular with respect to their ingenuity and great labour in the construction of their habitations, which are conical pyramids about three or four feet high, constructed with dry branches, which they collect with great labour and perseverance, and pile up without any apparent order, yet they are so interwoven with one another, that it would take a bear or wild-cat some time to pull one of these castles to pieces, and allow the animals sufficient time to secure a retreat with their young.

THE noise of the crocodiles kept me awake the greater part of the night, but when I arose in the morning, contrary to my expectations, there was perfect peace; very few of them to be seen, and those were asleep on the shore, yet I was not able to suppress my fears and apprehensions of being attacked by them in future; and indeed yesterday's combat with them, notwithstanding I came off in a manner victorious, or at least made a safe retreat, had left sufficient impression on my mind to damp my courage, and it seemed too much for one of my strength, being alone in a very small boat to encounter such collected danger. To pursue my voyage up the river, and be obliged every evening to pass such dangerous defiles, appeared to me as perilous as running the gauntlet betwixt two rows of Indians armed with knives and fire brands; I however resolved to continue my voyage one day longer, if I possibly could with safety, and then return down the river, should I find the like difficulties to oppose. Accordingly I got every thing on board, charged my gun, and set sail cautiously along shore; as I passed by Battle lagoon, I began to tremble and keep a good look out, when suddenly a huge alligator rushed out of the reeds, and [126] with a tremendous roar, came up, and darted as swift as an arrow under my boat, emerging upright on my lea quarter, with open jaws, and belching water and smoke that fell upon me like rain in a hurricane; I laid soundly about his head with my club and beat him off, and after plunging and darting about my boat, he went off on a strait line through the water, seemingly with the rapidity of lightning, and entered the cape of the lagoon; I now employed my time to the very best advantage in paddling close along shore, but could not forbear looking now and then behind me, and presently perceived one of them coming up again; the water of the river hereabouts, was shoal and very clear, the monster came up with the usual roar and menaces, and passed close by the side of my boat, when I could distinctly see a young brood of alligators to the number of one hundred or more, following after her in a long train, they kept close together in a column without straggling off to the one side or the other, the young appeared to be of an equal size, about fifteen inches in length, almost black, with pale yellow transverse waved clouds or blotches, much like rattle snakes in colour. I now lost sight of my enemy again.

STILL keeping close along shore; on turning a point or projection of the river bank, at once I beheld a great number of hillocks or small pyramids, resembling hay cocks, ranged like an encampment along the banks, they stood fifteen or twenty yards distant from the water, on a high marsh, about four feet perpendicular above the water; I knew them to be the nests of the crocodile, having had a description of them before, and now expected a furious and general attack, as I saw several large cro[127]codiles swimming abreast of these buildings. These nests being so great a curiosity to me, I was determined at all events immediately to land and examine them. Accordingly I ran my bark on shore at one of their landing places, which was a sort of nick or little dock, from which ascended a sloping path or road up to the edge of the meadow, where their nests were, most of them were deserted, and the great thick whitish egg-shells lay broken and scattered upon the ground round about them.

THE nests or hillocks are of the form of an obtuse cone, four feet high and four or five feet in diameter at their bases; they are constructed with mud, grass and herbage: at first they lay a floor of this kind of tempered mortar on the ground, upon which they deposit a layer of eggs, and upon this a stratum of mortar seven or eight inches in thickness, and then another layer of eggs, and in this manner one stratum upon another, nearly to the top: I believe they commonly lay from one to two hundred eggs in a nest: these are hatched I suppose by the heat of the sun, and perhaps the vegetable substances mixed with the earth, being acted upon by the sun, may cause a small degree of fermentation, and so increase the heat in those hillocks. The ground for several acres about these nests shewed evident marks of a continual resort of alligators; the grass was every where beaten down, hardly a blade or straw was left standing; whereas, all about, at a distance, it was five or six feet high, and as thick as it could grow together. The female, as I imagine, carefully watches her own nest of eggs until they are all hatched, or perhaps while she is attending her own brood, she takes under her care and protection, as many as she can get at one time, ei[128]ther from her own particular nest or others: but certain it is, that the young are not left to shift for themselves, having had frequent opportunities of seeing the female alligator, leading about the shores her train of young ones, just like a hen does her brood of chickens, and she is equally assiduous and courageous in defending the young, which are under their care, and providing for their subsistence; and when she is basking upon the warm banks, with her brood around her, you may hear the young ones continually whining and barking, like young puppies. I believe but few of a brood live to the years of full growth and magnitude, as the old feed on the young as long as they can make prey of them.

THE alligator when full grown is a very large and terrible creature, and of prodigious strength, activity and swiftness in the water. I have seen them twenty feet in length, and some are supposed to be twenty-two or twenty-three feet; their body is as large as that of a horse; their shape exactly resembles that of a lizard, except their tail, which is flat or cuniform, being compressed on each side, and gradually diminishing from the abdomen to the extremity, which, with the whole body is covered with horny plates or squamae,[28] impenetrable when on the body of the live animal, even to a rifle ball, except about their head and just behind their fore-legs or arms, where it is said they are only vulnerable. The head of a full grown one is about three feet, and the mouth opens nearly the same length, the eyes are small in proportion and seem sunk deep in the head, by means of the prominency of the brows; the nostrils are large, inflated and prominent on the top, so that the head in the water, resembles, at a distance, a great [129] chunk of wood floating about. Only the upper jaw moves, which they raise almost perpendicular, so as to form a right angle with the lower one. In the fore part of the upper jaw, on each side, just under the nostrils, are two very large, thick, strong teeth or tusks, not very sharp, but rather the shape of a cone, these are as white as the finest polished ivory, and are not covered by any skin or lips, and always in sight, which gives the creature a frightful appearance; in the lower jaw are holes opposite to these teeth, to receive them; when they clap their jaws together it causes a surprising noise, like that which is made by forcing a heavy plank with violence upon the ground, and may be heard at a great distance.

BUT what is yet more surprising to a stranger, is the incredible loud and terrifying roar, which they are capable of making, especially in the spring season, their breeding time; it most resembles very heavy distant thunder, not only shaking the air and waters, but causing the earth to tremble; and when hundreds and thousands are roaring at the same time, you can scarcely be persuaded, but that the whole globe is violently and dangerously agitated.

AN old champion, who is perhaps absolute sovereign of a little lake or lagoon (when fifty less than himself are obliged to content themselves with swelling and roaring in little coves round about) darts forth from the reedy coverts all at once, on the surface of the waters, in a right line; at first seemingly as rapid as lightning, but gradually more slowly until he arrives at the center of the lake, when he stops; he now swells himself by drawing in wind and water through his mouth, which causes a loud [130] sonorous rattling in the throat for near a minute, but it is immediately forced out again through his mouth and nostrils, with a loud noise, brandishing his tail in the air, and the vapour ascending from his nostrils like smoke. At other times, when swollen to an extent ready to burst, his head and tail lifted up, he spins or twirls round on the surface of the water. He acts his part like an Indian chief when rehearsing his feats of war, and then retiring, the exhibition is continued by others who dare to step forth, and strive to excel each other, to gain the attention of the favourite female.

HAVING gratified my curiosity at this general breeding place and nursery of crocodiles, I continued my voyage up the river without being greatly disturbed by them: in my way I observed islets or floating fields of the bright green Pistia, decorated with other amphibious plants, as Senecio Jacobea, Persicaria amphibia, Coreopsis bidens, Hydrocotile fluitans, and many others of less note.

THE swamps on the banks and island of the river, are generally three or four feet above the surface of the water, and very level; the timber large and growing thinly, more so than what is observed to be in the swamps below Lake George; the black, rich earth is covered with moderately tall, and very succulent tender grass, which when chewed is sweet and agreeable to the taste, somewhat like young sugar-cane: it is a jointed decumbent grass, sending out radiculae at the joints into the earth, and so spreads itself, by creeping over its surface.

THE large timber trees, which possess the low lands, are Acer rubrum, Ac. nigundo, Ac. glaucum, Ulmus sylvatica, Fraxinus excelsior, Frax. aquatica, Ulmus [131] suberifer, Gleditsia monosperma, Gledit. triacanthus, Diospyros Virginica, Nyssa aquatica, Nyssa sylvatica, Juglans cinerea, Quercus dentata, Quercus phillos, Hopea tinctoria, Corypha palma, Morus rubra, and many more. The Palm grows on the edges of the banks, where they are raised higher than the adjacent level ground, by the accumulation of sand, river-shells, &c. I passed along several miles by those rich swamps, the channels of the river which encircle the several fertile islands, I had passed, now uniting, formed one deep channel near three hundred yards over. The banks of the river on each side, began to rise and present shelly bluffs, adorned by beautiful Orange groves, Laurels and Live Oaks. And now appeared in sight, a tree that claimed my whole attention: it was the Carica papaya, both male and female, which were in flower; and the latter both in flower and fruit, some of which were ripe, as large, and of the form of a pear, and of a most charming appearance.

THIS admirable tree, is certainly the most beautiful of any vegetable production I know of; the towering Laurel Magnolia, and exalted Palm, indeed exceed it in grandeur and magnificence, but not in elegance, delicacy and gracefulness; it rises erect, with a perfectly strait tapering stem, to the height of fifteen or twenty feet, which is smooth and polished, of a bright ash colour, resembling leaf silver, curiously inscribed with the footsteps of the fallen leaves, and these vestiges, are placed in a very regular uniform imbricated order, which has a fine effect, as if the little column were elegantly carved all over. Its perfectly spherical top, is formed of very large lobe-sinuate leaves, supported on very long footstalks; the lower leaves are the largest as well as their petioles the longest, and make [132] a graceful sweep or flourish, like the long S on the branches of a sconce candlestick. The ripe and green fruit are placed round about the stem or trunk, from the lowermost leaves, where the ripe fruit are, and upwards almost to the top; the heart or inmost pithy part of the trunk is in a manner hollow, or at best consists of very thin porous medullae or membranes; the tree very seldom branches or divides into limbs, I believe never unless the top is by accident broken off when very young: I saw one which had two tops or heads, the stem of which divided near the earth. It is always green, ornamented at the same time with flowers and fruit, which like figs come out singly from the trunk or stem.

AFTER resting and refreshing myself in these delightful shades, I left them with reluctance, embarking again after the fervid heats of the meridian sun were abated, for some time I passed by broken ridges of shelly high land, covered with groves of Live Oak, Palm, Olea Americana, and Orange trees; frequently observing floating islets and green fields of the Pistia near the shores of the river and lagoons.

HERE is in this river and in the waters all over Florida, a very curious and handsome bird, the people call them Snake Birds, I think I have seen paintings of them on the Chinese screens and other India pictures: they seem to be a species of cormorant or loon (Colymbus cauda elongata) but far more beautiful and delicately formed than any other species that I have ever seen. The head and neck of this bird are extremely small and slender, the latter very long indeed, almost out of all proportion, the bill long, strait and slender, ta[133]pering from its ball to a sharp point, all the upper side, the abdomen and thighs, are as black and glossy as a raven's, covered with feathers so firm and elastic, that they in some degree resemble fish-scales, the breast and upper part of the belly are covered with feathers of a cream colour, the tail is very long, of a deep black, and tipped with a silvery white, and when spread, represent an unfurled fan. They delight to sit in little peaceable communities, on the dry limbs of trees, hanging over the still waters, with their wings and tails expanded, I suppose to cool and air themselves, when at the same time they behold their images in the watery mirror: at such times, when we approach them, they drop off the limbs into the water as if dead, and for a minute or two are not to be seen; when on a sudden at a vast distance, their long slender head and neck only appear, and have very much the appearance of a snake, and no other part of them are to be seen when swimming in the water, except sometimes the tip end of their tail. In the heat of the day they are seen in great numbers, sailing very high in the air, over lakes and rivers.

I DOUBT not but if this bird had been an inhabitant of the Tiber in Ovid's days, it would have furnished him with a subject, for some beautiful and entertaining metamorphoses. I believe they feed intirely on fish, for their flesh smells and tastes intolerably strong of it, it is scarcely to be eaten unless constrained by insufferable hunger.

I HAD now swamps and marshes on both sides of me, and evening coming on apace, I began to look out for high land to encamp on, but the extensive marshes seemed to have no bounds; and it was almost dark when I found a tolerable suitable place, [134] and at last was constrained to take up on a narrow strip of high shelly bank, on the West side.[29] Great numbers of crocodiles were in sight on both shores: I ran my bark on shore at a perpendicular bank four or five feet above the water, just by the roots and under the spreading limbs of a great Live Oak: this appeared to have been an ancient camping place by Indians and strolling adventurers, from ash heaps and old rotten fire brands, and chunks, scattered about on the surface of the ground; but was now evidently the harbour and landing place of some sovereign alligator: there led up from it a deep beaten path or road, and was a convenient ascent.

I DID not approve of my intended habitation from these circumstances; and no sooner had I landed and moored my canoe to the roots of the tree, than I saw a huge crocodile rising up from the bottom close by me, who, when he perceived that I saw him, plunged down again under my vessel; this determined me to be on my guard, and in time to provide against a troublesome night: I took out of my boat every moveable, which I carried upon the bank, then chose my lodging close to my canoe, under the spreading Oak; as hereabouts only, the ground was open and clear of high grass and bushes, and consequently I had some room to stir and look round about. I then proceeded to collect firewood which I found difficult to procure. Here were standing a few Orange trees. As for provisions, I had saved one or two barbecued trout; the remains of my last evenings collection in tolerable good order, though the sultry heats of the day had injured them; yet by stewing them up afresh with the lively juice of Oranges, they served well enough for my supper: having by this time but little relish or appe[135]tite for my victuals; for constant watching at night against the attacks of alligators, stinging of musquitoes and sultry heats of the day; together, with the fatigues of working my bark, had almost deprived me of every desire but that of ending my troubles as speedy as possible. I had the good fortune to collect together a sufficiency of dry sticks, to keep up a light and smoke, which I laid by me, and then spread my skins and blankets upon the ground, kindled up a little fire and supped before it was quite dark. The evening was however, extremely pleasant, a brisk cool breeze sprang up, and the skies were perfectly serene, the stars twinkling with uncommon brilliancy. I stretched myself along before my fire; having the river, my little harbour and the stern of my vessel in view, and now through fatigue and weariness I fell asleep, but this happy temporary release from cares and troubles I enjoyed but a few moments, when I was awakened and greatly surprised, by the terrifying screams of Owls in the deep swamps around me, and what encreased my extreme misery was the difficulty of geting quite awake, and yet hearing at the same time such screaming and shouting, which increased and spread every way for miles around, in dreadful peals vibrating through the dark extensive forests, meadows and lakes, I could not after this surprise recover the former peaceable state and tranquility of mind and repose, during the long night, and I believe it was happy for me that I was awakened, for at that moment the crocodile was dashing my canoe against the roots of the tree, endeavouring to get into her for the fish, which I however prevented. Another time in the night I believe I narrowly escaped being dragged into the river by him, for when again through excessive fatigue I had fal[136]len asleep, but was again awakened by the screaming owl, I found the monster on the top of the bank, his head towards me not above two yards distant, when starting up and seizing my fuzee well loaded, which I always kept under my head in the night time, he drew back and plunged into the water. After this I roused up my fire, and kept a light during the remaining part of the night, being determined not to be caught napping so again, indeed the musquitoes alone would have been abundantly sufficient to keep any creature awake that possessed their perfect senses, but I was overcome, and stupified with incessant watching and labour: as soon as I discovered the first signs of day-light, I arose, got all my effects and implements on board and set sail, proceeding upwards, hoping to give the musquitoes the slip, who were now, by the cool morning dews and breezes, driven to their shelter and hiding places; I was mistaken however in these conjectures, for great numbers of them, which had concealed themselves in my boat, as soon as the sun arose, began to revive, and sting me on my legs, which obliged me to land in order to get bushes to beat them out of their quarters.

IT is very pleasing to observe the banks of the river ornamented with hanging garlands, composed of varieties of climbing vegetables, both shrubs and plants, forming perpendicular green walls, with projecting jambs, pilasters and deep apartments, twenty or thirty feet high and compleatly covered, with Glycine frutescens, Glyc. apios, Vitis labrusca, Vitis vulpina, Rajana, Hedera quinquifolia, Hedera arborea, Eupatorium scandens, Bignonia crucigera, and various species of Convolvulus, particularly an amazing tall climber of this [137] genus, or perhaps an Ipomea. This has a very large white flower, as big as a small funnel, its tube is five or six inches in length and not thicker than a pipe stem; the leaves are also very large, oblong and cordated, sometimes dentated or angled, near the insertion of the foot-stalk; they are of a thin texture, and of a deep green colour: it is exceedingly curious to behold the Wild Squash climbing over the lofty limbs of the trees; their yellow fruit somewhat of the size and figure of a large orange, pendant from the extremities of the limbs over the water.[30]

TOWARDS noon, the sultry heats being intolerable, I put into shore, at a middling high bank, five or six feet above the surface of the river; this low sandy testaceous ridge along the river side was but narrow, the surface is light, black and exceedingly fertile, producing very large venerable Live Oaks, Palms and grand Magnolias, scatteringly planted by nature: there being no underwood to prevent the play of the breezes from the river, afforded a desirable retreat from the sun's heat: immediately back of this narrow ridge, was deep wet swamps, where stood some astonishingly tall and spreading Cypress trees; and now being weary and drowsy, I was induced to indulge and listen to the dictates of reason and invitations to repose, which consenting to, after securing my boat and reconnoitring the ground, I spread my blanket under the Oaks near my boat, on which I extended myself, where, falling to sleep, I instantaneously passed away the sultry hours of noon, what a blissful tranquil repose! undisturbed I awoke, refreshed and strengthened; I chearfully stepped on board again and continued to ascend the river. The [138] afternoon being cool and pleasant, and the trees very lofty on the higher Western banks of the river, by keeping near that shore I passed under agreeable shades the remaining part of the day.

During almost all this day's voyage, the banks of the river on both shores were midling high, perpendicular, and washed by the brisk current; the shores were not lined with the green lawns of floating aquatics, and consequently not very commodious resorts or harbours for crocodiles, I therefore was not disturbed by them, and saw but few, but those were very large. I however did not like to lodge on those narrow ridges, invested by such dreary swamps, and evening approaching, I began to be anxious for high land for a camping place; it was quite dark before I came up to a bluff, which I had in view a long time, over a very extensive point of meadows. I landed however at last, in the best manner I could, at a magnificent forest of Orange groves, Oaks and Palms. I here, with little labour or difficulty, soon collected a sufficient quantity of dry wood: there was a pleasant vista of grass betwixt the grove and the edge of the river bank, which afforded a very convenient, open, airy camping place, under the protection of some spreading Oaks.[31]

THIS was a high perpendicular bluff, fronting more than one hundred yards on the river, the earth black, loose and fertile, it is a composition of river-shells, sand, &c. back of it from the river, were open Pine forests and savannas. I met with a circumstance here, that, with some, may be reckoned worthy of mentioning, since it regards the monuments of the ancients; as I have already observed, when I landed it was quite dark, and in collecting [139] wood for my fire, strolling in the dark about the groves, I found the surface of the ground very uneven, by means of little mounts and ridges; in the morning I found I had taken up my lodging on the border of an ancient burying ground; sepulchres or tumuli of the Yamasees, who were here slain by the Creeks in the last decisive battle, the Creeks having driven them into this point, between the doubling of the river, where few of them escaped the fury of the conquerors. These graves occupied the whole grove, consisting of two or three acres of ground; there were near thirty of these cemeteries of the dead, nearly of an equal size and form, they were oblong, twenty feet in length, ten or twelve feet in width and three or four feet high, now overgrown with Orange trees, Live Oaks, Laurel Magnolias, Red bays and other trees and shrubs, composing dark and solemn shades.

I HERE, for the first time since I left the trading house, enjoyed a night of peaceful repose; I arose, greatly refreshed and in good spirits, stepped on board my bark and continued my voyage. After doubling the point I passed by swamps and meadows on each side of me. The river here is something more contracted within perpendicular banks, the land of an excellent quality, fertile, and producing prodigiously large timber and luxuriant herbage.

THE air continued sultry and scarcely enough wind to flutter the leaves on the trees. The Eastern coast of the river now opens, and presents to view ample plains, consisting of grassy marshes and green meadows, and affords a prospect almost unlimited and extremely pleasing. The opposite shore presents to view a sublime contrast; a high bluff bearing magnificent forests of grand Magnolia, glori[140]ous Palms, fruitful Orange groves, Live Oaks, Bays and others.[32] This grand elevation continues four or five hundred yards, describing a gentle curve on the river, ornamented by a sublime grove of Palms, consisting of many hundreds of trees together; they intirely shade the ground under them. Above and below the bluff the grounds gradually descend to the common level swamps on the river: back of this eminence opens to view, expansive green meadows or savannas, in which are to be seen glittering ponds of water, surrounded at a great distance, by high open Pine forests and hommocks, and islets of Oaks and Bays projecting into the savannas. After ranging about these solitary groves and peaceful shades, I re-embarked and continued some miles up the river, between elevated banks of the swamps or low lands, when on the East shore in a capacious cove or winding of the river, were pleasing floating fields of Pistia, and in the bottom of this cove opened to view a large creek or branch of the river, which I knew to be the entrance to a beautiful lake, on the banks of which was the farm I was going to visit, and which I designed should be the last extent of my voyage up the river.

ABOUT noon the weather became extremely sultry, not a breath of wind stirring, hazy or cloudy, and very heavy distant thunder, which is answered by the crocodiles, sure presage of a storm![33]

SOON after ascending this branch of the river, on the right hand presents to view, a delightful little bluff, consisting chiefly of shells, and covered with a dark grove of Red Cedar, Zanthoxilon and Myrtle, I could not resist the temptation to stop here, although the tremendous thunder all around the [141] hemisphere alarmed me greatly, having a large lake to cross.[34] From this grove presents to view, an expansive and pleasing prospect. The beauteous long lake in front, about North East from me, its most distant East shores adorned with dark, high forests of stately trees; North and South almost endless green plains and meadows, embellished with islets and projecting promontories of high, dark forests, where the pyramidal Magnolia grandiflora, Palma elata and shady Oak conspicuously tower.

BEING heretofore so closely invested, by high forests and deep swamps of the great river, I was prevented from seeing the progress and increase of the approaching tempest, the terrific appearance of which now at once confounded me; how purple and fiery appeared the tumultuous clouds! swiftly ascending or darting from the horizon upwards; they seemed to oppose and dash against each other, the skies appeared streaked with blood or purple flame overhead, the flaming lightning streaming and darting about in every direction around, seems to fill the world with fire; whilst the heavy thunder keeps the earth in a constant tremor. I had yet some hopes of crossing the lake to the plantation in sight. On the opposite shore of the creek before me, and on the cape as we enter the lake, stood a large islet or grove of Oaks and Palms, here I intended to seek shelter and abide till the fury of the hurricane was overpast, if I found it too violent to permit me to cross the lake; in consequence of this precipitate determination I stepped into my boat and pushed off, what a dreadful rushing and roaring there is every where around me; and to my utter confusion and astonishment I could not find from what particular quarter its strongest current [142] or direction came, whereby I might have a proper chance of taking measures of securing a harbour or running from it. The high forests behind me bend to the blast, and the sturdy limbs of the trees crack; I had by this time got up a breast of the grove or hommock, the hurricane close by, pursuing me, I found it dangerous and imprudent in the highest degree to put in here, as the groves were already torn up, and the spreading limbs of the ancient Live Oaks were flying over my head, and carried about in the air as leaves and stubble; I ran by and boldly entered the lake, (being hurried in by a strong current, which seemed a prodigy, the violent wind driving the stream of the creek back again into the lake) and as soon as possible took shelter under the high reedy bank of the lake, made fast my bark to the boughs of a low shrubby Hickory, that leaned over the water: such was the violence of the wind, that it raised the waters on the opposite shores of the lake several feet perpendicular, and there was a rapid flow of water from the creek into it, which was contrary to its natural course; such floods of rain fell during the space of half or three quarters of an hour that my boat was filled, and I expected every moment, when I should see her sink to the bottom of the lake; and the violence of the wind kept the cable so constantly extended, that it was beyond my ability to get to her; my box which contained my books of specimens and other collections, was floating about in her; and for a great part of the time the rain came down with such rapidity and fell in such quantities, that every object was totally obscured, excepting the continual streams or rivers of lightning, pouring from the clouds; all seemed a frightful chaos. When the wind and rain abated, I was overjoyed to see the face of nature again appear.

[143] IT took me an hour or more to clear the water out of my bark. I then

crossed the lake before a brisk and favourable breeze (it was about a mile over) and landed safely at the plantation.[35]

WHEN I arrived my friend was affrighted to see me, and immediately enquired of me in what manner I came there, supposing it impossible (until I had shewed him my boat) that I could have arrived by water, through so tremendous a hurricane.

INDEED I saw plainly that they were greatly terrified, having suffered almost irreparable damages from the violence of the storm; all the buildings on the plantation except his own dwelling-house, were laid almost flat to the ground, or the logs and roof rent asunder and twisted about; the mansion-house shook and reeled over their heads. He had nearly one hundred acres of the Indigo plant almost ripe for the first cutting, which was nearly ruined, and several acres of very promising Sugar-cane, totally spoiled for the season. The great Live Oaks which had been left standing about the fields, were torn to pieces, their limbs lying scattered over the ground: and one very large one which stood near his house torn down, which could not have been done by the united strength of a thousand men. But what is incredible, in the midst of this devastation and ruin, providentially no lives were lost, although there were about sixty Negro slaves on the plantation, and most of them in their huts when the storm came on, yet they escaped with their lives, though several were badly wounded.

I CONTINUED here three days, indeed it took most of the time of my abode with him, to dry my books and specimens of plants. But with attention and [144] care I saved the greatest number of them; though some were naturally so delicate and fragile, that it was impossible to recover them. Here is a vast body of land belonging to this estate; of high ridges fit for the culture of Corn, Indigo, Cotton, Batatas, &c. and of low swamps and marshes, which when properly drained and tilled, would be suitable for Rice, these rich low grounds when drained and ridged, are as productive as the natural high land, and vastly more durable, especially for Sugar-cane, Corn and even Indigo; but this branch of agriculture being more expensive, these rich lands are neglected, and the upland only is under culture. The farm is situated on the East shore of the beautiful Long Lake, which is above two miles long, and near a mile broad, which communicates with the St. Juan, by the little river which I ascended; it is about one and an half mile in length, and thirty or forty yards wide; this river, as well as the lake, abounds with fish, and wild fowl of various kinds, and incredible numbers especially during the winter season, when the geese and ducks arrive here from the North.

NEW-SMYRNA,[36] a pretty thriving town, is a colony of Greeks and Minorquies, established by Mr. Turnbull, on the Musquito river and very near its [145] mouth, is about thirty miles over land from this farm.

MY friend rode with me, about four miles distance from the house, to shew me a vast fountain of warm or rather hot mineral water, which issued from a high ridge or bank on the river in a great cove or bay, a few miles above the mouth of the creek which I ascended to the lake; it boils up with great force, forming immediately a vast circular bason, capacious enough for several shallops to ride in, and runs with rapidity into the river three or four hundred yards distance.[37] This creek, which is formed instantly by this admirable fountain, is wide and deep enough for a sloop to sail up into the bason. The water is perfectly diaphanous, and here are continually a prodigious number and variety of fish; they appear as plain as though lying on a table before your eyes, although many feet deep in the water. This tepid water has a most disagreeable taste, brassy and vitriolic, and very offensive to the smell, much like bilge water or the washings of a gun-barrel, and is smelt at a great distance. A pale bluish or pearl coloured coagulum covers every inanimate substance that lies in the water, as logs, limbs of trees, &c. Alligators and gar were numerous in the bason, even at the apertures where the ebullition emerges through the rocks, as also many other tribes of fish. In the winter season several kinds of fish and aquatic animals migrate to these warm fountains. The forbiding taste and smell of these waters seem to be owing to vitriolic and sulphurious fumes or vapours, and these being condensed, form this coagulum, which represents flakes of pearly clouds in the clear cerulean waters in the bason. A charm[146]ing Orange grove, with Magnolias, Oaks and Palms; half surrounded this vast fountain. A delightful stream of cool salubrious water issues from the ridge, meandering along and enters the creek just below the bason. I returned in the evening, and next day sat off again down the river.

MY hospitable friend, after supplying me with necessaries, prevailed on me to accept of the company and assistance of his purveyor, one day's voyage down the river, whom I was to set on shore at a certain bluff, upwards of twenty miles below, but not above one third that distance by land; he was to be out in the forests one day, on a hunt for turkeys.

THE current of the river being here confined within its perpendicular banks, ran briskly down; we chearfully descended the grand river St. Juan, enjoying enchanting prospects.

BEFORE night we reached the destined port, at a spacious Orange grove. Next morning we separated, and I proceeded down the river. The prospects on either hand are now pleasing and I view them at leisure, and without toil or dread.

INDUCED by the beautiful appearance of the green meadows, which open to the Eastward, I determined not to pass this Elisium without a visit. Behold the loud, sonorous, watchful savanna crane (grus pratensis) with musical clangor, in detached squadrons. They spread their light elastic sail; at first they move from the earth heavy and slow, they labour and beat the dense air; they form the line with wide extended wings, tip to tip, they all rise and fall together as one bird; now they mount aloft, gradually wheeling about, each squadron performs its evolu[147]tion, incircling the expansive plains, observing each one their own orbit; then lowering sail, descend on the verge of some glittering lake; whilst other squadrons, ascending aloft in spiral circles, bound on interesting discoveries, wheel round and double the promontory, in the silvery regions of the clouded skies, where, far from the scope of eye, they carefully observe the verdant meadows on the borders of the East Lake; then contract their plumes and descend to the earth, where, resting awhile on some verdant eminence, near the flowery border of the lake, with dignified, yet slow, respectful steps, approach the kindred band; they confer and treat for habitation; the bounds and precincts being settled, they confederate and take possession.

THERE is inhabiting the low shores and swamps of this river and the lakes of Florida, as well as Georgia, a very curious bird, called by an Indian name (Ephouskyca) which signifies in our language the crying bird.[38] I cannot determine what genus of European birds to join it with. It is about the size of a large domestic hen; all the body, above and beneath, is of a dark lead colour, every feather edged or tipped with white, which makes the bird appear speckled on a near view; the eye is large and placed high on the head, which is very prominent; the bill or beak is five or six inches in length, arched or bent gradually downwards, in that respect to be compared to one half of a bent bow, it is large or thick near the base, compressed on each side, and flatted at top and beneath, which makes it appear four square for more than inch, where the nostrils are placed, from whence to their tips, both mandibles are round, gradually lessening or tapering to [148] their extremities, which are thicker for about half an inch than immediately above, by which the mandibles never fit quite close their whole length; the upper mandible is small matter longer than the under; the bill is of a dusky green colour, more bright and yellowish about the base and angles of the mouth; the tail is very short and the middle feather the longest, the others on each side shorten gradually, and are of the colour of the rest of the bird, only somewhat darker; the two shortest or outermost feathers are perfectly white, which the bird has a faculty of flirting[39] out on either side, as quick as a flash of lightning, especially when he hears or sees any thing that disturbs him, uttering at the same instant an extreme harsh and loud shriek; his neck is long and slender, and his legs are also long and bare of feathers above the knee, like those of the bittern, and are black or of a dark lead colour.

THERE are two other species of this genus, which agree in almost every particular, with the above description, except in size and colour: the first[40] of these I shall mention is a perfect white, except the prime quill feathers, which are as black as those of a crow; the bill and legs of a beautiful clear red, as also a space clear of feathers about the eyes. The other species[41] is black on the upper side, the breast and belly white, and the legs and beak as white as snow; both these species are about half the size of the crying bird. They fly in large flocks or squadrons, evening and morning to and from their feeding places or roosts; both species are called Spanish curlews: these and the crying bird feed chiefly on cray fish, [149] whose cells they probe, and with their strong pinching bills drag them out: all the three species are esteemed excellent food.

IT is a pleasing sight at times of high winds and heavy thunder storms, to observe the numerous squadrons of these Spanish curlews driving to and fro, turning and tacking about, high up in the air, when by their various evolutions in the different and opposite currents of the wind high in the clouds, their silvery white plumage gleams and sparkles like the brightest chrystal, reflecting the sun-beams that dart upon them between the dark clouds.

SINCE I have turned my observation upon the birds of this country, I shall notice another very singular one, which though already most curiously and exactly figured by Catesby, yet it seems to be nearly allied to those before mentioned, I mean the bird which he calls the wood pelican.[42] This is a large bird, perhaps near three feet high when standing erect. The bill is very long and strong, bending with a moderate curve, from the base to the tip, the upper mandible is the largest, and receives the edges of the nether one into it its whole length; the edges are very sharp and firm, the whole of a dark ash or horn colour; the forehead round the base of the beak, and sides of the head is bare of feathers, and of a dark greenish colour, in which space is placed the eyes, which are very large; the remainder of the head and neck is of a nut brown colour; the back of a light bluish grey; upper part of the wings, breast and belly almost white, with some slight dashes of grey; the quill-feathers and tail, which are very short, are of a dark slate colour, almost black; the legs which are ve[150]ry long, and bare of feathers a great length above the knees, are of a dark dull greenish colour: they have a small bag or pouch under their throat: they feed on serpents, young alligators, frogs and other reptiles.

THIS solitary bird does not associate in flocks, but is generally seen alone; commonly near the banks of great rivers, in vast marshes or meadows; especially such as are caused by inundations, and also in the vast deserted Rice plantations; he stands alone on the topmost limb of tall dead Cypress trees, his neck contracted or drawn in upon his shoulders, and beak resting like a long scythe upon his breast: in this pensive posture and solitary situation, they look extremely grave, sorrowful and melancholy, as if in the deepest thought. They are never seen on the salt sea coast, and yet are never found at a great distance from it. I take this bird to be of a different genus from the tantalus, and perhaps approaches the nearest to the Egyptian ibis of any other bird yet known.

THERE are two species of vultures[43] in these regions I think not mentioned in history: the first we shall describe is a beautiful bird, near the size of a turkey buzzard;[44] but his wings are much shorter, and consequently, he falls greatly below that admirable bird in sail. I shall call this bird the painted vulture. The bill is long and strait almost to the point, when it is hooked or bent suddenly down and sharp; the head and neck bare of feathers nearly down to the stomach, when the feathers begin to cover the skin, and soon become long and of a soft texture, forming a ruff or tippet, in which the bird by contracting his neck can hide that as [151] well as his head; the bare skin on the neck appears loose and wrinkled, which is of a deep bright yellow colour, intermixed with coral red; the hinder part of the neck is nearly covered with short, stiff hair; and the skin of this part of the neck is of a dun-purple colour, gradually becoming red as it approaches the yellow of the sides and forepart. The crown of the head is red; there are lobed lappets of a redish orange colour, which lay on the base of the upper mandible. But what is singular, a large portion of the stomach hangs down on the breast of the bird, in the likeness of a sack or half wallet, and seems to be a duplicature of the craw, which is naked and of a redish flesh colour, this is partly concealed by the feathers of the breast, unless when it is loaded with food, (which is commonly, I believe, roasted reptiles) and then it appears prominent. The plumage of the bird is generally white or cream colour, except the quill-feathers of the wings and two or three rows of the coverts, which are of a beautiful dark brown; the tail which is large and white is tipped with this dark brown or black; the legs and feet of a clear white; the eye is encircled with a gold coloured iris; the pupil black.

THE Creeks or Muscogulges construct their royal standard of the tail feather of this bird, which is called by a name signifying the eagle's tail; this they carry with them when they go to battle, but then it is painted with a zone of red within the brown tips; and in peaceable negociations it is displayed new, clean and white, this standard is held most sacred by them on all occasions; and is constructed and ornamented with great ingenuity. These birds seldom appear but when the deserts are set on fire (which happens almost every day throughout the year, in [152] some part or other, by the Indians, for the purpose of rousing the game, as also by the lightning): when they are seen at a distance soaring on the wing, gathering from every quarter, and gradually approaching the burnt plains, where they alight upon the ground yet smoking with hot embers; they gather up the roasted serpents, frogs and lizards; filling their sacks with them; at this time a person may shoot them at pleasure, they not being willing to quit the feast, and indeed seem to brave all danger.

THE other species may very properly be called the coped vulture, and is by the inhabitants called the carrion crow; as to bulk or weight, he is nearly equal to either of the others before mentioned. His wings are not long and sharp pointed, but broad and round at their extremities, having a clumsy appearance; the tail is remarkably short, which he spreads like a little fan, when on the wing; they have a heavy laborious flight, flapping their wings, then sail a little and then flap their wings again, and so on as if recovering themselves when falling; the beak is very long and strait, until it makes a sudden hook at the point, in the manner of the other vultures; the whole bird is of a sable or mourning colour; the head and neck down to the breast is bare of feathers, and the skin wrinkled, this unfeathered skin is of a deep livid purple, appearing black and thinly set with short black hair; he has a ruff or tippet of long soft feathers, like a collar bearing on his breast, in which he can conceal his neck and head at pleasure.

HAVING agreeably diverted away the intolerable heats of sultry noon in fruitful fragrant groves, with renewed vigour I again resume my [153] sylvan pilgrimage. The afternoon and evening moderately warm, and exceeding pleasant views from the river and its varied shores. I passed by Battle lagoon and the bluff, without much opposition; but the crocodiles were already assembling in the pass. Before night I came to, at a charming Orange grove bluff, on the East side of the little lake, and after fixing my camp on a high open situation, and collecting a plenty of dry wood for fuel, I had time to get some fine trout for supper and joyfully return to my camp.

WHAT a most beautiful creature is this fish before me! gliding to and fro, and figuring in the still clear waters, with his orient attendants and associates: the yellow bream[45] or sun fish. It is about eight inches in length, nearly of

William Bartram, "Great Yellow Bream calld Old Wife" (aka Warmouth, *Lepomis gulosus*), watercolor sent to John Fothergill in 1774. By permission of the Natural History Museum, London.

the shape of the trout, but rather larger in proportion over the shoulders and breast; the mouth large, and the branchiostega opens wide; the whole fish is of a pale gold (or burnished brass) colour, darker on the back and upper sides; the scales are of a proportionable size, regularly placed, and every where variably powdered with red, russet, silver, blue and green specks, so laid on the scales as to appear like real dust or opaque bodies, each apparent particle being so projected by light and shade, and the various attitudes of the fish, as to deceive the sight; for in reality nothing can be of a more plain and polished surface than the scales and whole body of the fish; the fins are of an Orange colour; and like all the species of the bream, the ultimate angle of the branchiostega terminate by a little spatula, the extreme end of which represents a crescent of the finest ultramarine blue, encircled with silver, [154] and velvet black, like the eye in the feathers of a peacock's train; he is a fish of prodigious strength and activity in the water; a warrior in a gilded coat of mail, and gives no rest or quarters to small fish, which he preys upon; they are delicious food and in great abundance.

THE Orange grove, is but narrow, betwixt the river banks and ancient Indian fields, where there are evident traces of the habitations of the ancients, surrounded with groves of Live Oak, Laurel Magnolia, Zanthoxilon, Liquidamber, and others.[46]

HOW harmonious and soothing is this native sylvan music now at still evening! inexpressibly tender are the responsive cooings of the innocent dove, in the fragrant Zanthoxilon groves, and the variable and tuneful warblings of the nonparel; with the more sprightly and elevated strains of the blue linnet and golden icterus; this is indeed harmony even amidst the incessant croaking of the frogs; the shades of silent night are made more chearful, with the shrill voice of the whip-poor-will[47] and active mock-bird.

My situation high and airy, a brisk and cool breeze steadily and incessantly passing over the clear waters of the lake, and fluttering over me through the surrounding groves, wings its way to the moon-light savannas, while I repose on my sweet and healthy couch of the soft Tillandsi ulnea-adscites, and the latter gloomy and still hours of night passed rapidly away as it were in a moment; I arose, strengthen[155]ed and chearful, in the morning. Having some repairs to make in the tackle of my vessel, I paid my first attention to them; which being accomplished, my curiosity prompted me to penetrate the grove and view the illumined plains.

WHAT a beautiful display of vegetation is here before me! seemingly unlimited in extent and variety; how the dew-drops twinkle and play upon the sight, trembling on the tips of the lucid, green savanna, sparkling as the gem that flames on the turban of the Eastern prince; see the pearly tears rolling off the buds of the expanding Granadilla;[48] behold the azure fields of cerulean Ixea! what can equal the rich golden flowers of the Cana lutea, which ornament the banks of yon serpentine rivulet, meandering over the meadows; the almost endless varieties of the gay Phlox, that enamel the swelling green banks, associated with the purple Verbena corymbosa, Viola, pearly Gnaphalium, and silvery Perdicium; how fantastical looks the libertine Clitoria, mantling the shrubs, on the vistas skirting the groves. My morning excursion finished, I returned to the camp, breakfasted, then went on board my boat, and gently descended the noble river and passed by several openings of extensive plains and meadows, environing the East Lake, charming beyond compare; at evening I came to at a good harbour, under the high banks of the river, and rested during the night, amidst the fragrant groves, exposed to the constant breezes from the river: here I made ample collections of specimens and growing roots of curious vegetables, which kept me fully employed the greatest part of the day, and in the forests, in tufts or clumps, a large conical strobile disclosing its large coral red fruit, which appears singularly beautiful amidst the deep green fern-like pinnated leaves.

THE Erythryna corallodendrum is six or eight feet high; its prickly limbs stride and wreathe about with singular freedom, and its spikes of crimson flowers have a fine effect amidst the delicate foliage.

[163] THE Cactus opuntia is very tall, erect and large, and strong enough to bear the weight of a man: some are seven or eight feet high: the whole plant or tree seems to be formed of great oval compressed leaves or articulations; those near the earth continually encrease, magnify and indurate as the tree advances in years, and at length lose the bright green colour and glossy surface of their youth, acquiring a ligenous quality, with a whitish scabrous cortex: every part of the plant is nearly destitute of aculea, or those fascicles of barbed bristles which are in such plenty on the common dwarf Indian Fig. The cochineal insects were feeding on the leaves: the female of this insect is very large and fleshy, covered with a fine white silk or cottony web, which feels always moist or dewy, and seems designed by nature to protect them from the violent heat of the sun. The male is very small in comparison to the female, and but very few in number, they each have two oblong pellucid wings. The large polypetalous flowers are produced on the edges of the last years leaves, are of a fine splendid yellow, and are succeeded by very large pear shaped fruit, of a dark livid purple when ripe: its pulp is charged with a juice of a fine transparent crimson colour, and has a cool pleasant taste, somewhat like that of a pomegranate; soon after eating this fruit the urine becomes of the same crimson colour, which very much surprises and affrights a stranger, but is attended with no other ill consequence, on the contrary, it is esteemed wholesome, though powerfully diuretic.

ON the left hand of those open forests and savannas, as we turn our eyes Southward, South-west and West, we behold an endless wild desert, the upper stratum of the earth of which is a fine white sand, with small pebbles, and at some distance appears entirely covered with low trees and shrubs of [164] various kinds, and of equal height, as dwarf Sweet Bay (Laurus Borbonia) Olea Americana, Morus rubra, Myrica cerifera, Ptelea, Æsculus pavia, Quercus Ilex, Q. glandifer, Q. maritima, foliis obcuneiformibus obsolete trilobis minoribus,[52] Q. pumila, Rhamnus frangula, Halesia diptera, & Tetraptera, Cassine, Ilex aquifolium, Callicarpa Johnsonia, Erythryna corallodendrum, Hibiscus spinifex, Zanthoxilon, Hopea tinctoria, Sideroxilum, with a multitude of other shrubs, many of which are new to me, and some of them admirably beautiful and singular. One of them particularly engaged my notice, which, from its fructification I take to be a species of Cacalia. It is an evergreen shrub, about six or eight feet high, the leaves are generally somewhat cuniform, fleshy and of a pale whitish green, both surfaces being covered with a hoary pubescence and vesiculae, that when pressed feels clammy, and emits an agreeable scent; the ascendent branches terminate with large tufts or corymbes of rose coloured flowers, of the same agreeable scent; these clusters of flowers, at a distance, look like a large Carnation or fringed Poppy flower (Syngenesia Polyg. Oqul. Linn.) Cacalia heterophylla, foliis cuniformibus, carnosis, papil. viscidis.

HERE is also another species of the same genus, but it does not grow quite so large; the leaves are smaller, of a yet duller green colour, and the flowers are of a pale rose; they are both valuable evergreens.

THE trees and shrubs which cover these extensive wilds, are about five or six feet high, and seem to be kept down by the annual firing of the desarts, rather than the barrenness of the soil, as I saw a few large Live Oaks, Mulberry trees and Hicko[165]ries, which evidently have withstood the devouring flames. These adjoining wild plains, forests and savannas, are situated lower than the hilly groves on the banks of the lake and river, but what should be the natural cause of it I cannot even pretend to conjecture, unless one may suppose that those high hills, which we call bluffs, on the banks of this great river and its lakes, and which support those magnificent groves and high forests, and are generally composed of shells and sand, were thrown up to their present height by the winds and waves, when the bed of the river was nearer the level of the present surface of the earth; but then, to rest upon such a supposition, would be admitting that the waters were heretofore in greater quantities than at this time, or that their present channels and receptacles are worn deeper into the earth.

I NOW directed my steps towards my encampment, in a different direction. I seated myself upon a swelling green knoll, at the head of the chrystal bason.[53] Near me, on the left, was a point or projection of an entire grove of the aromatic Illisium Floridanum; on my right and all around behind me, was a fruitful Orange grove, with Palms and Magnolias interspersed in front, just under my feet was the inchanting and amazing chrystal fountain, which incessantly threw up, from dark, rocky caverns below, tons of water every minute, forming a bason, capacious enough for large shallops to ride in, and a creek of four or five feet depth of water, and near twenty yards over, which meanders six miles through green meadows, pouring its limpid waters into the great Lake George, where they seem to remain pure and unmixed. About twenty yards from the upper edge of the bason, [166] and directly opposite to the mouth or outlet to the creek, is a continual and amazing ebullition, where the waters are thrown up in such abundance and amazing force, as to jet and swell up two or three feet above the common surface: white sand and small particles of shells are thrown up with the waters, near to the top, when they diverge from the center, subside with the expanding flood, and gently sink again, forming a large rim or funnel round about the aperture or mouth of the fountain, which is a vast perforation through a bed of rocks, the ragged points of which are projected out on every side. Thus far I know to be matter of real fact, and I have related it as near as I could conceive or express myself. But there are yet remaining scenes inexpressibly admirable and pleasing.

BEHOLD, for instance, a vast circular expanse before you, the waters of which are so extremely clear as to be absolutely diaphanous or transparent as the ether; the margin of the bason ornamented with a great variety of fruitful and floriferous trees, shrub and plants, the pendant golden Orange dancing on the surface of the pellucid waters, the balmy air vibrates the melody of the merry birds, tenants of the encircling aromatic grove.

AT the same instant innumerable bands of fish are seen, some cloathed in the most brilliant colours; the voracious crocodile stretched along at full length, as the great trunk of a tree in size, the devouring garfish, inimical trout, and all the varieties of gilded painted bream, the barbed catfish, dreaded sting-ray, skate and flounder, spotted bass, sheeps head and ominous drum; all in their separate bands and communities, with free and unsus[167]picious intercourse performing their evolutions: there are no signs of enmity, no attempt to devour each other; the different bands seem peaceably and complaisantly to move a little aside, as it were to make room for others to pass by.

BUT behold yet something far more admirable, see whole armies descending into an abyss, into the mouth of the bubbling fountain, they disappear! are they gone forever? is it real? I raise my eyes with terror and astonishment,—I look down again to the fountain with anxiety, when behold them as it were emerging from the blue ether of another world, apparently at a vast distance, at their first appearance, no bigger than flies or minnows, now gradually enlarging, their brilliant colours begin to paint the fluid.

NOW they come forward rapidly, and instantly emerge, with the elastic expanding column of chrystalline waters, into the circular bason or funnel, see now how gently they rise, some upright, others obliquely, or seem to lay as it were on their sides, suffering themselves to be gently lifted or born up, by the expanding fluid towards the surface, sailing or floating like butterflies in the cerulean ether: then again they as gently descend, diverge and move off; when they rally, form again and rejoin their kindred tribes.

THIS amazing and delightful scene, though real, appears at first but as a piece of excellent painting; there seems no medium, you imagine the picture to be within a few inches of your eyes, and that you may without the least difficulty touch any one of the fish, or put your finger upon the crocodile's eye, when it really is twenty or thirty feet under water.

[168] AND although this paradise of fish, may seem to exhibit a just representation of the peaceable and happy state of nature which existed before the fall, yet in reality it is a mere representation; for the nature of the fish is the same as if they were in lake George or the river; but here the water or element in which they live and move, is so perfectly clear and transparent, it places them all on an equality with regard to their ability to injure or escape from one another; (as all river fish of prey, or such as feed upon each other, as well as the unwieldy crocodile, take their prey by surprise; secreting themselves under covert or in ambush, until an opportunity offers, when they rush suddenly upon them): but here is no covert, no ambush, here the trout freely passes by the very nose of the alligator and laughs in his face, and the bream by the trout.

BUT what is really surprising, that the consciousness of each others safety or some other latent cause, should so absolutely alter their conduct, for here is not the least attempt made to injure or disturb one another.

THE sun passing below the horizon, and night approaching, I arose from my seat, and proceeding on arrived at my camp, kindled my fire, supped and reposed peaceably. And rising early, employed the fore part of the day in collecting specimens of growing roots and seeds. In the afternoon, left these Elisian springs and the aromatic graves, and briskly descend the pellucid little river, re-entering the great lake; the wind being gentle and fair for Mount Royal, I hoisted sail and successfully crossing the N. West bay, about nine miles, came to at Rocky Point, the West cape or promontory, as we enter the river descending towards Mount Royal: [169] these are horizontal slabs or flat masses of rocks, rising out of the lake two or three feet above its surface, and seem an aggregate composition or concrete of sand, shells and calcarious cement; of a dark grey or dusky colour; this stone is hard and firm enough for buildings, and serve very well for light hand mill-stones; and when calcined affords a coarse lime; they lay in vast horizontal masses upon one another, from one to two or three feet in thickness, and are easily separated and broke to any size or form, for the purpose of building. Rocky Point is an airy cool and delightful situation, commanding a most ample and pleasing prospect of the lake and its environs; but here being no wood, I re-embarked and sailed down a little farther to the island in the bay, where I went on shore at a magnificent grove of Magnolias and Oranges, desirous of augmenting my collections. Arose early next morning, and after ranging the groves and savannas, returned, embarked again, and descending, called at Mount Royal, where I enlarged my collections; and bidding adieu to the gentleman and lady, who resided here, and who treated me with great hospitality on my ascent up the river; arrived in the evening at the lower trading house.

## 3

## Correspondence

Letter writing was at the heart of scientific discovery and exchange. Letters shared information, covered specimens and seeds, accompanied journals and drawings, and served purposes of introduction. They were sometimes folded whole-cloth into publication, and they served as a medium for intimate exchange, even between people who had never met. As the son of an indefatigable correspondent, William Bartram understood the importance of maintaining contacts, and more than two hundred of his letters survive today. The letters to and from him are by turns personal, scientific, philosophical, and legal; they take care of business, they inform, and they are often artful.

This brief selection offers a window into Bartram's correspondence, with particular emphasis on the St. Johns years. A 1766 note from John to William, written shortly after their tour, accounts for supplies and slaves purchased for William's plantation near Picolata Creek. John, who was ill at the time, clearly had misgivings about his son's decision to stay in Florida. An attempt at reconciliation by the statesman, planter, and slave trader Henry Laurens, who was investigating land in Florida, shows that John's misgivings were prescient. William was never meant to be a planter, and he did not last long in the situation that Laurens described. A scientific epistle to Benjamin Rush, then in Scotland, focuses on the *Calydorea coelestina* (Bartram's Ixia), then being described for the first time. Probably intended for publication, this account of the rare flower ranks among Bartram's finest writing and serves as an early example of the nature essay. A long overdue update from William to John, written in 1775 but dated 1774, ends the long silence between the two Bartrams. As he describes the St. Johns and overland tours of Florida, the younger Bartram seems to brim with a belated sense of accomplishment. William announces that he will continue to West Florida, or Pensacola, and onto the Mississippi River, journeying well beyond the range of his father's own vast travels.

John Bartram to William Bartram[1]

[Charleston, S.C.]
April 5, 1766

I have procured 4 good yams two white ones & two red, a present from the colonel, & sent. A west india gentleman said thay cut of one half of the yam & planted the upper part of it in a pretty large hill of loose earth prety deep & when the vine shot up a foot high thay set a pole deep in the hill 8 or 9 foot high for the vine to run up he says the whole root planted dont do so well as the upper part cut off the lower part thay eate    how this will do I cant say    to make the pumkins & cowcumbers large thay cut of the top when thay run several yards which makes them branch & bear prodigiously. thay say the potatoes is the best that is raised from the cuttings of the vines    if so here surely in florida this method will produce well. I believe if the setts fire to the 20 acre marsh will be the place to plant rice in this year if it be two wett how it up in narrow ridges & plant the rice on the ridge for all agree if the water covers the young blade it will kill it: most here thinks that where the grass grows so rank as about thy house amongst tall pines such ground will bear good corn when the pines is fallen & the tops burnt    but above all take care the negroes dont fall the trees upon one another. thee hath had sufficient warning    its supposed here that half a bushel of rice will plant an acre of rich new land but ould land takes twice as much I have packed up a rice barrel marked B containing 3 bushels of seed rice one covered pot one heavy pensylvenia ax by M[r] Lambol 2 leading chisel a broad ax, adze, shovel, much better then any spade, saw, rag, whestone    bass line & hook, & mistris Lambol hath sent 3 stone cups a bed Cloath for thee to fill with feathers of ducks & turkey, a kettle a bushel & half or two of pease, taniers a pot of sugar ground nuts & several garden seeds beans &c: I have sent 20 yards of crocus & hesing[2] for bags to fill with moss which the people here say makes good beds I have ordered by the procurement of Col. Laurance two barrels of corn one of rice   a barrel of poark & the Colonel sent thee a cask of salt gratis. provisions here is strangly risen within a week or two. rice is double what it was indian corn twenty shillings per bushel & both it & peas wholy prohibited sending out   but by the Col. favour he spared us some Captain hardy did bring thy watch to be mended & took it away to Philadelphia promised to leave it with thy mother. Narny saith it will not go long well. that it is not worth much. all thy friends here laments thy resolute choice to live at St Johns & leave off drawing or writeing thay say the negros will run away or murther thee. thay all seem to have a miserable opinion of negroes & recons the new the best as not yet haveing learnt the mischievous practices of the negroes born in the country & town which the people generaly represents as if thay was all either murderers, runawas   robers, or theeves; espetialy the Plantation negros   I have at last by the dayly assitance & choice of Doctor garden, Major Moultrey, M[r]. Sanders & Col: Lawrans all which tooke a great deal of pains to examin them the Colon[el] is owned by all to be the best Judge in town as to thair appearance & the doctor examined thair health[3]   thay chose these out of several hundred of both publick & private sail: ould M[r] Lambol hath been very sick & could do nothing but give his advice which runs all upon haveing nothing to do with them & declares thay are the greatest curse that ever came to america yet owns that there is no raiseing rice without them   this is Menegots & Narneys story.[4] Colonel Lawrance bought the two new negroes for me & the doctor examined them as to thair health   thay have chose each other for man & wife & she is with child & the other woman I chose for a wife for Jacob. she is allso supposed to be with child so that if thay do well thee may boldly claim a Pattent from the Governour.

I have shiped on board the East Florida Captain Bachop[5] 6 likely negroes called Jack a lusty man a new negro 5 foot 8 inches high & ¼: Siby his wife new 5 foot one inch ¾ Jacob 5 foot high & Sam 4 foot 7 inches ½ allso Flora a lusty woman not so black as many a cromantee[6] which her master & mistris solemny declares to be incorupted with the vices of the town being never sufered to go aut at night nor any negroes to come to her but the family she has a general good character & Bachus her son is a pretty boy 3 or 4 years ould   I have allso sent a pair of good millstones & a grind stone; & a pair of smoothing irons delivered to the care of the slaves   half a dozen Sickles or hooks a choice good Jack plain, a bar of lead for to make slugs which many guns will shoot truer then a round bullet we cutt it about a quarter longer then its thickness which should slip down the barrel pretty easy: our friend Lambol tells me the way to catch mullets is to take the cano in the night with a stick of lightwood 3 or 4 foot long well lighted which one must hould in his hand as far as he can reach toward the grass or reed about 2 or 3 foot, water where the mullets sleep the other strikes on the side of the canoe to waken them    thay seeing the light Jumps from it into the canoe which must be heded where by multitudes is catched    if thee thinks thee can safely let the negroes blood let me know & I will send thee a lancet    John Bartram

[on back] Doctor garden & others say that when the negros pounds rice thay will be all in a sweat then they run out or to the dore with thair brest open then they catch cold & often fall into a pleurisey which he recons with the flux two of the most dangerous diseases & adviseth thee to take great care of them & thair cloaths which thay are now well furnished with for thay will not take any care of themselves

Henry Laurens to John Bartram[7]

Charlestown, S.C.<br>August 9, 1766

Sir,

I have had the pleasure of hearing from some of our acquaintance here that you were safely arrived in Philadelphia but that good news has been somewhat abated by Capt Eastwick's account that you were very sick when he left that City. I hope soon to know from your own hand that you are recovered & as well re:establish'd as we poor brittle clay-shells can expect to be at threescore and ten.

Since you left Carolina I have prosecuted my long intended Voyage & journey through the southern parts of this country & Georgia to East Florida & was near five weeks in the last mentioned Province in which time I thrice visited the River S<sup>t</sup> John, often landed upon each shore, exploring the Swamps & Hummocks Pine barrens & Sand barrens between the great Lake & the Ocean & you may be sure that I did not carelessly pass by your Son's habitation—I called upon him twice & as a confirmation of it you will find enclosed in this a Letter from him wrote after my second visit.

Your knowledge of that Country together with the addition of M<sup>r</sup>. William Bartram's remarks upon his further experience renders it unnecessary as it would be unedifying for me to trouble you with my few general observations—but I hope you will not think me quite impertinent if I detain you to say a word or two touching the particular situation & circumstances of that poor Young Man & the less so when you know that it is done partly as his request.

His situation on the River is the least agreeable of all the places that I have seen, on a low sheet of sandy pine barren verging on the swamp, which before his door is very narrow in a bite or Cove of the River so shoal & covered with umbrelloes that the common current is lost & the Water almost stagnated, exceedingly foul & absolutely stank when stirred up by our Oars on both days of my landing there—tho at the same times the River was said to be rather high & the stream running down strong beyond that Cove—this I should think must make the place always unhealthy as well as troublesome to come at by Water carriage especially in dry seasons.—the swamp & adjoining Marsh which I walked into, will without doubt produce good Rice when properly cleared & cultivated but both seem to be narrow & will require more strength to put them in tolerable order than M<sup>r</sup>. W Bartram is at present possessed of to make any progress above daily bread & that of a coarse kind too. there is some Cypress which if he had a little more strength he might soon convert to Shingles & ready Money—The Pine land (I am sorry to differ in opinion with you) is very ordinary—indeed I saw none good in the whole country but that peice of his may justly be ranked in an inferior class even there.

At my first visit your Son shewed me the growth of some pease Beans Corn & Yams, planted only four days before in the Land on the swamp edge, which then looked very flourishing, but when I called three Weeks after, altho there had been much Rain in the mean time, the progress was barely perceptible—a remark that we both concurred in—I found that he had according to my advice continued to clear the Swamp & in that time cut down part of an Acre of Trees but that sort of work goes on very heavily for want of strong hands—he assured me that he had but two among the Six Negroes that you gave him that could handle an Axe tolerably & one of those two had been exceedingly insolent—I encouraged & pressed him to put a little Rice in the ground even at that late day (5<sup>th</sup> or 6<sup>th</sup> July) & he promised to do so the day following.

The House or rather hovel that he lives in is extremely confined & not proof against the weather, he has not proper assistance to make a better & from its situation it is very hot. The only disagreeably hot place that I found in East

Florida, but it should be remarked that the weather had been uncommonly temperate—His provision of Grain, Flesh & Spirits are scanty even to penury, the latter article very much so—His own health very imperfect—he had the fever when I was first with him & looked very poorly in the second visit—I am determined by the next conveyance to send him a little Rum, Wine, Sugar, Tea, Cheese, Biscuit & other trifles & charge the small amount to your Account tho I would most freely give him the whole but for fear that you should take it amiss.

Possibly Sir, your Son tho a worthy ingenious Man may not have resolution enough, or not that sort of resolution that is necessary to encounter the difficulties incident to & unavoidable in his present state of Life—You & I probably could surmount all those hardships without much chagrin—I verily believe that I could—but at the same time I protest that I should think it less grievous, to disinherit my own Son & turn him into the wide world, if he was of a tender & delicate frame of Body & intelects as yours seems to be, than to restrict him, in my favour just in the state that your Son is reduced to—this is, no doubt, more than even you apprehended & admitting that my account is in part erroneous (which I do not admit, meaning to speak nothing but truth) yet the general outlines of the foregoing description must affect & grieve you—but it is by no means my design or intention to compass any particular end by colouring too strongly—in fact according to my ideas no colouring can do justice to the forlorn state of poor Billy Bartram—A gentle mild Young Man—no Wife—no Friend—no Companion—no Neighbour—no Human inhabitant within nine miles of him the nearest by Water—no Boat to come at them & those only common Soldiers—Seated upon a beggarly spot of Land—scant of the bare necessaries & totally void of all the comforts of Life except an inimitable degree of patience for which he deserves a thousand times better fate—an unpleasant unhealthy situation—Six Negroes rather plagues than aid to him—of whom one so insolent as to threaten his Life—one a useless expence—one a helpless child in arms—one a pregnant Woman without prospect of any female help—distant 30 long Miles from the Metropolis—no Money to pay the expence of a journey there upon the most important occasions—over a Road always bad & in wet weather wholly impassible—to which might be enumerated a great many smaller & perhaps some imaginary evils the natural offspring of so many substantial ones—these I say are discouragements enough to break the spirits of any Modest Young Man & more than any Man should be exposed to without his own free acceptance, unless his crimes had been so great as to merit a state of exile.—

I had been inform'd indeed before my visit to M$^r$. W. B. that he had felt the pressure of his solitary & hopeless condition so heavily as almost to drive him to dispondency, he expressed an inclination to decamp from the place that I have endeavoured to describe—but was supported by advice of a friend to wait until he should see me who was then daily expected in E. Florida—He did not open his mind so fully to myself, but rather modestly appealed to me upon his circumstances & situation accompanying his complaints with the most dutiful & affectionate mention of his Father, to whom he requested I should take some notice of them in my next Letter—in answer to which I gave him my sentiments very candidly, encouraging him at the same time to persevere until he should hear from you—

I have presum'd to say so much in consequence of my promise to him upon that request as well as from a natural & irresistable inclination to relieve every virtuous Man in distress; and as the foregoing representation can have no evil effects, however it may be imperfect or appear to be officious, I trust that I shall not suffer under your candid interpretation.

After this account of your Son's circumstances, I might add that a list of several necessary articles besides exchange of good Negroes in place of almost useless ones that are wanting & will be wanted to mend them a little, but no doubt he has given some needful hints on that head & if his modesty has restrained his pen—you will if you pay any regard to what I have been so bold as to write upon so slight an acquaintance as ours—chearfully & quickly give orders to supply him with such things as shall be necessary to make his banishment less galling & after present him with some prospect of reaping the fruit of his Labours. Here I shall drop the subject & presenting M$^{rs}$. Laurens's & my own hearty good wishes put an end to this long letter subscribing myself,

Sir, Your most obedt. Servt.—
Henry Laurens


## William Bartram to Benjamin Rush[8]

December 5, 1767

Purple Flower'd Ixia of S$^t$ Johns Riv$^r$ E$^t$. Florida.

Every Species or variety of this Tribe of Plants exhibet very eminent beauties; but this with applause claims the preeminence, its elegant form of groath with the brilliant colouring of its Flowers strikes on the imagination delight; and one

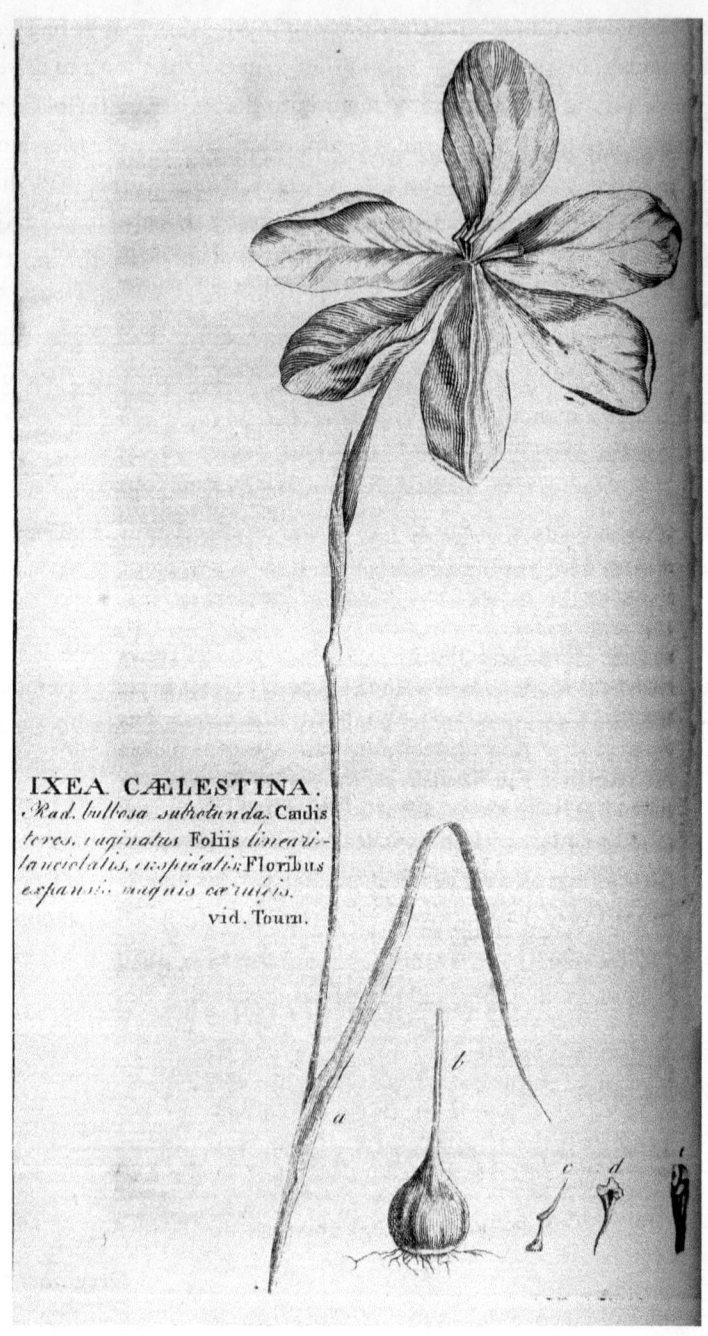

William Bartram's celestial lily, *Ixia coelestina* or "Bartram's ixia," now called *Calydorea coelestina*. This plate appeared in *Travels* but is given no further description there. For a lovely watercolor of the same flower, see Hallock and Hoffmann, *William Bartram, the Search for Nature's Design* (69).

can't look on it but with admiration.—The flowers open in the Morning soon after the day breaketh, whose Petals appear as a transparent Film framed with singular beauty consisting of a number of longitudinal Fibres, which take their rise from the bottom departing from each other gradually to near the middle, then they divide, thus again to the end, and are so very minute preventing altogether an appearance of the finest webby membrane, of so tender and delicate an excellence, they are bruised and ruffled, by the gentlest breathe of wind, and no sooner then the slightest glance of the Sunbeams pass over them then they disappear, the Acres of ground were partly cover'd in such manner as to cast a glowing purple around soon after the sun is above the horison, it would be almost imposeble to find a flower; and one would be apt to conjecture all the beauty seen this moment to be mere delution—

The colour of this most delightfull of Flowers is a lively blue reflecting a slite cast of purple. The delicate texture of these Flowers is admirable beyond anything that Vigitation presents besides. Having crop't a many plants with a view of preserving a specimin of such rare beauty, but was as often baffled in the attempt, for as often as they were placed in the Book its leaves quickly absorbed the purple juice from the Petals, leaving the transparent film colourless, This purple tinct is of such strength and penitration; I have Gen$^a$: Plant$^m$: by me at prisent wherein a specimen had been laid, the Juice of which has struck thro' and colour'd five leaves, & remains a fixt and most perfect purple colour.[9]

But tho' these flowers are of so short a durance, that seeming difect is amply compensated by a most liberal sucession for the next morning the curious Botanist is delighted by a seeming return of those fugitives, or he would rather emagin himself beholding a new creation & in the midst of thousands.—

The Root is a small and nearly round Bulb, with a brown scaley covering from whence rises first one or 2 leaves 6 inches in length and very narrow very like a blade of common Grass, soon after the stalk for Flowers which is very small and round, rising 8 or 9 inches high a single Flower breaks out from a Spath formed of a single lanciolated leaf the footstalk of the Flower is more then an inch long bending downards The Flower is composed of six equal oblong petals narrower towards their bases. The [Stamen] are three very short bending a little inward & on their sharp points are placed the Anthera, which are long and crooked. The Germen is partly oval swelling near the top & three cornered, seated beneath the receptacle of the Flower. The Stile is in the midst rising from the apex of the Germen very small but inlarging upwards when it devides into three Stigma which are thick. [Pericarpum] is suboval shaped composed of three valves & contains three Cells each having several seeds.—

The maner which Nature hath assigned this Plant in producing the wonderfull succession of Flowers which presents to the sight every morning a new, continuing for the space of three Weeks is very singular and perticular to it.

The root is a nearly round Bulb, & from the center of which rises the Flowering Stalk producing commonly one tho' sometimes two flowers there being one [*illeg.*] on a spatha & if two the stalk then shoots forward terminated[10] by the second flower proceding from a spatha, there being never more than one flower from a Spatha, & the Stalk never divides—. Wether this sucession of flowers, may not be caus'd by the Older Roots flowering first, & so the next in Succession, according as their situation of groath may be more or less favourable for Nature to bring them forward to proper season

The preceeding descriptions and observations are the result of repeated opertunaties of Tryal, and was there no nothing in this rare plant exclusive of its beauty, that would recommend it to perticular notice, I hope its merit on that head will gain the attention of the curious, and in some degree plead the excuse, of one who in every object finds the greatest pleasure in following [nature's steps] in serch of knowledge that may tend to publick advantage or speculation

William Bartram


## William Bartram to John Bartram[11]

Charleston, S.C.
March 27, 1775

Honour$^d$. & Benevolent Father

I am happy by the blessings of the Almighty God by whose care I have been protected, & led safe through a Pilgrimage these three & twenty months, till my return to Charlestown, two days since. I am now lodged most kindly in the Family of your deceased Friend Lambol: his Daughter M$^{rs}$. Thomas excellent in goodness beyond her sex with expressions of the same affable & cordial Friendship so perticular in the character of her antient excellent Parent asked me to her house while I stayed in this Province which believe will be but a fiew days. I wrote to my Father soon after my return to Savanah from Tugilo River, which letter give an account of my proceedings there in that journey which I traveled upwards of 300 Miles, I collected a large number of Specimens I sent to Doct$^r$. Fothergill with some drawings in answer to which the Doct$^r$. was pleased to send me a List of the new & nondescript which I was glad to find were many & here he was pleased to express his satisfaction with the success of my labours & his willingness that I should continue my reserches. this Packet I received in E$^t$. Florida. Soon after my return to Savana in order to forward my collections to Doct$^r$. Fothergill, I intended to go back into the Cheroke & Creek Countries; When the Alarm from the Frontiers of hostilities commencing between the Indians & the whites put a stop to that scheme; I then turned my views towards E$^t$. Florida & prepared for it   I put my baggage onboard a vessell bound from Savanah to M$^r$. Spaldings Store on S$^t$. Johns intending to go by land there, & set off accordingly got safe to the Alatamaha, where I was taken Ill of a Fever of which I did not recover so as to be able to travel for near 2 Months, when I sett off again, but was turn'd back again by expresses from E$^t$. Florida that the Indians were up in Arms against us in that Province having killed & captivated several White People, & the Inhabitants were flying in to Augustine, & all the Indian Stores except one were robed & broken up so I stayed in the So$^n$ Parts of Georgia waiting for a favourable turn, & here I discovered & collected many Valuable & new Vigitables; hearing that the Lower Creeks were treating with the Governor of S$^t$. Augustine for Peace I resolved to make the second attempt. I left my horse in Georgia, & went down the Alatamaha, to Fredrica on the Island S$^t$. Simons, waited on M$^r$. Spalding who was pleas'd to give me Letters to his Agent in E$^t$. Florida &, in a fiew Days went onboard his Vessell bound to his Store on S$^t$. Johns, 2$^d$ day after we left Fredrica we met another of his Vessells we come too, went onboard. This Vessell was return'd from the Store, having onboard Numbers of Traders returning from the Indian Country being drove away by the Indians. they brot very bad talks & had onboard the Vessell all the Goods of the Trading houses except a fiew which the Goverer of Florida purchased of M$^r$. Spaldings agent, at the request of the Siminole Indians they being desireous to have the lower store kept up   these Goods were relanded on an Island a fiew Miles below the Store in the River S$^t$. Johns where my Chest & baggage was with them; the Vessell returnd back to Fredrica & I prevaled on them to sett me on Amelia Island near the mouth of S$^t$. Marys, being determined to pursue my journey into Florida at all events; & having some Papers & Books in my Chest which I stood in need of so, I walked the Beech untill I come to a Plantation, where I was friendly rec$^d$. by Lord Egmont's Agent[12] & stay'd with him 3 or 4 days on his promising me a passage to S$^t$. Johns in a boat, he going to S$^t$. Augustine went onboard a boat rowed by 5 Negroes & in about thirty hours arived at S$^t$. Johns near the Cowford, & here I was again put to my shifts being once more left alone, however this Gentleman sent me to a plantation in his Boat higher up the River where I purchased a small Canoe, & having furnished myself with a Sail & Paddle set off on my Voiage up the River S$^t$. Johns & got safe to the Island where I found my Chest went to the Store where I heard much more favourable accounts of the Indian affairs & on conferring with M$^r$. Spaldings Agent he encouraged me to stay a while untill the Indians were quiet, a short time after this some of the Traders thought fit to risque a journey out to Alatchua in quest of horses which they had amongst the Indians & having an inclination to see the Siminole Indian Town of Cuscoela on the great Alatchua Savanah I went with them. The Savanah is vast & beautifull beyand description. The Chief of the Town[13] recieved us most friendly assured us of his protection & gave the Traders liberty to hunt up their horses I rode with them near 50 Miles round the green Verge of this beautiful Savanah & went to the sink or Vortex where the waters are discharged    the Savanah is sorounded by hamocks of rich land planted with Orange Groves, Palm Trees Morus Magnolia grandiflora Telea Laurus vera Laurus Cærasus & a variety of other Trees & shrubs. after a week or ten days we returnd from Alatchua to the Store continued my excursions about this country, took A trip in my Canoe up S$^t$. Johns about, 100 Miles above the Store, to the uppermost Plantation, returned down to the Store & after some time an opertunaty offered to an Indian Town, on Little S$^t$. Juane River at the Bay of Apalache, about 100 Miles W$^t$. from the Store across the Istmous this was a pleasant Journey & afforded me a many Curiosities    The face & constitution of this country is Indian wild new & pleasing—

 The Indians at the Town received us with the complaisance & good breeding peculiar to them    treated us with the best they had & assured us of their protection whilst with them return'd to the Store, & took another Voiage up S$^t$. Johns returnd with some fine Roots & Seeds which together with my former Collections made up 3 large boxes of Roots & One of Seeds, which I caried safe with me to Sundbery in Georgia where I put them onboard a Vessell to London for Doct$^r$. Fothergill, having collected a number of curious roots in Georgia.

 Dear Father it is the greater pleasure that I hear by my Worthy Doct$^r$. Chalmers that you are alive & well, with my dear Mother which I pray may continue. I beg leave to acquaint my benevolent Parents that I am resolved with the concurence of Doct$^r$. Chalmers to continue my travels another year    Intend to go through the Cheroke & Creek Countries to Pensacola where I shall send my necessary baggage, & if it please God to spare me life & health I may go to the Messisipe River, I have been often with the Doct$^r$. concerning it & he promises to assist me with proper Recommendatorry Letters through the Nations. please to excuse this long tedious Letter

I am ever Your faithfull Son
William Bartram

    I have not had the favour of a Line from
    my Father or Mother whome God ever preserve.

# Part II

# 4

## Through Their Eyes

The Bartrams Explore the St. Johns River Valley

RICHARD FRANZ

John Bartram (1699–1777) and his son, William Bartram (1739–1823), were visionaries in a golden age of scientific discovery. They were not only explorers and plant collectors but also natural historians and scientists. Imagine their life in small open boats on the St. Johns River (SJR) in the 1700s, not knowing what perils might lie ahead and without accurate maps, GPS devices, ice chests with cold beverages, cameras, bug repellent, plant and wildlife field guides, or binoculars. Their mission was to reconnoiter the assets of Florida, England's latest provincial acquisition. Part II endeavors to acquaint readers with the natural and cultural landscapes that John and William Bartram encountered as they wandered the uncharted St. Johns River valley and beyond.

### Francis Harper, William Bartram's Chronicler

As part of this account, I acknowledge the phenomenal contributions of Francis Harper (1886–1972), who made William Bartram's writings accessible for interpretation. Harper's obsession with Bartram began at least eight decades ago. He was obviously influenced by his famous older brother, Roland Harper (1878–1966), who served as staff botanist for the Geological Survey of Alabama and helped Francis retrace Bartram's routes there and through the Florida Panhandle. Francis Harper began offering up his thoughts on Bartram with a series of publications beginning in the 1930s. He eventually condensed his findings in his "Travels" of William Bartram: Naturalist's Edition, published in 1958, with a second edition available in 1967.

One of Harper's greatest contributions was to identify William Bartram's routes, camping sites, and places of special events. It was indeed fortunate that Harper's fascination with Bartram began when it did, a time when local folks still remembered the early byways and historic landmarks. Today this kind of reconstruction would be practically impossible, since the world that Bartram explored, and Harper traveled, has been so totally reshaped, and the old people and their memories are gone.[1]

## Bartram Landscapes

The term *landscape* is used here, in lieu of more restrictive ecological concepts such as habitat, biological community, and ecosystem, to imply a more flexible portrayal of natural scenes that the Bartrams witnessed as they explored Florida.

The landscape narratives I use here consist of brief sketches of scenery and a sampling of dated excerpts from John Bartram's *Diary* (Stork ed., 1769) and William Bartram's 1791 *Travels* (Harper ed., 1967, with page numbers). These textual materials and others garnered from my personal experiences in North Florida and elsewhere are supplemented by professional literature and information from knowledgeable reviewers. This treatment offers readers the experience of viewing natural history through the eyes of modern natural historians and those of our intrepid explorers.

The narratives are limited to places encountered by the Bartrams in the St. Johns River valley. They are grouped into four general geographic regions.

L-SJR: lower reaches of the St. Johns River (Cowford to the present-day location of Palatka)
M-SJR: middle reaches of the St. Johns River (Palatka to Spalding's upper store at present-day Astor)
U-SJR: upper reaches of the St. Johns River (Astor to Puzzle and Loughman Lakes west of Mims)
I-Trek: interior treks (Spalding's lower store to Cowpen Lake and the vicinity of the Putnam–Alachua county line).

These regions do not conform to those used by the St. Johns River Water Management District or other political entities, but rather are the travel routes of the Bartrams, local geologic features, and landscape considerations. Specific sites are named when appropriate. Stopping the narrative of the I-Trek at the county line was an arbitrary decision to focus attention on the St. Johns River valley, although William Bartram traveled farther west to the Alachua Savanna and Suwannee River during his interior wanderings.

## St. Johns River

The St. Johns River basin is the third largest in the state, after the Apalachicola and Suwannee Rivers, and it lies completely within the bounds of Florida. The contemporary St. Johns River is relatively young, with its probable origins associated with rebounding sea levels in the latest Pleistocene.

The river flows north for 310 miles originating at Blue Cypress Lake marsh, just north of Lake Okeechobee, entering the Atlantic Ocean at Mayport near Jacksonville, Florida. The total drop between its origin and its end is only 27 feet (about an inch per mile). Most of that drop occurs within the first third of its route. The river tends to be flat-bottomed, shallow, 4–15 feet deep, with occasional deeper holes: for example, Croaker Hole in Little Lake George, water depth 52 feet; Possum Bluff Hole, 42 feet; Rice Creek, Murphy Island, and Black Creek Holes, 35 feet each, based on navigation charts. Multitudes of clear-water springs and dark-water streams pour freshwater into the river. Major tributaries are Julington Creek, Black Creek, Rice Creek, Dunn's Creek, the Ocklawaha River, and, farther upstream, the Wekiva and Econlockhatchee Rivers.

The boundaries of the St. Johns valley are controlled by north–south trending Pleistocene beach ridges. Occasional offsets shift the direction of the valley, suggesting great complexity in its subsurface geology. These shifts may have resulted from earlier faulting events and subsequent weathering of local limestones. Prehistoric wetlands between the relict ridges drained as sea levels fell during the last Ice Age, exposing the valley floor and the river's future path.

The river follows a meandering path through the valley. In the middle reaches, the river generally hugs the shoreline of the prehistoric eastern bluffs. The western bank intercepts broad expanses of near-level plains, often supporting river swamps, pine flatwoods, shallow ponds, intermittent streams, and bayheads. These flatwoods landscapes suggest the presence of underlying, less-porous sediments that serve as a hardpan, keeping water near the surface.

In the middle and upper regions the river forms immense pools. The largest of these is Lake George, 14 miles long and 6 miles wide, making it the second largest pool of water in Florida behind Lake Okeechobee. Daily tidal wedges extend southward upriver to at least Palatka, affecting local river levels and sa-

Memorial Bridge over the St. Johns River at Palatka, Florida. The river is about .8 mile wide here. Photo by Richard Franz.

linities. Tannic-stained water gives the river its dark red color. Springs along the banks of the St. Johns River also contribute sufficient clear, mineral-rich waters into the river, which together with the tidal water enables marine fishes, bluecrabs, and shrimps to penetrate into the middle reaches of the St. Johns River and Lake George.

The bottom of the river consists of organic silt or sand, with fields of tapegrass growing in the shallows on firmer bottoms. Several large flooded sand bars occur in the river shallows, the most prominent of which are located south of Lake George (Volusia Bar) and north of Buffalo Bluff (Miller's Bar). These bars can become navigational hazards during periods of low water. Strangely, exposed sandbars, typical of other southeastern coastal plain rivers, are missing from this river.

In the Bartrams' writings, one of the unresolved paradoxes is why they never penetrated the largest tributary of the St. Johns, the Ocklawaha River. The only mention of its existence in their writings was this brief comment by William Bartram in *Travels*: "The traders informed me . . . of a great lake, many miles in length, in magnitude exceeding Lake George, and communicates with St. Juan's by a river, its confluence above the lower store at the Little Lake" (182). Harper suggests that Bartram's "a river" refers to the Ocklawaha. Perhaps the exploration of the Ocklawaha was not part of their agenda. It is hard to imagine that they missed it as they sailed past the mouth of the Ocklawaha multiple times as they navigated the St. Johns River, and William Bartram passed within a mile of it four times when he crossed Deep Creek on his way to and from the Alachua Savanna and beyond. Even more puzzling, William Bartram must have been aware of the name Achlawaugh (presumably an earlier spelling of Ocklawaha), which appeared in British documents with commentaries concerning an important Seminole encampment along the river near Orange Springs. This village apparently was under the watchful eye of William Bartram's friend Long Warrior.[2]

> *Diary*, 19 Dec 1765 (L-SJR, Greenwood house, possibly Marshall's Plantation, near Julington Creek, at Mandarin): "surface of the river, which rises here 18 inches at high water, and in dry seasons is sometimes brackish, but in wet is drinkable to Cow-ford, which is 12 miles below this, and about 24 from its mouth."
>
> *Diary*, 25 Dec 1765 (M-SJR, Charlotia, also called Rollestown): "the river is very deep near the bluff, tho there is a great barr opposite to the town."
>
> *Diary*, 30 Dec 1765 (M-SJR, Lake George): "Arrived at the head of the great lake 20 or more miles long, one and a half fathom deep, and 12 miles wide."
>
> *Diary*, 30 Jan 1766 (L-SJR, JB's Gray's Creek, probably Rice Creek): "we rowed 8 miles, crossing the river to Gray's creek, which is 60 yards wide, and two fathom and a half deep; we went about 7 miles up it; its general course is west by south, and generally pretty straight, good high swamps on each side . . . we could not pass near so far, as we had depth of water, by reason of many old trees fallen across the creek."
>
> *Travels*, 78 (L-SJR, near Mandarin): "the shores of this great river St. Juan, are very level and shoal, extending in some places, a mile or two, into the river, betwixt the high land, and the clear waters of the river, which is so level, as to be covered not above a foot or two deep, with water, and at a little distance appears as a green meadow having water-grass and other amphibious vegetables, growing in the oozy bottom, and floating upon the water."

## River Islands

The middle and upper reaches of the St. Johns River include numerous islands of many sizes and features; they may be completely independent islands in the main river channel, such as Drayton, Hog, Murphy, and Turkey, or islands of low relief surrounded by narrow meandering creeks, including Tick and Dexter along the southern margins of lakes Dexter and Woodruff. Many of the larger elevated islands have long histories of human occupation, indicated by human-generated shell mounds that extend back thousands of years. Drayton Island continues to be occupied today, having a ferry that transports residents between Georgetown and the island.

Vegetation on the islands reflects responses to elevations above the river, available soil moisture, and disturbance. Mixed pine and hardwood hammocks occur on the more elevated parts of the islands, often with weedy understories, presumably reflecting previous human activity. Like the riverside banks, elevated areas are associated with shell midden materials; wet hammock or swamp species occur in the low swampy areas. Lightning strikes are a reality, with ignitions associated with the taller pines, but lightning-generated wildfires are probably uncommon because burnable surface fuels are sparse. Murphy Island has been burned in recent years by the St. Johns River Water Management District managers. There is also a report of a wildfire there in the early 2000s.

> *Diary*, 26 Dec 1765 (M-SJR, Dunn's Island, now called Murphy Island): "landed on Dunn's Island on a large snail shell ridge, the adjacent swamp excellent, and the middle ground rich for corn, turkeys, and alligators plenty, saw a middling sized Indian tumulus, 20 yards diameter and 6 or 8 foot high."

> *Diary*, 6 Jan 1766 (U-SJR): "We rowed by a very large island on the eastside and another on the west, the best I have seen in Florida; the river, for these two days, has run very crooked."

> *Diary*, 27 Jan 1766 (M-SJR, Bear Island in the middle of Crescent Lake): "landed on a small island of near 100 acres, part cypress-swamp, part marsh, and piney palmetto, a very rotten black soil, mixed with white sand: We landed on a low bluff of muscle and snail-shells, generally broken and powdered by the surges of the lake; here, as well as in most other places on any high dry bank on the river or its branches where the soil is good, are found fragments of old Indian pots and orange-trees, which clearly demonstrates, that the Florida Indians inhabited every fertile

spot on the St. John's river, lakes and branches; now the ash, maple, elm, and pavia, are all green, and shot out several inches, the cypress is in full bloom, the water-oak begins to look yellow, and the sweet-gum just casting its leaves."

*Travels,* 103–4 (M-SJR, Drayton Island): "There grows on this island, many curious shrubs, particularly a beautiful species of Lantana. It grows in coppices in old fields, about five or six feet high, the branches adorned with rough serrated leaves, which sit opposite, and the twigs terminate with umbelliferous tufts of orange coloured blossoms, which are succeeded by a cluster of small blue berries: the flowers are of various colours, on the same plant . . . crimson, scarlet, orange, and golden yellow."

*Travels,* 104 (M-SJR, Drayton Island): "rich swamps on the shores of the island . . . covered entirely with tall grass, rushes, and herbaceous plants; amongst these are several species of Hibiscus, particularly the Hibiscus coccineus . . . are embellished with large expanded crimson flowers."

## Floating Mats and Islets of Vegetation

Rooted and floating aquatic plants form huge living mats along the middle and upper reaches of the St. Johns River. They are important retreats for game fishes, alligators, turtles, and other wildlife. The mats often extend out from the river's banks dozens of feet into the open channel in protected coves and river bends. They can clog smaller channels between groups of islands, such as the Seven Sisters, often preventing boats from passing through. These mats include masses of water lettuce, spatterdock, pennywort, smartweed, and beautiful flowering species, such as cardinal flower, scarlet hibiscus, saltmarsh mallows, and string lilies. There are also remnant patches of the introduced purple-flowered water hyacinth, which have been largely controlled by herbicide spraying and foraging by introduced weevils. As a result, current vegetation mats are surely more similar to those described by the Bartrams than at any time since the introduction of the water hyacinths to the St. Johns River in the mid-1880s.[3]

*Diary,* 31 Dec 1765 (M-SJR, Lake George): "at the entrance of the river into the great lake there floats prodigious quantities of the pistia, which grows in great plenty most of the way from hence to the head of the river, and is continually driving down with the current . . . entangled with a large species of water-numularia, persicaria, water-grass, and saxifrage, all which send down very long fibrous roots deep into the water . . . all together gather mud, by the daily accumulation of which they are formed into islands."

*Diary*, 8 Jan 1766 (U-SJR): "banks in many places are raised, a foot or more, by the trash [vegetation] floating down the river, which being drove on shore by the wind, there rots and is converted into stiff soil, on which the alligators love to bask."

*Travels*, 117–18 (U-SJR, Lake Dexter): "The mouth or entrance from the river to it was narrow, but the waters soon after spread and formed a little lake, extending into the marshes, its entrance and shores within I observed to be verged with floating lawns of the Pistia and Nymphea and other aquatic plants; these I knew were excellent haunts for trout" [Large-mouth bass].

## Bluff Hammocks

John Bartram reported "very rich hammocks" growing in "light black shelly soil" along river bluffs on the SJR. His term *hammock* is still in common usage today in Florida to distinguish hardwood woodlands from pinelands. The Bartrams mention cabbage palms, magnolias, water oak, live oaks, hickories, red cedars, a "curious zanthoxilon," bays, celtis, and orange groves in these river bluff forests.

Elevated banks often rise up from the river's edge; some ascend gradually, while others form sheer eroded walls. William Bartram referred to the vertical walls as "perpendicular" banks. The Bartrams reported some steep banks reaching 20 feet in height, such as those they saw at Charlotia. Trees and shrubs, growing on bank edges, often have their roots exposed and cling precariously to available layers of clay, sands, and shell midden materials. These roots help stabilize the river banks, thus limiting riverside erosion.

Hammock plants ascend the bluff slopes, responding to slope gradients, soil types, available soil moistures, fire frequencies, and disturbances. Today, most riverside hammocks have been converted to human-derived landscapes. In a natural state, wetland plants dominate the moist bottoms and seepage slopes, where they are exposed to periodic inundation and occasional fires (water oaks, laurel oaks, Virginia live oaks, cabbage palms, dahoon hollies, sweet bay, Walter's viburnum, green hawthorn). These moisture-loving species are replaced farther up the slopes by species that favor drier soil conditions (sweetgums, American beech, basswood, pignut hickories, magnolias, longleaf pines). The most drought-resistant plants (sand live and sand post oaks, shrub evergreen oaks, saw palmetto, longleaf pines, sparkleberry, Florida rosemary, wiregrass, gopher apple) occur on the driest, higher slopes, often positioned adjacent to upland pinelands. These species live with frequent fires that often originate with lightning strikes in adjoining upland pinelands.

Certain riverside hammocks offer high humidity and moderate temperatures by virtue of living in close proximity to the St. Johns River and having closed forest canopies. These variables enable some tropicals, particularly epiphytic orchids, bromeliads, ferns, and wild coffee, to range much farther north, well beyond the expected tropical environs of their native South Florida. It is so intriguing to spot shoestring ferns, golden polypody ferns, and Bartram's air plants encrusting palm trunks, or unusual orchids growing on spreading oaks, as one paddles the braided branches of the St. Johns River and its tributaries.[4]

> *Diary*, 28 Dec 1765 (M-SJR): "banks of this fine river are a continual alternate change of pine-land, bluffs, cypress, swamps, marshes, and rich ash, swamps, and maple: the hammocks of live-oaks and palmettos are generally surrounded either with swamp or marsh."

> *Diary*, 11 Jan 1766 (U-SJR, Puzzle Lake): "came to a bluff where we could set our feet on dry ground; this being a very rich hammock of 6 acres of light black shelly soil producing red-cedar, celtis, a curious zanthoxylium, and several others we never observed before, a few large orange-trees, and some young ones."

> *Diary*, 20 Jan 1766 (U-SJR, vicinity of the Spalding's upper store): "we walked from the landing directly towards the pine-lands, at first over a rich level, then ascended a hill 6 feet perpendicular, formed all of shells mixed with a little black sandy mould, ... shells diminishing gradually, and the fine sand appearing more and more ... we still came to rising ground producing hiccory, magnolia, bay, and water-oak, then ground-oak, chamaerops, then pine-lands."

> *Travels*, 114–15 (U-SJR, near Manhattan): "perpendicular bluff, ten or twelve feet high, consisting of a black sandy earth, mixed with a large proportion of shells, chiefly various species of fresh water Cochlea and Mytuli. Near the river, on the high shore, grew Corypha palma, Magnolia grandiflora, Live Oak, Callicarpa, Myrica cerifera, Hibiscus spinifex, and the beautiful evergreen shrub called Wild lime or Tallow nut. ... At the upper end of this bluff is a fine Orange grove."

## River Swamps

River swamps are forested wetlands that grow on floodplains along the St. Johns River and its larger tributaries. Hydroperiods of these swamps tend to be short, fluctuating with water levels. Saturated soils, flowing water, and high dissolved oxygen levels control swamp landscapes by speeding up the removal of organic matter and reducing fire frequencies.

The interiors of swamp areas can be flooded or laced with small pools and meandering streams depending on local water levels. They are heavily shaded and difficult to traverse because of mucky, organic soils, fallen trees, exposed roots, and cypress knees. Scattered shallow depressions in the swamp during low water periods commonly serve as reservoirs for shade-tolerant ferns, emergent aquatic plants, shrubs, small trees, poison ivy, and spiny vines, which concentrate in patches of dappled sunlight.

Swamps along the east side of the St. Johns River. Photo by Richard Franz.

River swamps are commonly timbered with bald cypress, red maple, cabbage palm, blackgum, green ash, pop ash, laurel oak, and Florida elm. Shrubs at the river's margin include wax myrtle, dahoon holly, Virginia willow, swamp dogwood, swamp bay, climbing hemp-vine, and climbing aster.[5]

*Diary,* 25 Dec 1765 (L-SJR, Palatka): "in the swamp grows the swamp or northern kind 18 inches diameter, and 60 foot high, liquid-amber and red-maple 3 foot diameter, elm, ash, and bays; the plants were most sorts of the northern ferns, saururus, iris, pancratium, large long flowering convolvolus running 20 foot high, chenopodium as high, and 4 inches diameter, pontedereia and dracontium."

*Diary,* 2 Jan 1766 (U-SJR): "We observed many short willows, but the woody swamps are chiefly black and white ash, with red maple next the river, and generally a cypress-swamp interposed between the pine-lands and swamps of ash."

*Travels,* 116 (U-SJR, Lake Dexter): "a little lake, which is an expansion of the river . . . lined with vast Cypress swamps, both coasts gradually approaching each other, to the opening of the river again."

*Travels,* 122 (U-SJR, Lake Dexter): "at a distance of about two hundred yards from my encampment, on the land side, were invested by a large Cypress swamp, covered with water."

## Riverside Palm Forests and Isle of Palms

Mature sabal palm hammocks occur in fragmented stands along the low shorelines of Lake George and Little Lake George. A riverside palm forest, across from Drayton Island and north of Rocky Point, has dense stands of huge cabbage palms, many 50–60 feet in height, a few scattered large oaks, and smaller ash trees filling in beneath them. The ground cover consists mostly of small palms and ash saplings. The trees are all shallow-rooted, growing on shell midden heaps and limestone rock. The larger oaks are subjected to occasional uprooting, bringing up with them masses of shell material and limestone chunks that become exposed in their root balls. The riverside palm hammocks are also often inundated with river water, based on the amount of human-derived flotsam and jetsam littering the forest floor. The flooding, shallow soils, and wind probably account for uprooted trees. William Bartram mentions a palm landscape existing on an island in Lake George that he encountered during his 1774 visit. He referred to it as the Isle of Palms and stated that it was located off Cedar Point, but this island with its palm forest completely disappeared sometime after his visit. Wyman reported "Rope Island" in 1868 as located off the right bank, near the entrance to Lake George. Rope Island is considered identical to Bartram's Isle of Palms (Harper, 157), but the island has now also completely disappeared from Lake George.

*Travels*, 115–16 (U-SJR, near Manhattan): "I set sailed alone. The coast on each side had much the same appearance.... The Palm trees here seem to be of a different species from the Cabbage trees; their strait trunks are sixty, eighty or ninety feet high, with a beautiful taper of a bright ash colour, until within six or seven feet of the top, where it is a fine green colour, crowned with an orb of rich green plumed leaves." (Bartram's Palma elata is listed as royal palm [*Roystonea elata*] in Harper's 1967 edition of *Travels*, 586, and as Florida royal palm [*Roystonea regia*] in Wunderlin and Hansen. Bartram also reported this palm from below Palatka, at Charlotia, and near Huntoon Island.)

*Travels*, 157 (M-SJR, Isle of Palms in Lake George): "I was however induced to deviate a little from my intended course, and touch at the inchanting little Isle of Palms. This delightful spot, planted by nature, is almost an entire grove of Palms, with a few pyramidal Magnolias, Live Oaks, golden Orange, and the animating Zanthoxilon; what a beautiful retreat is here!"

## River Marshes

River marshes are open wetlands that are associated with shallow water and often occur as backwaters of the river. As part of the river floodplain, they are hydrologically connected to the river. Marshes differ from river swamps by lacking dense stands of large trees. St. Johns River marshes often open into large panoramas of sky and distant tree-lines.

River marshes consist of thick growths of emergent grasses and other herbaceous plants that are rooted in shallow water. They form a patchwork of emergent maidencane, sawgrass, cattails, and bulrushes, with adjoining areas of more open water with pickerelweed, white water lilies, spatterdock, and pennywort. At Tick Island and the Salt Spring run, these marshes have dense stands of sand cordgrass.

River marsh on the back side of Tick Island, showing tussocks of sand cordgrass. Photo by Richard Franz.

Fires are common in river marshes, ignited by summer lightning. These fires usually burn when moisture levels are greatest in the marsh, and as a consequence they consume mostly above-water parts of the plants, leaving roots and soils intact. River marshes occasionally include scatterings of isolated young trees and woody shrubs, particularly red maple and Carolina willows, but the invasions of woody species are probably kept in check by fires and periodic flooding.[6]

> *Diary*, 2 Jan 1766 (U-SJR): "very extensive marshes on each side (with several short cypress-trees and maple-hammocks interspersed). . . . We observed many short willows."

> *Diary*, 3 Jan 1766 (U-SJR): "then fell back to a fine rich grassy swamp, chiefly ash, elm, and cypress, but much more open than down the river below the great lake, with more frequent patches of marsh and high grass and small maples, willows, and cephalanthus thinly scattered upon them."

*Diary,* 6 Jan 1766 (U-SJR): "very different swamp and marsh joining it [Mount Joy, in the vicinity of Volusia Blue Spring Landing], some dry, others middling moist, and some very wet, some reedy soil, some myrtle, oak, cypress, and lastly pine; then we came a little farther to tall water-reeds on both sides, and much elder grew next the river and close to the reeds, which last grew very thick close to the bank."

*Diary,* 7 Jan 1766 (U-SJR): "it being generally good reed-marsh and some cypress-swamps, we came to the middle lake 1, 2 or 3 miles broad, and 8 long."

## Rocky Shores

William Bartram visited Rocky Point at the northern end of Lake George with plans of stopping there to camp, but he moved on when he found no firewood present. He described this site as "the West cape or promontory" (*Travels,* 169). The USGS Salt Springs Quad Map places Rocky Point at the end of a small peninsula jutting out from the west bank of the river. The rocks at "West cape" are inundated, visible as a submerged rocky shelf during periods of high water, but may become partially exposed during low water.

Rocks are also exposed at Kinsley Point on the southern end of Drayton Island, even during high water, which may have been William Bartram's landing site after finding Rocky Point unsuitable for camping. The name Kinsley Point on the USGS topo map is probably a misspelling of Kingsley, for Zephaniah Kingsley, who occupied this island in the early 1800s. The rocky shoals at Drayton Island and Rocky Point appear to be near the same elevation as the floor of the spring basin at Salt Springs. This rock represents dolostone (carbonate rock with high percentage of the mineral dolomite) probably associated with the Coosawhatchee Formation in the Hawthorn Group (Miocene-aged sediments). Other dark, smaller rocklike chunks found in the water with the limestone might be mineralized peat nodules.

The vegetation on Rocky Point and the rocky prominence at Drayton consist of mostly red maples, sugarberry, sabal palms, bald cypress, and shrubs. Marsh grasses, cattails, bulrushes, and sawgrass extend out from their shores, where sufficient soil development occurs. The rocks in the water are often seated in sand, which apparently helps to scour them of algae and other vegetation.[7]

*Travels*, 168–69 (M-SJR, north of Lake George): "Rocky Point, the West cape or promontory, as we enter the river descending towards Mount Royal: these are horizontal slabs or flat masses of rocks, rising out of the lake two or three feet above its surface, and seem an aggregate composition or concrete of sand, shells, and calcareous cement; of a dark grey or dusty colour; this stone is hard and firm enough for buildings. . . . Rocky Point is an airy cool and delightful situation, commanding a most ample and pleasing prospect of the lake and its environs; but here being no wood, I re-embarked and sailed down a little farther to the island in the bay, where I went on shore."

## Shelly Banks, Shelly Knolls, and Shelly Prominences

Numerous deposits of freshwater shells occur along both banks of the St. Johns River and larger river islands. These high, dry shelly sites were sought out as camping places by the Bartrams.

During the Bartram times and later, it was not known how these freshwater shell deposits accumulated, although many attributed them to actions of the river. By the 1870s, Jeffries Wyman (1814–74) had determined that the mounds were human refuse deposits, containing shells and animal bones from meals. He thought human remains in the mounds were the result of cannibalism on the part of the inhabitants. In the 1890s, Clarence Moore (1852–1936), a wealthy businessman, educated at Harvard, who turned archaeologist in his later years, found historic objects as well as mortuaries in St. Johns River shell mounds, thus dispelling the cannibalism idea.

Information from the lower layers of the shell deposits suggests people began intensively harvesting and eating freshwater mollusks around 6,000–7,000 years ago. The most common shells, found as midden debris along the middle reaches of the St. Johns River, are freshwater banded mystery snails in the family Viviparidae. About 3,000 years ago, the native peoples shifted away from a snail-based economy (perhaps caused by a collapse in the fishery) to growing food crops on shell mounds. In modern times, many of these shell accumulations have been lost to mining for road fill and other construction purposes.

Shell mounds are composed of very rich calcareous soils that develop from the leaching of the freshwater shells. These soils support diverse hardwoods including elms, ashes, orange trees, and wild coffee. Oyster mounds in coastal Florida are known to support nearly two hundred kinds of plants. Informa-

Banded mystery shells washing out from an extensive shell midden along the banks of the St. Johns River. Photo by Richard Franz.

tion is limited on shell mound vegetation on the St. Johns River, except for the brief account by Laessle (1942), who noted the presence of 16 species on the Orange Point shell mound near the town of Welaka on the east side of the river.[8]

> *Diary*, 25 Dec 1765 (M-SJR, Charlotia): "a bluff point 17 foot high, more or less, of which 5 foot is composed of snail and muscle-shells, mixed with black mould or rotten vegetables, intermixed with sand, 20 paces distant from the shore."

> *Diary*, 28 Dec 1765 (M-SJR): "Mount Hope is 50 yards long and 30 wide, near 20 foot high, composed all of fresh water snails and muscle-shells of various dimensions, the small ones drove into the large, and the broken and powdered ones into the interstices of both; these are very fertile soils as far as the shells reach, and if not the only, yet the common planting grounds of the former Florida Indians."

*Diary*, 28 Dec 1765 (M-SJR): "Landed at Mount-Royal, where there are 50 acres of cleared old fields, fine oranges in the woods; the bank and for 50 yards back is composed of sandy soil mixed with snail-shells; encamped on the east-side of the river opposite to the island, from whence we heard a bear roaring in the night; we lay on a low bluff of snail shells."

*Diary*, 30 Dec 1765 (M-SJR, Lake George): "We landed on a fine shelly bluff 10 foot above the water; here grows red-cedar, live-oak, great palmetto, and good oranges, behind which is a high rich clear marsh producing grass as high as one's head, reaching to the pine-lands."

*Diary*, 1 Jan 1766 (M-SJR, below the upper store): "Landed at a high shelly bluff, where thousands of orange-trees surrounded us, with red cedars and live-oaks."

*Diary*, 5 Jan 1766 (U-SJR): "Staid at Mount-joy; this mount is formed of snail and muscle-shells, and is 8 or 10 foot perpendicular, about 150 yards long and 20 broad, on the south-east side of the river, declining gradually at each end to an extensive stiff moistish marsh."

## High Pine

Upland longleaf pine savannas occur on well-drained sandy soils in Florida. These pine forests consist of diffuse stands of longleaf pine and turkey oak, with herbaceous ground covers of wiregrass and more than a hundred other low-growing shrubs and herbaceous plants. Wiregrass and other high pine plants serve as fire promoters that carry the fire through the stand. Frequent fires are responsible for maintaining the open, grassy aspects of this habitat; exclusions of fire enable encroaching hardwoods to choke these open landscapes and encourage the buildup of combustible fuels from unburned plant litter. Fires not only influence landscape structure, plant composition, and species abundance but also promote flowering, seed germination, and longleaf pine regeneration.

Even though longleaf sandhills appear rather unremarkable, they possess unique xeric-adapted faunas and very rich herbaceous floras. Sandhills are also the primary landscape where burrowing gopher tortoises (reptile), pocket gophers (mammal), old field mice, and numerous burrowing snakes, lizards, and arthropods live. Burrowing activities churn up droughty soils, thus having a significant role in recycling sequestered nutrients. Excavated soils can also provide

High pine landscape with large longleaf pines and a grassy understory. Photo by Richard Franz.

nesting spots for gopher tortoises, proper soil conditions for small burrowing arthropods, lizards and snakes, and ideal nursery sites for the germination of rare plants. The burrowing gopher tortoise, described and illustrated for the first time by William Bartram from between Halfway Pond and Alachua Savanna, is often referred to as a "keystone" species, critical for the well-being of a landscape. This apt title was conferred on the gopher tortoise because of its ability to construct burrows that provide retreats for more than 350 other animal species, including 20 burrow obligates, many of which would likely perish without these protective structures.[9]

> *Travels*, 173 (I-Trek, west of Deep Creek): "where it gently rises the higher sand hills. . . . A magnificent grove of stately Pines, succeeding to the expansive wild plains we had a long time traversed, had a pleasing effect."

> *Travels*, 173–74 (I-Trek, Cowpen Lake): "The Pine groves passed, we immediately find ourselves on the entrance of the expansive airy Pine forests, on parallel chains of low swelling mounds, called the Sand Hills. . . . but yet, as we approach them, they insensibly disappear, and seem to be lost, and we should be ready to conclude all to be a visionary scene, were it not for the sparkling ponds and lakes, which at the same time gleam through the open forests."

> *Travels*, 179–80 (I-Trek, near Lochloosa): "From Halfway pond, we proceed Westward, through the high forests of Cuscowilla. . . . Now the sand ridges become higher, and their bases proportionably more extensive; the savannas and ponds more expansive; the summit of the ridges more gravelly; here and there, heaps or piles of rocks, emerging out of the sand and gravel; these rocks are the same sort of concrete of sand and shells as noticed on St. Juan and the great lake."

## Scrub

Scrub is a xeric evergreen shrub landscape that occupies well-drained, sandy soils (for example, sand live oak, Chapman's oak, myrtle oaks, scrub hickory, rusty lyonia, saw palmetto, and Florida rosemary). Fires are crucial to the survival of the scrub community, but unlike high pine and other pine landscapes, scrubs are subjected to infrequent catastrophic fires, where essentially all of the above-ground plant growth is destroyed. Scrub plants regenerate following fires, either by root sprouting or germination of seeds stored in the soil. One type of sand pine (Ocala sand pine) restricted to peninsular Florida requires intense heat from fires to open their serotinous (resinous) cones and release their seeds.

William Bartram visited "sandy pine barrens" along what is now the upper part of the Ft. Gates Ferry Road, just northeast of the town of Salt Springs; he reported coontie (as Zamia pumila), garberia (as Cacalia), the Ocala tree form of prickly-pear cactus (as Opuntia), American beautyberry (as Callicarpa), and Cherokee bean (as Erythrina) from these scrubs. Today, the American beautyberry, garberia, and tree cacti, as well as the Ocala sand pine, big-flowered pawpaw, pink-flowered lady lupines, and other scrub plants grow in great profusion along this road.

Florida scrubs are homes to a wide variety of endemic plants, invertebrates, and vertebrates. These plants and animals now occur as isolated pockets in scrub habitats, which correspond to remote Pleistocene islands that periodically became stranded during worldwide sea level changes, beginning 2.6 million years ago. This episodic isolation provided a mechanism for subsequent speciation to occur on these remote scrub islands. Some endemics, confined to these sand islands, include scrub lizards, sand skinks, and red widow spiders.[10]

*Diary*, 27 Dec 1765 (M-SJR): "Lodged at Johnson's Bluff, where for a mile the sandy pine-barren comes close or near the shore."

*Travels*, 163–64 (M-SJR, Salt Springs): "an endless wild desert, the upper stratum of the earth of which is a fine white sand, with small pebbles, and at some distance appears entirely covered with low trees and shrubs of various kinds, and of equal height."

## Pine Flatwoods

Flatwoods are associated with near-level topography and poorly drained soils; light-textured fine sands occur at or near the surface; clay hardpans often lie beneath the sands. Flatwoods are composed of scattered or dense stands of pine, including slash, pond, and longleaf pines, with understories of wiregrass, pineywoods dropseed, saw palmetto, gallberry, fetterbush, tarflower, and other low-growing shrubs. Fire is essential in pine systems in Florida for reducing encroaching hardwood competitors, releasing nutrients from consumed plants and litter, and increasing the vigor of plant species. Flatwoods sites with frequent fires often produce open, grassy vistas.

Bay swamps, or Bartram's so-called bay-galls, are forested wetlands with evergreen species such as loblolly bays, red bays, pond pines, slash pines, and titi. These swamps are situated on lower slopes or in low, swampy peat-filled depressions in the midst of pine flatwoods. The swamps are fed by groundwater seepage and rainwater, and they are often drained by shallow black-water creeks. Hydroperiod may be controlled by underlying clay hard-pans, which keep the

Pine flatwoods with shallow flatwoods pond. Breeding pond for rare amphibians. Photo by Sandra Kokernoot reproduced by permission.

water near the surface. Bay swamps have acidic soils, often remain moist or wet, and can be irregularly covered with standing water. Because of moist conditions, fires are often excluded from these swamps. Ferns and sphagnum moss are common in areas of standing water. Vines, especially greenbrier and grapes, may be abundant at the edges of the bays.[11]

*Travels,* 94 (M-SJR, Charlotia): "green and delightful, being covered with grass and the Corypha repens, and thinly planted with trees of the long leaved, or Broom Pine, and decorated with clumps or coppices of... aromatic shrubs, and enameled with patches of the beautiful little Kalmea ciliata."

*Travels*, 170 (I-Trek, 4 or 5 miles west of Spalding's lower store): "we travelled Westward, over a perfectly level plain, which appeared . . . as a charming green meadow, thinly planted with low spreading Pine trees (*P. palustri*). The upper stratum of the earth is a fine white crystalline sand, the very upper surface of which being mixed or incorporated with the ashes of burnt vegetables, renders it of sufficient strength or fertility to clothe itself perfectly, with a very great variety of grasses, herbage and remarkably low shrubs, together with a very dwarf species of Palmetto (*Corypha pumila stipit. serratius*)."

*Travels*, 173 (I-Trek, west of Deep Creek): "path descends to a wet baygale; the ground is hard, fine white sand, covered with black slush, which continued above two miles, when it gently rises the higher sand hills. . . . The ascent of the hill, ornamented with a variety and profusion of herbaceous plants and grasses, particularly Amaryllis atamasco, Clitoria, Phlox, Ipomea, Convolvulus, Verbena corymbosa, Ruellia, Viola, etc."

## Deep Creek

William Bartram and his trader companions crossed Deep Creek, and possibly Cabbage Creek and Little Orange Creek, on their way to Halfway Pond, the Alachua Savanna, and points west in 1774. The precise location of their crossing points are not specifically known, although they may have been in the vicinity of SR 310, 315, 21, and 20. The Deep Creek crossing, west of Rodman, is now covered with the waters of Rodman Pool, which flooded the lower part of the creek as a result of damming the Ocklawaha River. The head waters of Deep Creek originate as seepages and shallow springs flowing from the elevated Interlachen highlands. A section of Deep Creek, south of the town of Interlachen, is noteworthy because of its stand of the rare Atlantic white cedar in its floodplain. This stand represents one of two white cedar swamps in peninsular Florida.

*Travels*, 172–73 (I-Trek, Deep Creek): "we crossed a fine brook or rivulet; the water cool and pleasant; its banks adorned with varieties of trees and shrubs, particularly the delicate Cyrilla racemiflora, Chionanthus, Clethra, Nyssa sylvatica, Andromeda nitida, Andromeda formosissima: and here were great quantities of a very large and beautiful Filex osmunda, growing in great tufts or clumps."

## Upland Ponds and Lakes

John Bartram noted in his diary the presence of grassy ponds behind the elevated banks of the St. Johns River. Later his son described other ponds and lakes, including Halfway Pond, as he and his trader companions traversed western Putnam County on their westward treks.

According to limnologists Mark Brenner, Michael Binford, and Edward Deevey in *Ecosystems of Florida*, Florida has at least "7,800 lakes with surface areas greater than 0.4 acres."[12] There are probably at least that many pools smaller than that. Most are shallow with maximum water depths less than 16 feet; most lack overland outflows; many leak water through their porous bottoms. Ponds and lakes are often circular, reflecting their sinkhole origins. They tend to derive their water from seepage that flows through the bordering upland soils. Deeper pools may have direct connections with surficial or deeper aquifers. For example, Devil's Hole near Interlachen is more than 100 feet deep and connects with a small cave system. Shallow pools tend to be ringed with saw palmettos, pond cypress, and black gum, or they merge directly with the surrounding pinelands. Many are subject to dramatic water level fluctuations, with many shallow pools completely drying up during droughts. Some shallow pools are deepened by alligator activities, enabling these pools to persist, after other nearby ponds dry up. Fires can sweep through pine wetlands during droughts, often igniting peat deposits in their bottoms. The burning of the peat deepens and resuscitates filling pond bottoms. Shallows of these pools are often vegetated with exquisite growths of maidencane, southern cutgrass, pickerelweed, sandweed, and buttonbush during periods of high water.

The ephemeral nature of the small ponds are important to the health of the pineland communities. Since they are often dry, these pools lack populations of predatory fishes and other large aquatic predators. These fishless ponds, as a consequence, provide breeding sites for rare upland amphibians, such as Florida gopher frogs and striped newts, as the ponds refill. Their larvae lack the means to escape predatory fish; hence these fishless ephemeral pools are essential for the conservation of these rare species.

William Bartram and his trader companions camped on the shores of Halfway Pond, which was populated with predatory fish, alligators, and softshell turtles. No one knows its precise location. Bartram aficionados have long pondered its position as key to locating the trader's path across north Florida and its importance as the origin for Bartram's new species of bream (sunfish) and the Florida softshell turtle. Harper speculated that Halfway Pond was located in the Cowpen Lake basin. So finding it somewhere in this morass of dozens of ponds and lakes, near the village of Johnson, represents a serious challenge. Harper thought Drummer's Pond might be the campsite area; unfortunately, no one has been successful in locating this pond, despite intense efforts. Blue Pond, on the north side of SR-20A, across from Lake McMeekin, is another candidate. It fits with Bartram's description of having crystal clear water, submerged rocky ledges, and sunfish and softshell turtles. The rocks that Bartram reported are actually consolidated fine-grained white clays (kaolin) that outcrop in the area as horizontal ledges. These exceptionally high quality clays have been mined at Edgar and Johnson since 1896; current mining operations continue at Edgar, a few miles east of Johnson. There is a distinct possibility that Halfway Pond may have been obliterated by more than 100 years of kaolin mining operations in the area.[13]

> *Diary*, 20 Jan 1766: "in the afternoon our host went over the river to shoot geese in the pine-land ponds, where they generally feed on the grass growing there; for they don't frequent the river, as we did not see one all the way, but multitudes of ducks... then pine-land, dwarf-myrtle, kalmia, vaccinium, andromeda, small pines and long grass in the ponds, where the water was about knee-deep more or less, some of which contain from one to 10 acres;... some surrounded close with the adjacent pine-lands, and others with large savannahs at one or both sides."

> *Travels*, 174 (I-Trek, Halfway Pond): "Arrived early in the evening at the Halfway pond, where we encamped and stayed all night. This lake spreads itself in a spacious meadow, beneath a chain of elevated sand-hills, ... the upper end, and just under the hills, are surrounded by a crescent of dark groves, which shaded a rocky grotto. Near this place, was a sloping green bank, terminating by a point of flat rocks, which projected into the lake, and formed one point of the crescent that partly surrounded the vast grotto or bason of transparent waters, which is called by the traders a sinkhole."

## Limestone Springs and Spring Runs

The Bartrams visited at least ten calcareous spring basins along the St. Johns River. Three are large, first magnitude springs, with recorded flow rates exceeding 100 $feet^3$/sec: William Spring (Silver Glen Springs) and Six-mile Spring

(Salt Springs), both on the west side of Lake George (Marion County), and Volusia Blue Spring, a *"vast Fountain of mineral water"* south of DeLand (Volusia County). Other Bartram springs are smaller, with flows of 1.55 to 12.4 feet$^3$/sec: Johnson Spring (Saratoga Harbor), Satsuma Spring and Nashua Spring (along the base of Magnolia Bluff), Welaka Spring (in the river, at the base of Johnson Bluff, north of the town of Welaka), Beecher Springs (south of Welaka), all on the east side of the St. Johns River (Putnam County); Gemini Springs on the north side of Lake Monroe (Volusia County); and finally Clifton Springs on the southeast side of Lake Jessup, near the town of Oviedo (Seminole County).

Florida's calcareous springs are windows into groundwater reservoirs flowing in cave conduits that thread their way through limestone rocks. Spring discharges flow from fissures, cracks, or other breaches in the limestone. Springs with sufficient hydrostatic pressure can have turbulent discharges called "spring boils" visible at the water surface; water exiting from smaller sand-covered spring vents produce continuous suspensions of sand particles in the water column, causing "sand-boils" at the openings. Spring vents can occur in the bottoms of the St. Johns River and its tributaries, river bank alcoves, and inland springs that flow to the river by way of spring runs. Most springs along the St. Johns River are rich in calcium, magnesium, sodium, chlorides, and sulfates; pH is usually near neutral to slightly alkaline; dissolved oxygen levels are often low. Salt, Satsuma, Nashua Springs, springs on Lake Monroe, and Clifton springs that were visited by the Bartrams have distinctive chemical signatures; their waters contain extremely high levels of calcium, magnesium, sodium, sulfates, and chlorides, making their waters odiferous and salty or bitter to the taste.

Many springs along the St. Johns River emit foul-smelling hydrogen sulfide gas. These springs are often referred to as "sulfur springs." The hydrogen sulfide gas is produced by highly specialized sulfate-reducing bacteria. The sulfates in groundwater originate from dissolution of gypsum deposits that lie deeply buried in Avon Park limestones hundreds of feet below the land surface. This mineral-rich water gradually travels through interconnected spaces in the Upper Floridan Aquifer, eventually reaching shallow limestones where it discharges through local spring vents.

Other chemoautotrophic (sulfur) bacteria occur in spring caves and shaded sulfur spring outflows, where they form extensive threadlike mats on plants, wood, rocks, and other debris. Collectively known as purple sulfur bacteria, they thrive under anoxic conditions and oxidize hydrogen sulfide to produce granules of elemental sulfur that collect inside their cells. The resulting accumulations of sulfur are responsible for the whitish color of the bacterial mats. The mats, as well as the odor, dissipate downstream as the hydrogen sulfide is vented and the spring water becomes more oxygenated.

The St. Johns River springs, their spring pools, and spring runs are hot spots for biotic diversity. They provide essential wintering retreats for temperature-sensitive manatees. The spring waters are important fisheries, feeding areas for wading birds, and specialized habitats for rare invertebrates. The unique nature of the St. Johns River springs, isolated from one another by river water and by land, have become centers of evolution for specialized aquatic mollusks and crustaceans. All of these species are limited to specific springs, where their total world distributions are measured in feet. There are fourteen species of aquatic snails, called hydrobes or siltsnails, with each confined to a specific spring. In addition, there may be as many as a dozen species of cave-adapted white crustaceans, living in dark portions of the spring caves, rarely appearing in the open waters of spring pools (cave crayfish, cave amphipods, and cave isopods), many of which remain undescribed at this time. Most of these spring-associated invertebrates are targeted for conservation efforts because of their very restricted distributions, specialized life histories, sensitivity to environmental changes, and at least with the cave species, their longevity (living decades).[14]

> *Diary*, 27 Dec 1765 (M-SJR, Saratoga Harbor-to-Welaka): "landed on a high bluff... at Johnson's Spring, a run of clear and sweet water.... [Satsuma Spring] issued out a large fountain (big enough to turn a mill) of warm clear water of a very offensive taste, and smelt like bilge-water, or the washings of a gun-barrel; ... [Nashua Spring] at the foot of the last issued out another warm spring of clear water like the other, but not so large. Then travelling alternately over hills and swamps, in all about 3 or 4 miles, came to a great cove, near a quarter of a mile from the river, out of the head of which arose a prodigious large fountain of clear water of loathsome taste, like the other two beforementioned; it directly formed a large deep creek 40 or 50 yards wide to the river [Welaka Spring]."

> *Diary*, 4 Jan 1766 (U-SJR, Volusia Blue Spring): "we soon came to a creek, up which we rowed a mile, in 4 and 6 foot water and 30 yards broad, of the colour of the sea, smelled like bilge-water, tasting sweetish and loathsome, warm and very clear, but a whitish matter adhered to the fallen trees near the bottom; the spring-head is about 30 yards broad, and boils up from the bottom like a pot: plummed it, and found about five fathom

water. . . . what a great space of ground must be taken up in the pine-lands, ponds, savannahs, and swamps, to support and maintain so constant a fountain, continually boiling right up from under the deep rocks."

*Diary*, 7 Jan 1766 (U-SJR, probably Gemini Springs on Lake Monroe): "here is a pretty stream of sweet water, small enough to run through the bung-hole of a barrel, and at about 200 yards distance from it runs out a large stream of water, so warm as to support the thermometer at 71 in it, feels warm to a coolish hand, tastes more loathsome than the others beforementioned of the same kind, and may be smelt at some roods distant; hereabout is drove on shore, the most delicate crystalline sand I ever saw, except what is got on an island near our capes, tho this is still finer: A few 100 yards from the last spring is another much like it in taste, but much larger, and near 30 yards broad, having three heads within 30 yards; the water is very loathsome and warm, but not so hot as one's blood: This differs from the other in having most of its surface covered with duck-meat; its banks full of shelly stone of the snail-shell kind, and running level with the river; the last had some fall; they are not above 200 yards from the lake."

*Diary*, 23 Jan 1766 (M-SJR, Silver Glen Springs): "Set out early, and coasted the west-side of the lake . . . until we came to William's Spring, a creek of very clear warm water, 30 yards broad and 2 foot deep, the spring heads even with the river; we landed near its mouth on a shelly-bluff amongst thousands of orange-trees, growing so thick that we could hardly pass between them for a quarter of a mile; we walked near a mile up to two or three of its heads, and left one on the right hand which we did not search, because we could not get at it without a boat. . . . About noon we set out from this place, and coasted still on the west-side."

*Diary*, 24 Jan 1766 (M-SJR, Salt Springs): "came to the main springs, where a prodigious quantity of very clear warm brackish water boiled up between vast rocks of unknown depth, we could not reach the bottom by a very long pole; . . . we walked round the west-end towards the south-bank, where the bare flat rocks appeared above water, and a great stream boiled up of a salt and sourish taste, but not near so loathsome as several before-described, nor had it any bad smell, or whitish sediment as they; we examined the composition of the rocks, and found some of them to be a concrete reddish sand, some whitish mixed with clay, others a ferruginous irregular concrete, ... with sea-shells, clams, and cockles.... my son found a lovely sweet tree, with leaves like sweet bay, which smelled like sassafras, and produce a very strange kind of seed-pod [discovery of the Yellow anise].... We saw near the spring numbers of large garr, cats, mullets, trouts, and several other kinds unknown to us."

*Travels*, 159–60 (M-SJR, Salt Springs, nine years later): "I set sail with a favourable breeze, coasting along the shores; when on a sudden the waters became transparent, and discovered the sandy bottom, and the several nations of fish, passing and repassing each other. Following this course I was led to the cape of the little river, descending from Six mile Springs, and meandering six miles from its source, through green meadows. I entered this pellucid stream, sailing over the heads of innumerable squadrons of fish.... As I approached the distant high forest on the main, the river widens, floating fields of the green Pistia surrounded me, the rapid stream winding through them. What an alluring scene was now before me! A vast bason or little lake of crystal waters, half encircled by swelling hills, clad with Orange and odoriferous Illisium groves."

## Ruderal Sites

The Bartrams encountered trading houses, Indian villages, and English plantations during their river travels. They saw remnants of abandoned Spanish farms, old fields, citrus groves, hunting shelters, and other human-derived disturbances, many of them overgrown and melting back into the local landscape. Contrasting the observations of John Bartram's diary entries with those of William Bartram nine years later demonstrates how quickly human landscapes can revert to "old habitations ... mouldering to earth."[15]

*Diary*, 25 Dec 1765 (L-SJR, Forrester Point): "we landed at a point of high ground, which has been an ancient plantation of Indians or Spaniards."

*Diary*, 25 Dec 1765 (M-SJR, Charlotia, also known as Rollestown): "small Spanish intrenchment on the bluff about 20 paces square, and pieces of Indian pots."

*Travels*, 80 (L-SJR, Fort Picolata, 1774): "I landed, but to my disappointment, found the fort dismantled and deserted.... It is a square tower, thirty feet high, invested with a high wall, without bastions, about breast high, pierced with loop holes and surrounded with a deep ditch. The upper story is open on each side, with battlements, supporting a cupola or roof.... The works are constructed with hewn stone, cemented with lime. The stone was cut out of quarries, on St. Anastatius Island, opposite St. Augustine."

*Travels*, 92–93 (L-SJR, Palatka, 1774): "coasting the Indian shore of this bay, on doubling a promontory, I suddenly saw before me an Indian settlement, or village. It was a fine situation, the bank rising gradually from the water. There were eight or ten habitations, in a row, or street, fronting the water, and about fifty yards distance from it.... They were civil, and appeared happy in their situation. There was a large Orange grove at the upper end of the village; ... and the ground under them clean, open, and airy. There seemed to be several hundred acres of cleared land, about the village; a considerable portion of which was planted, chiefly with corn (Zea), Batatas, Beans, Pompions, Squashes (Cucurbita verrucosa), Melons (Cucurbita citrullus), Tobacco (Nicotiana), etc. abundantly sufficient for the inhabitants of the village."

*Travels*, 95 (M-SJR, Charlotia, 1774): "The remaining old habitations, are mouldering to earth, except the mansion house, which is a large frame building, of Cypress wood, yet in tolerable repair, and inhabited by an overseer and his family. There is also a black-smith with his shop and family, at a small distance from it.... The aborigines of America had a very great town, in this place, as appears from the great tumuli, and conical mounts of earth and shells, and other traces of a settlement which yet remain. There grew in the old fields on these heights great quantities of Callicarpa and the beautiful shrub Annona: the flowers of the latter are large, white, and sweet scented."

*Travels*, 96 (M-SJR, Spalding's lower store at Stokes Landing): "I was received with great politeness, and treated during a residence of several months, with the utmost civility and friendship, by Mr. C. M'Latche, Messrs. Spalding and Kelsall's agent."

John and William Bartram visited the lower store on their first excursion to the St. Johns River in 1765–66. The lower store later provided lodging and support for William on his return trip in 1774. The store's manager, Charles McLatchie, loaned him a horse and saddle for his two trips with the traders as they traveled to Creek and Seminole villages west of the St. Johns River.[16]

*Travels*, 260 (Spalding's lower store): "busy in my apartment in the council-house, drawing some curious flower." [This leads up to the rattlesnake incident in the adjoining Seminole village.]

*Travels*, 253 (M-SJR, Lake George): "I reconnoitered the adjacent groves and lawns; here is a deserted plantation, the property of Dr. Stork, where he once resided. I observed many lovely shrubs and plants in the old fields and Orange groves."

*Travels*, 253 (M-SJR, east shore of Lake George): "Came to again, at an old deserted plantation, the property of a British gentleman, but some years since vacated. A very spacious frame building was settling to the ground and mouldering to earth; here are very extensive old fields, where were growing the West-Indian or perennial Cotton and Indigo, which had been cultivated here, and some scattered remains of the ancient Orange groves, which had been left standing at the clearing of the plantation."

*Diary*, 19 Jan 1766 (U-SJR, Spalding's upper store at Astor): "crossed the mouth of the east lake, and in an hour or two arrived at Spalding's Upper-store, where we staid all night, which was very warm, and the muskitoes very troublesome, as much so as any time since I left Charles-Town."

*Travels*, 111 (Spalding's upper store, 1774): "in the evening [we] reached the trading-house, Spalding's upper store, where I took up my quarters for several weeks."

William Bartram stayed at the trading post while he was exploring the upper reaches of the St. Johns River. His companion on several St. Johns River journeys, Job Wiggins, was the chief trader at the store during that time (Schafer, "New World").

## River's End

Both John and William Bartram followed the St. Johns River along its journey between its headwaters in southeast Florida and its final destination at the edge of the Atlantic Ocean. In the more than 250 years since they originally documented the natural wonders of East Florida, other explorers have followed their routes and recorded more adventures. Among them, naturalist Bill Belleville, like the Bartrams, has contributed further testimony to the river's incredible diversity and resiliency:

The water around us is now full of swirling eddies where the outgoing downstream current introduces itself full force to the incoming tides, the last noble molecule of upland St. Johns marsh meeting the indomitable sea. Some months ago, I stood in the headwaters of this river, up to my waist in a matrix of sawgrass and rain-driven water and peat. . . . I have gone from where there is no measureable current . . . to a place where hydrologists say 58.4 million gallons of water a minute swirl back and forth, between the river and the ocean.[17]

## List of Plants and Animals from Landscape Descriptions

Species are listed in order of appearance. Names are not repeated if they appear more than once in descriptions. Species names from John and William Bartram's quotations, extracted from the *Diary* and *Travels*, are listed in the Annotated Lists of Bartram Species at the end of the chapter.

Tapegrass (*Vallisneria americana*)
Water lettuce (*Pistia stratiotes*)
Spatterdock (*Nuphar advena*)
pennywort (*Hydrocotyle* sp.)
smartweed (*Polygonum* sp.)
Cardinal flower (*Lobelia cardinalis*)
Scarlet hibiscus (*Hibiscus coccineus*)
Saltmarsh mallow (*Kosteletzkya pentacarpos*)
String lily (*Crinum americanum*)
Water hyacinth (*Eichhornia crassipes*)
Cabbage palm (*Sabal palmetto*)
Southern magnolia (*Magnolia grandiflora*)
Water oak (*Quercus nigra*)
Virginia live oak (*Quercus virginiana*) hickories (*Carya* sp.)
Red cedar (*Juniperus virginiana*)
"curious zanthoxilon" Prickly ash (*Zanthoxylum clava-herculis*)
"celtis" Sugarberry (*Celtis laevigata*)
orange tree (*Citrus* sp.)
Laurel oak (*Quercus laurifolia*)
Dahoon holly (*Ilex cassine*)
Sweet bay (*Magnolia virginiana*)
Walter's viburnum (*Viburnum obovatum*)

Green hawthorn (*Crataegus viridis*)
Sweetgum (*Liquidambar styraciflua*)
American beech (*Fagus grandifolia*)
Basswood (*Tilia americana*)
Pignut hickory (*Carya glabra*)
Sand live oak (*Quercus geminata*)
Sand post oak (*Quercus margaretta*)
Evergreen shrub oak (*Quercus myrtifolia*)
Saw palmetto (*Serenoa repens*)
Longleaf pine (*Pinus palustris*)
Sparkleberry (*Vaccinium arboreum*)
Florida rosemary (*Ceratiola ericoides*).
Wiregrass (*Aristida stricta*)
Gopher apple (*Licinia michauxii*)
Shoestring fern (*Vittaria lineata*)
Golden polypody fern (*Phlebodium aureum*)
Bartram's airplant (*Tillandsia bartramii*)
Poison ivy (*Toxicodendron radicans*)
Bald cypress (*Taxodium distichum*)
Red maple (*Acer rubrum*)
Blackgum (*Nyssa sylvatica*)
Green ash (*Fraxinus pennsylvanica*)
Popash (*Fraxinus caroliniana*)
Florida elm (*Ulmus floridana*)
Wax myrtle (*Myrica cerifera*)
Virginia willow (*Itea virginica*)
Swamp bay (*Persea palustris*)
Climbing hemp-vine (*Mikania scandens*)
Climbing aster (*Aster carolinianus*)
Florida royal palm (*Roystonea regia*)
Maidencane (*Panicum hemitomon*)
Sawgrass (*Cladium jamaicense*)
cattails (*Typha* sp.)
bulrushes (*Scirpus* sp.)
Pickerelweed (*Pontederia cordata*)
White water lily (*Nymphaea odorata*)
Sand cordgrass (*Spartina bakeri*)
Carolina willow (*Salix caroliniana*)

Banded mystery snail (*Viviparia georgianus*)
Wild coffee (*Psychotria nervosa*)
Turkey oak *(Quercus laevis)*
Gopher tortoise (*Gopherus polyphemus*)
Pocket gopher (*Geomys pinetis*)
Old field mouse (*Peromyscus polionotus*)
Chapman's oak (*Quercus chapmanii*)
Florida hickory (*Carya floridana*)
Rusty lyonia (*Lyonia ferruginea*)
Ocala sand pine (*Pinus clausa*)
Coontie (*Zamia pumila*)
Garberia (*Garberia heterophylla*)
Prickly-pear cactus, Ocala scrub form (*Opuntia humifusa* var. *ammophila*)
American beautyberry (*Callicarpa americana*)
Cherokee bean (*Erythrina herbacea*)
Big-flowered pawpaw (*Asimina obovata*)
Pink-flowered lady lupines (*Lupinus villosus*)
Scrub lizard (*Sceloporus woodi*)
Sand skink (*Neoseps reynoldsi*)
Red widow spider (*Latrodectus bishopi*)
Pineywoods dropseed (*Sporobolus junceus*)
Gallberry (*Ilex glabra*)
Fetterbush (*Lyonia lucida*)
Tarflower (*Bejaria racemosa*)
greenbriers (*Smilax* sp.)
grapes (*Vitis* sp.)
sphagnum moss (*Sphagnum* sp.)
Loblolly bay (*Gordonia lasianthus*)
Redbay (*Persea borbonia*)
Pond pine (*Pinus serotina*)
Slash pine (*Pinus elliottii*)
Titi (*Cyrilla racemiflora*)
Atlantic white-cedar (*Chamaecyparis thyoides*)
Pond cypress (*Taxodium ascendens*)
Southern cutgrass (*Leersia hexandra*)
Sandweed (*Hypericum fasciculatum*)
Buttonbush (*Cephalanthus occidentalis*)
Florida gopher frog (*Lithobates capito*)

Striped newt (*Notophthamus perstriatus*)
bream (sunfish) (*Lepomis* sp.)
Florida softshell turtle (*Apalone ferox*)
hydrobes or siltsnails (*Aphaostracon* sp. and *Floridobia* sp.)
cave crayfish (*Procambarus* sp. and *Troglocambarus* sp.)
cave amphipods (*Crangonyx* sp.)
cave isopods (*Caecidotea* sp.)

## Naming Plants and Animals

Names are rooted deep in every language. They are coupled with action and modifying words, allowing us precise communication with our fellow humans. As with any language, people with specialized interests generate vocabularies to accommodate their specific needs. Science is an excellent example, creating special words dedicated to its objects, organisms, processes, methods, and theories. Early naturalists in Europe endeavored to invent a system to identify their objects, but their attempts led to lengthy complex names consisting of Latin words strung together. The use of Latin offered naturalists, born to different cultures, traditions, and languages, access to information in what was, at the time, a shared language among classically educated individuals. Long series of descriptive words were used as formal names for organisms, such as *Grus pratensis, corpore cinereo, vertice papillosa* (large bird or crane of the meadows, with a grey body and humped head) for the sandhill crane. But this system was faulty, cumbersome, and a major impediment in communicating taxonomic information. This practice needed reform, and that's where Carl Linnaeus, a Swedish botanist, stepped in.

## The Linnaean Legacy

Carl Linnaeus (1707–78) had already introduced his new plant classification system to the world by the time that the Bartrams made their first trip to Florida in 1765. Carl had also used his new binomial terminology to describe hundreds of plants and animals. Linnaeus's innovations were instrumental in allowing John Bartram, and later his son, to interpret and identify their Florida plant and animal discoveries. Their use of the Linnaean system has given modern taxonomists and Bartram historians access to their natural history writings.

Linnaeus began articulating a new classification system for organisms and minerals based on a hierarchical system in his published works beginning in

1735. This classification was summarily voiced in his 1753 edition of *Species Plantarum* for plants and in the 1758 edition (10th) of *Systema Naturae* for plants and animals. Hence the year 1753 is now acknowledged as the starting date for modern botanical nomenclature and 1758 for zoological nomenclature.

Departing from past practices, Linnaeus instituted a simplified arrangement for naming organisms that used a two-part (binomial) epithet, which consisted of a genus and species. This binomial became the valid scientific name for each described kind of organism. This two-part system recognized related organisms united by similar features. This arrangement places similar types together in the same "genus" (pl. genera); the second name, "species," separates unique related populations, thought to represent members of the same genus. As you might imagine, there was resistance by other practitioners, particularly those in England, to accepting new ways. However, early scientists, including the Bartrams in North America, saw merit in this new approach and many started using it.

In practice, the Linnaean name for the water oak consists of the genus name "Quercus," which identifies it as an oak, and "nigra" to distinguish it from other oaks. Together, the binomial name *Quercus nigra* identifies the plant specifically as the water oak. The first letter of the genus name Quercus is capitalized, and the entire scientific name *Quercus nigra* is either italicized or underscored when presented in print. To extend this concept further, the genus *Quercus*, based on Linnaeus's hierarchical interpretation, is a kind of angiosperm (flowering plants), placed within the order Fagales and the family Fagaceae (oak and beech trees). Linnaeus named literally thousands of plant and animal species.

The new methodology eventually pushed biological practitioners of the eighteenth century on both continents toward the modern era of taxonomy. Acknowledgment of the Linnaean system provided stability in scientific nomenclature.[18]

## Scientific Names versus Common Names

The Bartrams used both scientific and vernacular names in their writings. Many of their scientific names originated with Linnaeus's publications. By convention, modern scientific names are penned from Latin or are Latinized words from other languages. New generic and species names most often recognize either some unique feature possessed by the new organism or individual people (patronyms), who in some way contributed to the discovery or classification of that organism. These names become accepted and then used by authorities around the world, no matter where the scientist calls home.

They enable scientists to communicate with one another in both their conversations and writings.

Common or colloquial names, on the other hand, spring from local lore or some obvious physical aspect of the species that targets morphological, behavioral, or distributional information. They are not in Latin but in regional dialects and languages. Vernacular names, by their very nature, can change through time or from one geographic location or tradition to another. Common names for *Dryocopus pileatus*, a large woodpecker in the Southeast, for example, include pileated woodpecker [standard name], great red crested black woodpecker [William Bartram's name], and about a half a dozen others. In recent years, biologists and informed amateurs have attempted to standardize common names for many groups of organisms (bird names are perfect examples), thus providing a gateway for communication between these two interest groups. Common names will never replace the scientific epithet, but they certainly will offer common ground for engaging interactions.

## The New Taxonomy

As scientific thought matures and new technologies emerge, scientific endeavors escalate to meet the challenges of expanding information and ideas. In the field of taxonomy (evolutionary and biological classification), taxonomists are contending with an explosion of new information. As a result, modern taxonomy is moving away from the traditional hierarchical Linnaean system to a more phylogenetic approach that depicts relationships based on evolutionary histories. Linnaean ranks (e.g., families and orders), however, continue to be employed. This emerging field is now referred to as cladistics or phylogenetics. This method aligns lineages of organisms believed to have similar origins, based on shared derived characters (synapomorphies) that originate with the most recent common ancestor. These relationships are constructed with the help of detailed morphological assessments, DNA studies, fossil discoveries, computer simulations, and other kinds of information. These related phylogenetic groupings are called clades, and diagrams that portray the position of these clades are cladograms or evolutionary trees.

Novel approaches often require taxonomists to change how they view classic taxonomic groupings. This can result in shifts in taxonomic alignments, causing organisms to be moved from one genus or one family to another. These transferals may require the establishment of completely new names to accommodate emerging arrangements. Take, for example, the removal of maples from the traditionally recognized Maple Family to the Soapberry Family. Such transferals are evident in the name changes in the Annotated List of Bartram Species below.

## Science Is Progressive

It's difficult to keep up with changes within the field of biological classification, but be assured, there will be a continual supply of new names, ideas, alignments, and methodologies in its future. There will be new ways of communicating these ideas, too. Like the European naturalists and horticulturalists of the mid-1700s, there are those modern taxonomists who cling to the older, more conventional taxonomic approaches, while others totally embrace the newer phylogenetic ideas.

## Bartram Species

The following plant and animal lists are constructed from annotations in John Bartram's *Diary* (with dates) and William Bartram's *Travels* (with page numbers). I followed Harper's interpretations of Bartram names from his *Naturalist's Edition* (1967) in the development of the current lists. I changed Harper's names, when appropriate, to reflect recent changes in the modern taxonomic literature. Animals in William Bartram's list in *Travels* (part 2, chapter 10) are not included here because they are not part of his Florida travelogue.

The initial bolded names in the accompanying accounts are shown as the Bartrams presented them in their writings. Redundant references to species are listed when they contain unique information. Each species account includes the specific Bartram source. Bartram localities are placed in general regions (L-SJR, M-SJR, U-SJR, I-Trek), but in many situations I include precise localities. The currently accepted scientific names are based on Wunderlin and Hansen (2011) for plants, and standard scientific names for animals. Explanations appear at the end of some accounts when scientific names, used by Harper (1967) or Fry (2010), are at variance with those used here. I also employed notes for supplemental information that enhances the reader's appreciation of unique species. Harper used the term *nomen nudum* (nude names) in some of his annotations for certain Bartram plant names, because these names never made it into the mainstream taxonomic literature and therefore were never formally accepted. Harper also listed taxonomic synonyms (syn) for certain taxa. Synonyms refer to once-accepted scientific names that, for one reason or another, are no longer in common use.

Lists in Harper and Fry extend well beyond the reaches of this book, which focuses on the Bartrams in the St. Johns River valley of north Florida; readers should consult *Wildflowers of Florida and the Southeast* by Hall et al. (2011) and *Florida Wildflowers* by Taylor for flowering-plant descriptions with photographs.

## Annotated Lists of Bartram Species

### PLANTAE

FERNS (PTERIDOPHYTES)

Royal Fern Family (OSMUNDACEAE)

**Filex osmunda.** *Travels,* 173 (I-Trek, Deep Creek). Cinnamon fern, *Osmunda cinnamomea* and/or Royal fern, *Osmunda regalis,* according to Harper, 504. Both ferns currently occur along Deep Creek.

CONE-BEARING PLANTS (GYMNOSPERMS)

Cedar Family (CUPRESSACEAE)

**Red Cedar.** *Travels,* 140 (U-SJR). Red cedar, *Juniperus virginiana.* Listed as *Juniperus* sp. by Harper, 468.

**Red cedar.** *Diary,* 9 Jan 1766 (U-SJR).

**Cypress (or Cupressus disticha).** *Travels,* 90, 91, 93, 137 (L-SJR, U-SJR). Bald cypress, *Taxodium distichum.* Listed as either River cypress or Pond cypress (*Taxodium ascendens*) in Harper, 491. Probably Bald cypress based on habitat. Cypress was formerly placed in the Cypress Family (Taxodiaceae), but now has been moved to the Cedar Family (Wunderlin and Hansen).

**Cypress in full bloom.** *Diary,* 27 Jan. 1766 (M-SJR). Bald cypress.

Pine Family (PINACEAE)

**Longleaved Pines (or Broom).** *Travels,* 94, 161, 170, 173, 179 (M-SJR, I-Trek). Longleaf pine, *Pinus palustris.* Listed as *Pinus australis* by Harper, 594.

Zamia Family (ZAMIACEAE)

**Zamia pumila.** *Travels,* 162 (M-SJR, Salt Springs). Coontie, *Zamia pumila.*

Listed as *Zamia integrifolia* by Harper, 666–67. The name *Zamia integrifolia* is not recognized by Wunderlin and Hansen. *Zamia* was previously placed in the family Cycadaceae.

FLOWERING PLANTS (ANGIOSPERMS)

Wild Petunia Family (ACANTHACEAE)

**Ruellia.** *Travels,* 173, 180 (I-Trek). Presumably Wild petunia, *Ruellia caroliniensis*. Listed "as a genus of Acanthaceae, comprising the ruellias," in Harper, 616.

Moschatel or Elderberry Family (ADOXACEAE)

**Sambucus (or Sambuces).** *Travels,* 94 (M-SJR). Elderberry, *Sambucus nigra*. Listed as Southern elderberry, *Sambuscus simpsonii* in Harper, 618. Wunderlin and Hansen placed *Sambuscus simpsonii* in syn. of *Sambucus nigra*.

**Elder-trees.** *Diary,* 3 Jan 1766 (U-SJR). Elderberry.

Agave Family (AGAVACEAE)

**Yucca gloriosa.** *Travels,* 157 (M-SJR). Spanish dagger, *Yucca aloifolia*. Listed as Spanish bayonet, *Yucca gloriosa*, by Harper, 666. *Yucca gloriosa* is a coastal species, not occurring in SJR valley (Wunderlin and Hansen). See comments by Fry.

Amaranth Family (AMARANTHACEAE)

**Chenopodium.** *Diary,* 25 Dec 1765 (M-SJR). Probably Pigweed or Southern water-hemp, *Amaranthus australis*. This herb occurs in salt and fresh water in mostly coastal areas, grows to 30 feet tall, with a base up to a foot in diameter.[19] John compared his chenopodium to the size of *"flowering convolvulus running 20 foot high, chenopodium as high, and 4 inches diameter."* This plant was not listed in William's *Travels*.

Amaryllis Lily Family (AMARYLLIDACEAE)

**Amaryllis atamasco.** *Travels,* 173 (I-Trek, west of Deep Creek). Atamasco lily or Rain lily, *Zephyranthes atamasca* .

**Perfumed Crinum.** *Travels,* 157 (M-SRJ, Lake George). Swamp lily or String lily, *Crinum americanum*.

**Odorous Pancratium.** *Travels,* 105 (M-SJR, Drayton Island). Listed as Spider lily, *Hymenocallis* sp. by Harper, 587. Either *Hymenocallis crassifolia*, or a closely related species . The Bartram name "pancratium" probably refers to the genus *Pancratium*, European lily genus bearing a resemblance to North American spider lilies.

**Pancratium.** *Diary,* 25 Dec 1765 (Palatka). Spider lily.

Pawpaw Family (ANNONACEAE)

**Dwarf decumbent Annona with narrow leaves, and various flowers, already noticed at Alatamaha (Annona pigmea).** *Travels,* 171 (I-Trek, vicinity of Rodman). Dwarf pawpaw, *Asimina pygmea*. The plant was still common in the uplands at Rodman in 2015. The pawpaw genus *Asimina* includes ten species and at least six named hybrids in Florida (Wunderlin and Hansen). The distributions of these taxa are incompletely defined, as are the ecological factors that control their occurrences.

**Beautiful shrub Annona: the flowers ... large, white and sweet scented.** *Travels,* 95 (M-SJR, Charlotia). Listed as Woolly pawpaw, *Asimina incana* by Harper, 440 and Fry.

**Annona alba.** *Travels,* 303 (near Palatka). Probably Woolly pawpaw, *Asimina incana*. Listed as *nomen nudum* by Harper, 440.

**New species of Annona (Annona incana or "incarna"): Anona grandiflora: showy pawpaw.** *Travels,* 171 (I-Trek, vicinity of Rodman). Possibly Big-flowered pawpaw, *Asimina obovata*.

**Species of Annona** (Annona incarna, floribus grandiorbis paniculata). *Travels,* 171 (I-Trek, vicinity of Rodman). Big-flowered pawpaw, *Asimina obovata*. Fry suggests that this was the Big-flowered pawpaw. The Bartram illustration, labeled as *Anon grandiflora*, figured in Harper (15), may also be this species. Bartram provides detailed descriptions of the flowers, leaves, and fruits for pawpaw plants near Rodman. Several features of his *Annona incarna* fit *Asimina obovata*, specifically "this grows three, four, or five feet high ... flowers very large, perfectly white." The illustration from Harper (15) shows both mature leaves and flowers on the same plant, another feature common to *obovata,* not *incana*. Both *Asimina incana* and *Asimina pygmea* currently occur on the Rodman upland, east of Deep Creek, and *Asimina obovata,* in a small scrub patch near Kenwood, west of Deep Creek. Both sites are located along Harper's proposed Trader's Path between the lower store and Halfway Pond.

Holly Family (AQUIFOLIACEAE)

**Cassine.** *Travels,* 164, 171 (M-SJR, I-Trek). Yaupon, *Ilex vomitoria*. See comments by Harper, 466. William Bartram applied the names Cassine yapon, Yaupon, and Cassine to this species of *Ilex*. He implicated this holly as the source of the ritual "black drink" beverage, used in Native American purification rites. This tea contains massive quantities of caffeine, antioxidants, and other nutrients and is reported to have emetic qualities.[20] The exact recipe for the black drink is unknown, although it has been suggested that it was likely made either from boiling Yaupon leaves or as a concoction with various hollies and other plants. Accounts indicate that vomiting often accompanied drinking copious quantities of the black drink, which led to the current scientific name for Yaupon, *Ilex vomitoria*.

**Ilex aquifolium.** *Travels*, 84, 164 (L-SJR, M-SJR). American holly, *Ilex opaca*.

Arum Family (ARACEAE)

**Pistia stratiotes** (also listed as **Pistia**). *Travels*, 106, 118, 130, 132, 140, 160 (M-SJR, U-SJR). Water lettuce, *Pistia stratiotes*. Often considered an exotic, this floating plant appears to be native, since it was seen by the Bartrams during both trips to Florida, and fossil seeds have been found near Vero Beach and fossil pollen from Lake Annie in peninsular Florida.[21]

**Pistia.** *Diary*, 31 Dec 1765 (M-SJR).

**Dracontium.** *Diary*, 25 Dec 1765 (Palatka). Undetermined. John Bartram probably saw Green dragon, *Arisaema dracontium*, or one of several other arums: Jack-in-the-pulpit, *Arisaema triphyllum*, Spoonflower, *Peltandra sagittifolia*, or Green arrow arum, *P. virginica*.

Ginseng Family (ARALIACEAE)

**Hydrocotile fluitans.** *Travels*, 130 (SJR). Listed as *nomen nudum*—water pennywort, *Hydrocotyle* sp., by Harper, 530. Probably either Manyflower marshpennywort *Hydrocotyle umbellata*, or Floating marshpennywort, *Hydrocotyle ranunculoides*.

**Water-numularia.** *Diary*, 31 Dec 1765 (M-SJR). Probably a species of *Hydrocotyle*.

Palm Family (ARECACEAE)

**Dwarf creeping Chamaerops.** *Diary*, 20 Jan 1765 (M-SJR). Saw palmetto, *Serenoa repens*.

**Dwarf creeping Palmetto with stipes serrated.** *Travels*, 173, 181 (I-Trek). Saw palmetto.

**Corypha repens (dwarf saw palmetto).** *Travels,* 94 (M-SJR). Saw palmetto.

**Very dwarf species of Palmetto** (Corypha pumila stipit, serratis). *Travels,* 170 (I-Trek). Listed as *Serenoa repens* by Harper, 586.

**Corypha palma (or great cabbage palm).** *Travels,* 93 (M-SJR, U-SJR). Cabbage palm, *Sabal palmetto*. Listed Corypha palma as *nomen nudum* in Harper, 93

**Palms.** *Travels,* 60, 92, 99, 102, 103, 106, 116. 117, 131, 132, 137, 140, 146, 157 (Palatka, M-SJR, U-SJR). Most reports by William Bartram are Cabbage palms, *Sabal palmetto*. See Harper, 585.

**Tree palmetto . . . cabbage-tree . . . eaten raw and boiled.** *Diary,* 31 Dec 1765 (M-SJR). Cabbage palm.

**Corypha pumila.** *Travels,* 93 (M-SJR). Dwarf or Blue-stem palmetto, *Sabal minor*.

**Palma elata.** *Travels,* 90, 94, 141 (L-SJR, M-SJR, U-SJR). Florida royal palm, *Roystonea regia* by Wunderlin and Hansen. Listed as Royal palm, *Roystonea elata* by Harper, 484. J. H. Davis reported *Roystonea elata* at Paynes Prairie (Alachua Co.) before the 1895 freeze (D. Hall, pers. comm.).

Aster Family (ASTERACEAE)

**Cacalia heterophylla.** *Travels,* 164 (I-Trek, Salt Springs). Garberia, *Garberia heterophylla*.

**Another species of Cacalia.** *Travels,* 164 (I-Trek, Salt Springs). Undetermined. See comments in Harper, 460.

**Coreopsis bidens of floating islets in SJR.** *Travels,* 130 (SJR). Listed as beggar-ticks, *Bidens* sp., by Harper, 482.

**Coreopsis.** *Diary,* 3 Jan 1766 (U-SJR). Sunflowers growing along the SJR, possibly a coreopsis but more likely a species of yellow *Bidens*.

**Sun-flowers.** *Diary,* 6 Jan 1766 (U-SJR).

**Eupatorium scandens.** *Travels,* 136 (U-SJR). Climbing hemp-vine, *Mikania scandens*.

**Eupatorium.** *Diary,* 6 Jan 1766 (U-SJR). Undetermined.

**Gnaphalium.** *Travels,* 155 (U-SJR). Everlasting, *Gamochaeta* sp. Listed as *Gnaphalium* by Harper, 518

**Golden Corymbosus Jacobea (Senecio Jacobea).** *Travels,* 105, 130 (M-SJR). Butterwort, *Packera glabella* in Fry. Listed as probably Ragwort, *Senecio glabellus,* in Harper, 543.

**Silvery Perdicium.** *Travels,* 155 (U-SJR, Lake Dexter). Woolly sunbonnet, *Chaptalia tomentosa*.

Trumpet Creeper Family (BIGNONIACEAE)

**Bignonia crucigera.** *Travels*, 87, 136 (L-SJR, U-SJR). Probably Crossvine, *Bignonia capreolata*.

**Bignonia radicans.** *Travels*, 87 (L-SJR). Trumpet creeper or Trumpet-vine, *Campsis radicans*.

Pineapple Family (BROMELIACEAE)

**Tillandsia usneascites.** *Travels*, 87, 154 (L-SJR, U-SJR). Spanish moss, *Tillandsia usneoides*.

**Bed of long tree-moss.** *Diary,* 27 Jan 1766 (M-SJR). Spanish moss.

Cactus Family (CACTACEAE)

**Cactus opuntia.** *Travels*, 162, 163 (M-SJR, Salt Springs). Prickly-pear cactus, erect Ocala scrub form, *Opuntia humifusa* var. *ammophila*. Listed as a syn of *Opuntia humifusa* in Wunderlin and Hansen.

Senna Family (CAESALPINIACEAE)

**Guilandina.** *Diary,* 19 Dec 1765 (L-SJR). Undetermined. The name *guilandina*, as currently applied, refers to the coastal-growing Gray nicker, *Caesalpinia bonduc*, a vine-like climbing shrub with spiny stems, yellow flowers, and large gray seeds (nickernuts) in spiny pods. John Bartram's reference was later corrected (probably by William) to Kentucky coffee tree, *Gymnocladus dioicus*, a native to the Mississippi valley. John could have seen Water locust, *Gleditsia aquatica*, which has thorns and twice pinnately compound leaves.

Bell Flower Family (CAMPANULACEAE)

**Lobelia cardinalis.** *Travels*, 105 (M-SJR). Cardinal flower, *Lobelia cardinalis*.

Canna Lily Family (CANNACEAE)

**Canna lutea.** *Travels*, 155 (M-SJR). Golden canna, *Canna flaccida*.

Hackberry Family (CELTIDACEAE)

**Celtis.** *Diary,* 11 Jan 1766 (U-SJR). Sugarberry, *Celtis laevigata*.

White Alder Family (CLETHRACEAE)

**Clethra.** *Travels*, 172 (I-Trek). Coastal sweetpepperbush, *Clethra alnifolia*.

Morning-Glory Family (CONVOLVULACEAE)

**Ipomoea.** *Travels,* 173, 253 (I-Trek, M-SJR). Listed as morning glories, species of *Ipomoea* or related genera, by Harper, 541.

**Convolvulus.** *Travels,* 136, 173 (U-SJR, I-Trek). Listed as a genus of Convolvulaceae, comprising bindweeds, by Harper, 480.

**Convolvulus.** *Diary,* 25 Dec 1765, 3 Jan 1766 (Palatka, U-SJR). Undetermined. John Bartram's use of *convolvulus* could refer to any number of morning-glory species in the genus *Ipomoea* or other genera that grow along the St. Johns River.

**Convolvulus . . . having very large, white, sweet-scented flowers.** *Travels,* 253 (M-SJR, Lake George). Moon flower, *Ipomoea alba.* Listed as Moon flower, *Calonyction aculeatum* by Harper, 480.

**New and beautiful palmated leaved convolvulus (Convol. dissectus).** *Travels,* 104 (M-SJR, U-SJR). Probably Noyau vine, *Merremia dissecta.* Listed as morning glory, *Operculina dissecta,* by Harper, 481.

Dogwood Family (CORNACEAE)

**Nyssa aquatica.** *Travels,* 93, 131, 161, 172 (M-SJR, U-SJR, I-Trek). Likely Blackgum, *Nyssa sylvatica.* Black gum was formerly listed in the family Nyssaceae, but now placed in the Dogwood family (Wunderlin and Hansen).

**Nyssa sylvatica.** *Travels,* 131, 161, 172 (M-SJR, I-Trek). Blackgum, *Nyssa sylvatica.*

**Corau femina.** *Diary,* 14 Jan 1766 (U-SJR). Possibly Swamp dogwood, *Cornus foemina.*

Gourd Family (CUCURBITACEAE)

**Native gourd or squash.** *Diary,* 6 Jan 1766 (U-SJR). Undetermined. Possibly Okeechobee gourd or Indian-pumpkin, *Cucurbita okeechobeensis.* Listed as endangered by both Florida and the United States. Early reports indicate that it grew quite far north along the St. Johns .

Sedge Family (CYPERACEAE)

**Bull-rushes.** *Diary,* 24 Jan 1766 (M-SJR). Probably Woolgrass, *Scirpus cyperinus.*

**Tall water-reeds.** *Diary,* 6 Jan 1766 (U-SJR). Undetermined, but possibly Bulrush, *Scirpus* sp.

Titi Family (CYRILLACEAE)

**Cyrilla racemiflora.** *Travels*, 172 (I-Trek). Titi, *Cyrilla racemiflora*.

Yam Family (DIOSCOREACEAE)

**Rajana.** *Travels*, 164 (U-SJR). Possibly the native Florida yam, *Dioscorea floridana*. Listed as Eardrops, *Brunnichia cirrhosa*, by Harper, 607.

Ebony Family (EBENACEAE)

**Diospyros virginica.** *Travels*, 131 (U-SJR). Persimmon, *Diospyros virginiana*.
**Pishamins.** *Diary,* 14 Jan 1766 (U-SJR). Probably Persimmon.

Heath Family (ERICACEAE)

**Andromeda.** *Travels*, 181 (I-Trek). Harper, 437 states, "In Bartram's usage, a collective genus, more or less equivalent to the ericaceous tribe Andromedaceae, which included several genera of woody shrubs, specifically *Leucothoe, Pieris, Chamaedaphne, Oxydendron, Lyonia*." Harper's use of tribe Andromedaceae is incorrect: the ending -aceae is used to indicate a family level name, not a tribe name, which would end in -deae.
**Tall Andromeda.** *Diary,* 9 Jan 1766 (U-SJR). Undetermined.
**Andromeda axillaris.** *Travels*, 303 (Palatka). Presumably Coastal doghobble or Fetterbush, *Leucothoe axillaris*.
**Andromeda formosissima.** *Travels*, 172, 303 (I-Trek, Palatka). The names, *Agarista populifolia* and *Leucothoe populifolia*, have been applied to Florida hobble bush (Wunderlin and Hansen). Listed as Pipewood, *Leucothoe formosissima*, by Harper, 437.
**Andromeda calyculata.** *Travels*, 303 (Palatka). Undetermined.
**Andromeda ferruginea.** *Travels*, 172, 303 (I-Trek, Palatka). Rusty staggerbush or Stagger-bush, *Lyonia ferruginea*.
**Andromeda nitida.** *Travels*, 171, 172, 303 (I-Trek). Fetterbush or Hoorah bush, *Lyonia lucida*.
**Andromeda viridis.** *Travels*, 303 (Palatka). Undetermined. Listed as *nomen nudum* by Harper, 438.
**Empetrum.** *Travels*, 171 (I-Trek). Florida rosemary, *Ceratiola ericoides*. Formerly placed in the family Empetraceae, but now included in the Heath Family. (Wunderlin and Hansen).
**Kalmea ciliata.** *Travels*, 94, 171 (M-SJR). Wicky, *Kalmia hirsuta*. Bartram described this plant as the Calico-bush, *Kalmea ciliata*, in *Travels*. See comments in Harper, 545.

**Kalmea.** *Diary,* 30 Dec 1765 (M-SJR). JB recognized kalmia along the banks of the SJR.

**Halmea spuria.** *Travels,* 303 (Palatka). Listed as *nomen nudum* by Harper, 545. Probably Tarflower, *Befaria* (now *Bejaria*) *racemosa*, by Harper, 545.

**Vaccinium.** *Travels,* 171 (I-Trek). Blueberries and related genera.

Pea Family (FABACEAE)

**Clitoria.** *Travels,* 155, 173 (U-SJR, I-Trek). Atlantic pigeonwings or Butterfly pea, *Clitoria mariana.*

**Erythrina corallodendrum.** *Travels,* 162, 164 (M-SJR). Cherokee-bean, Coral-bean, or Cardinal spear, *Erythrina herbacea.*

**Gleditsia monosperma.** *Travels,* 131 (U-SJR). Listed as perhaps Water locust, *Gleditsia aquatica* by Harper, 517.

**Short-poded gleditsia.** *Diary,* 28 Dec 1765 (M-SJR). Probably Water locust. This tree is an important component of the bottomland floodplain forest along the SJR.

**Gleditsia triacanthus.** *Travels,* 84, 131 (L-SJR, U-SJR). Probably Water locust. Not Honey locust, *Gleditisa tricanthus*, since this plant does not occur in the Florida peninsula.

**Glycine apios.** *Travels,* 136 (U-SJR). Groundnut, *Apios americana.*

**Glycine frutescens.** *Travels,* 131 (U-SJR). American wisteria, *Wisteria frutescens.*

Oak-Beech Family (FAGACEAE)

**Fagus sylvatica.** *Travels,* 84 (L-SJR). American beech, *Fagus grandifolia.* Not the European *Fagus sylvatica*.

**Live Oaks.** *Travels,* 94, 99, 103, 105, 106, 114, 116, 117, 131, 132, 134, 137, 139, 142, 143, 152, 154, 160, 164, 259 (M-SJR, U-SJR). Virginia live oak, *Quercus virginiana*, in moist areas, or Sand live oak, *Quercus geminata*, in dry uplands.

**Dwarf Querci (Oaks).** *Travels,* 164, 171 (M-SJR, I-Trek). One or more of scrub oaks (*Quercus myrtifolia, Quercus chapmanii, Quercus virginiana* var. *maritima*), by Harper, 603. The name *Quercus virginiana* var. *maritima* listed as a syn of *Quercus geminata* by Wunderlin and Hansen.

**Quercus dentata.** *Travels,* 84, 131, 161 (Palatka, M-SJR, U-SJR). Laurel oak, *Quercus laurifolia.* The name dentata is considered a *nomen nudum.* Harper, 604 listed it as probably Darlington oak, *Quercus hemisphaerica.* Wunderlin and Hansen considered *Quercus hemispherica* to be a syn of *Quercus laurifolia.*

**Quercus Ilex.** *Travels,* 164 (M-SJR). Swamp chestnut oak, *Quercus michauxii.* Not the European *Quercus,* see Harper, 605.
**White swamp oaks.** *Diary,* 27 Dec 1765 (M-SJR). Swamp chestnut oak.
**Quercus maritima.** *Travels,* 164 (M-SJR). Sand live oak. Listed as Myrtle oak by Harper, 605.
**Quercus nigra.** *Travels,* 173 (I-Trek). Turkey oak, *Quercus laevis* (Hall et al.). Locals often call smaller oaks that grow in dry habitats black-jack oaks. Harper's comment on page 605, "doubtless Blackjack oak, *Quercus marilandica,*" is inaccurate, since this oak occurs in the Panhandle and not in the Florida peninsula.
**Quercus phellos.** *Travels,* 131 (U-SJR). Willow oak, *Quercus phellos.*
**Quercus pumila, oak runner.** *Travels,* 164 (M-SJR). Running oak, *Quercus pumila.*
**Quercus sinuataor scarlet oak.** *Travels,* 173 (I-Trek). Southern red oak, *Quercus falcata.*
**Water oaks.** *Diary,* 22 Dec 1765 (L-SJR). Water oak, *Quercus nigra.*
**Chinquapins.** *Diary,* 22 Dec 1765 (L-SJR). Chinquapin, *Castanea pumila.*

Witch Hazel Family (HAMAMELIDACEAE)

**Liquid-amber.** *Travels,* 84, 90, 94, 154 (L-SJR, U-SJR). Sweetgum, *Liquidambar styraciflua.*
**Liquid-amber.** *Diary,* 19 Dec 1765 (L-SJR). Sweetgum.

Frog's-Bit Family (HYDROCHARITACEAE)

**Green meadow having water-grass and other amphibious vegetables, growing in the oozy bottom.** *Travels,* 78 (L-SJR). Probably Tapegrass or American eelgrass, *Vallisneria americana.*

Iris Family (IRIDACEAE)

**Cerulean Ixea.** *Travels,* 155 (U-SJR, Lake Dexter). Bartram's ixia or Bartram's celestial lily, *Calydorea caelestina.* Listed as *Salpingoustylis caelestina* in Harper, 542. William Bartram's description of Ixia at Lake Dexter, "*prompted me to penetrate the grove and view the illumined plans . . . dewdrops twinkle and play upon the sight, trembling on the tips of the lucid, green savanna . . . behold the azure fields of cerulean Ixea!*"

Sweetspire Family (ITEACEAE)

**Saxifrage.** *Diary,* 31 Dec 1765 (M-SJR). Unidentified. Possibly the shrub

Virginia-willow, *Itea virginica*, in the Sweetspire family. This plant was once placed in the Saxifrage family (Saxifragaceae). Virginia-willow grows along streams, lake banks, and swamps throughout Florida.[22] John Bartram observed his saxifrage growing with accompanying aquatic plants along the St. Johns River, having their long fibrous roots deep in the water . . . growing all matted together.

Walnut Family (JUGLANDACEAE)

**Hiccory or hickories.** *Travels*, 93, 142, 164 (M-SJR, U-SJR). *Carya* species.
**Juglans hiccory also hickory.** *Travels*, 131 (L-SJR). Hickory, *Carya* species.
**Juglans cinerea.** *Travels*, 90, 131 (U-SJR). Pignut hickory, *Carya glabra*, or Water hickory, *C. aquatica*. Not *Juglans cinerea* of Bartram; not Bitternut hickory, *Carya cordiformis*, as suggested by Harper, 544. Neither species occurs in peninsular Florida.

Mint Family (LAMIACEAE)

**Callicarpa.** *Travels*, 95, 114, 164 (M-SJR). American beautyberry or French mulberry, *Callicarpa americana*.
**Callicarpa Johnsonia.** *Travels*, 164 (M-SJR). Syn of *Callicarpa*. See comment in Harper, 543.

Bay and Laurel Family (LAURACEAE)

**Laurus Borbonia or Red Bay.** *Travels*, 84, 93, 94, 139, 140, 160 (L-SJR, M-SJR, U-SJR). One of the red bays, *Persea borbonia* (listed by Harper, 450). Identity of the Bartram bays depends on whether he saw them in dry or wet habitats. *Persea borbonia* var. *borbonia* in dry; *Persea borbonia* var. *humilis* (Nash) in scrub; *Persea palustris* in wet. This tree produces bluish purple fruits, which may be John Bartram's purple-berried bay. Today these trees are under attack by the redbay ambrosia beetle, which infects the tree with laurel wilt fungal disease, eventually killing the plant.
**Red Bay.** *Diary*, 21 Dec 1765 (L-SJR).
**Dwarf sweet bay (Laurus Borbonia).** *Travels*, 164 (M-SJR). Silkbay, *Persea borbonia* var. *humilis*.

Duckweed Family (LEMNOIDACEAE or ARACEAE)

**Duck-meat.** *Diary*, 7 Jan 1766 (M-SJR, Gemini Springs). Duckweed, either *Lemna* sp. or *Spirodela polyrhiza*. *Lemna* was observed on a recent visit to

Gemini Springs. This group of tiny floating plants has traditionally been placed in either the family Lemnaceae.

Magnolia Family (MAGNOLIACEAE)

**Magnolia species differs very little from the Magnolia glauca.** *Travels,* 84, 141, 161 (Palatka, M-SJR, U-SJR). Sweetbay, *Magnolia virginiana.*

**Magnolia(s).** *Travels,* 81, 102, 103, 106, 117, 137, 139, 146, 165, 166, 169, 174 (L-SJR, M-SJR, U-SJR, I-Trek). Southern magnolia, *Magnolia grandiflora* suggested by Harper, 558.

**Laurels.** *Travels,* 99, 131, 139, 154 (M-SJR, U-SJR). Southern magnolia.

**Laurels (Magnolia grandiflora).** *Travels,* 84, 103, 106, 114, 116, 117, 141, 146, 165, 169 (L-SJR, M-SJR, U-SJR). Southern Magnolia.

**Very large great magnolia.** *Diary,* 27 Dec 1765 (M-SJR). Southern magnolia.

Mallow Family (MALVACEAE)

**Plant allied to Alcea ... with flowers of a fine damask rose colour.** *Travels,* 105 (M-SJR). Virginia saltmarsh mallow, *Kosteletzkya pentacarpos* (Wunderlin and Hansen). The name *Kosteletzkya virginica* listed by Harper, 433. Common along streams and spring runs.

**Another species of hibiscus, embellished with ovate lanceolate leaves covered with fine down ... flowers are very large and of a deep incarnate colour.** *Travels,* 105 (M-SJR). Swamp rosemallow, *Hibiscus grandiflorus,* which has extremely large pink flowers, or possibly rosemallow, *Hibiscus moscheutos,* with white medium-sized flowers. The latter was proposed by Harper, 526. Leaf descriptions would fit both.

**Hibiscus coccineus.** *Travels,* 104, 105 (M-SJR). Red hibiscus or Blazing star, *Hibiscus coccineus.*

**Orange flowered shrub Hibiscus, a shrub (perhaps Hibisc. spinifex of Linn.).** *Travels,* 104, 114, 164 (M-SJR, U-SJR). Gingerbush, *Pavonia spinifex,* suggested by Harper, 526.

**Tilia.** *Travels,* 94 (M-SJR, Charlotia). Carolina basswood, *Tilia americana* var. *caroliniana.* Listed as Basswood, *Tilia,* by Harper, 646.

Mulberry Family (MORACEAE)

**Morus rubra.** *Travels,* 94, 131, 164 (M-SJR, U-SJR). Red mulberry, *Morus rubra.*

Bayberry Family (MYRICACEAE)

**Myrica cerifera.** *Travels,* 114, 140, 157 (M-SJR, U-SJR). Wax myrtle, *Myrica cerifera.*

**Myrtles.** *Diary*, 5 Jan 1766 (U-SJR). Wax myrtle.

Lotus Family (NELUMBONACEAE)

**Nymphaea nilumbo.** *Travels*, 107 (M-SJR, U-SJR). American lotus or Water chinquapin, *Nelumbo lutea*. William Bartram commented, "*This bay, about the mouth of the creek, is almost covered with the leaves of the Nymphaea nilumbo: its large sweet-scented yellow flowers are lifted up two or three feet above the surface of the water.*"

Water Lily Family (NYMPHAEACEAE)

**Floating nymphaea.** *Travels*, 108, 118 (M-SJR). Spatterdock, *Nuphar advena*. William Bartram's comment—"*fishing for trout, round about the edges of the floating nymphaea*"—suggests spatterdock, rather than lotus, which is a major component of the floating mats on the St. Johns River.

Olive Family (OLEACEAE)

**Ash.** *Travels*, 93, 160 (M-SJR). Ash, *Fraxinus* sp.

**Chionanthus.** *Travels*, 172 (I-Trek). Fringe tree or Old man's beard, *Chionanthus virginica*.

**Fraxinus aquatica.** *Travels*, 130 (U-SJR). Water ash, *Fraxinus caroliniana*, or Pumpkin ash, *Fraxinus profunda* (Hall et al.).

**Fraxinus excelsior.** *Travels*, 94, 130 (M-SJR, U-SJR). Green ash, *Fraxinus pennsylvanica*. Not Old World *F. excelsior*. White ash, *Fraxinus americana*, by Harper, 511.

**Black-ash.** *Diary*, 28 Dec 1765 (M-SJR). Black ash, *Fraxinus nigra*, does not occur in Florida. Again it could be Green ash, Pop ash, or Pumpkin ash, all of which occur in moist or wet bottomlands in north Florida.

**Olea Americana.** *Travels*, 84, 132, 157, 164, 171 (M-SJR, U-SJR, I-Trek). Wild olive or Devil wood, *Osmanthus americanus*.

**Purple-berried bay.** *Diary*, 21 Dec 1765 (L-SJR). Possibly *Osmanthus americana*.

Grass Family (POACEAE)

**Cane(s).** *Travels*, 304 (Palatka). Giant cane, *Arundinaria gigantea*, or Small cane, *Arundinaria tecta*. Both are possible, but they are difficult to differentiate (D. Hall pers. comm.).

**Water-grass.** *Diary*, 31 Dec 1765 (M-SJR). Unspecific wetland grasses could be Water grass, *Luziola fluitans*.

Phlox Family (POLEMONIACEAE)

**Phlox.** *Travels*, 155, 173 (U-SJR, I-Trek). *Phlox* sp.

Buckwheat Family (POLYGONACEAE)

**Persicaria.** *Diary,* 31 Dec 1765 (M-SJR). Smartweed, *Polygonum* sp. This plant forms extensive mats along the margins and backwaters of the St. Johns River. John Bartram's use of persicaria probably stems from his familiarity with related Eurasian knotweeds in the genus *Persicaria*.

**Persicaria amphibia.** *Travels*, 130 (U-SJR). Listed as *nomen nudum*—Smartweed, *Polygonum* sp. in Harper, 591. In *Travels*, Bartram noted, "In my way observed islets or floating fields of bright green Pistia, decorated with other amphibious plants, as Senecia Jaobea, Persicaria amphibian, Coreopsis bidens, Hydrocotyle fluitans, and many others of less note."

Pickerelweed Family (PONTEDERIACEAE)

**Pontederia.** *Diary,* 25 Dec 1765 (Palatka). Pickerelweed or Blue bonnet, *Pontederia cordata*.

Buckthorn Family (RHAMNACEAE)

**Rhamnus frangula.** *Travels*, 157, 164, 171 (M-SJR, I-Trek). Carolina buckthorn, *Rhamnus caroliniana*. Not the European *Rhamnus frangula*. See comments in Harper, 611.

**Rhamnus volubilis.** *Travels*, 87 (L-SJR). Supplejack or Rattan-vine, *Berchemia scandens*. See comments by Harper, 611.

**Zizyphus scandens.** *Travels*, 94 (L-SJR). Rattan-vine, by Harper, 667.

Rose Family (ROSACEAE)

**Cluster-cherry.** *Diary,* 27 Dec 1765 (M-SJR). William Stork identified John Bartram's cluster cherry as the American bird cherry, *Prunus virginiana*. The Chokecherry, *Prunus virginiana*, is a northern tree and does not occur in Florida. The common Black cherry, *Prunus serotina*, however, has small black fruits in clusters and may have been John Bartram's cluster-cherry.

**Plum-tree in full blossom.** *Diary,* 26 Jan 1766 (M-SJR). John Bartram's plum might be either the American plum, *Prunus americana* (large flowers—2 cm) or Flatwoods plum, *Prunus umbellata* (small flowers—1 cm, teeth without glands). Both occur on the river bluffs along the St. Johns River. Both would have been in flower when the Bartrams were retreating back down the river in January 1766.

Madder Family (RUBIACEAE)

**Cephalanthus.** *Diary*, 3 Jan 1766 (U-SJR). Common buttonbush, *Cephalanthus occidentalis*.

Citrus Family (RUTACEAE)

**Ptelea.** *Travels*, 94, 157, 164 (M-SJR). Water or Wafer ash, *Ptelea trifoliata*.

**Zanthoxilon.** *Travels*, 88, 107, 140, 154, 157, 164 (L-SJR, M-SJR, U-SJR). Hercules' club or Toothache tree, *Zanthoxylum clava-herculis*. Hercules' clubs are spiny trees used by Native Americans and early settlers to numb the mouth, teeth, and gums for relief from toothaches.

**Zanthoxilon.** *Diary*, 21 Dec 1765 (L-SJR).

**Oranges.** *Diary* (L-SJR, M-SJR, U-SJR). Oranges, *Citrus* sp. John Bartram's diary makes scattered reference to oranges: "Orange-trees, either full of fruit or scattered on the ground" (27 Dec 1765) . . . "Thousands of orange-trees" (1 Jan 1766) . . . "A few large orange-trees and some young ones" (11 Jan 1766) . . . "Great quantities of what is called bitter sweets, which are next to goodness to the china" (18 Jan 1766) . . . "Good bitter-sweets, the sour ones lay scattered all over the ground" (21 Jan 1766) . . . "Thousands of orange-trees grow as thick as possible, and full of sour and bitter-sweet fruits . . . about 4 miles from Mr. Roll's" (30 Jan 1766).

Willow Family (SALICACEAE)

**Many short willows.** *Diary*, 3 Jan 1766 (U-SJR). Carolina willow, *Salix caroliniana*, common along the river. Two other species are possible: Black willow, *Salix nigra*, and the rare Florida willow, *Salix floridana*.

Soapberry Family (SAPINDACEAE)

**Acer rubrum.** *Travels*, 84, 130 (L-SJR, U-SJR). Red maple, *Acer rubrum*. Maples have been removed from Aceraceae and placed in the family Sapindaceae (Wunderlin and Hansen).

**Acer glaucum.** *Travels*, 130 (U-SJR). Probably Red maple.

**Acer negundo.** *Travels*, 130 (U-SJR). Boxelder or Ash-leaved maple, *Acer negundo*.

**Aesculus pavia.** *Travels*, 164 (M-SJR). Red buckeye, *Aesculus pavia*. Buckeye was formerly placed in the family Hippocastanaceae (Wunderlin and Hansen).

**Pavia.** *Diary*, 3 Jan 1766 (U-SJR). Red buckeye.

**Sapindus.** *Travels*, 75, 84, 94 (L-SJR, M-SJR). Soapberry, *Sapindus saponaria*.

Sapodilla Family (SAPOTACEAE)

**Sideroxilon.** *Travels*, 157, 164 (M-SJR). Buckthorn or Bully, *Sideroxylon* sp. Also known as *Bumelia*.

Lizard-tail Family (SAURURACEAE)

**Saururus.** *Diary*, 25 Dec 1765 (Palatka). Lizard-tail, *Saururus cernuus*.

Anisetree Family (SCHISANDRACEAE or ILLICIACEAE)

**Odoriferous Illicium groves.** *Travels*, 160 (M-SJR). Yellow anise, *Illicium parviflorum*. A lovely sweet tree with leaves like the sweet bay which smell like sassafras and produce a very strange seed pod. *Diary*, 24 Jan 1766 (M-SJR, Salt Springs). First description of Yellow anise.

**Illicium Floridanum.** William Bartram reported this anise near Lake George (presumably Salt Springs). Only Yellow anise occurs in the Lake George area. See comments by Harper, 532. Florida anise, *Illicium floridanum*, is a distinctive species with maroon instead of yellow flowers and is native to the Florida panhandle and westward (Wunderlin and Hansen).

Storax Family (STYRACACEAE)

**Halasia tetraptera.** *Travels*, 164 (M-SJR). Four-winged silverbells, *Halesia carolina*.

**Halesia diptera.** *Travels*, 164 (M-SJR). Probably *Halesia carolina*. Listed as Two-winged silverbells, *Halesia diptera*, by Harper, 523. But this species is not found in the SJR area. Two-winged silverbells range from the Suwannee River westward (Wunderlin and Hansen).

Sweet Leaf Family (SYMPLOCACEAE)

**Hopea tinctoria.** *Travels*, 131, 164 (U-SJR, M-SJR). Horse sugar, *Symplocos tinctoria*.

Tea Family (THEACEAE)

**Gordonia lasianthus.** *Travels*, 93, 161, 162, 171 (M-SJR, I-Trek). Loblolly bay, *Gordonia lasianthus*.

Cattail Family (TYPHACEAE)

**Cat-tails.** *Diary*, 24 Jan 1766 (M-SJR). Cattail, *Typha* sp. Two species occur in the area, Broadleaf cattail, *Typha latifolia*, and Southern cattail, *Typha domingensis*. (Wunderlin and Hansen).

Elm Family (ULMACEAE)

**Elm.** *Diary,* 28 Dec 1765 (M-SJR). John Bartram probably saw the Florida elm, *Ulmus floridana,* in the floodplain forest along the SJR.

**Elms.** *Travels,* 93 (M-SJR). *Ulmus* sp.

**Ulmus.** *Travels,* 84, 94 (Palatka, M-SJR). Elm.

**Ulmus suberifera.** *Travels,* 130, 131 (U-SJR). Probably American elm, *Ulmus americana.* Listed suberifera as *nomen nudum*—doubtless the Winged elm, *Ulmus alata,* according to Harper, 656.

**Ulmus sylvatica.** *Travels,* 130 (U-SJR). Sylvatica listed as *nomen nudum*—perhaps White elm *Ulmus americana,* or the closely related Florida elm, *Ulmus floridana,* by Harper, 656.

Vervain Family (VERBENACEAE)

**Beautiful species of lantana (perhaps lant. camerara).** *Travels,* 103 (M-SJR). Shrub verbena, *Lantana camara.* Bartram notes: "It grows in coppices in old fields, about five or six feet high, the branches adorned with rough serrated leaves, which sit opposite, and the twigs terminated with umbelliferous tufts of orange coloured blossoms." If introduced, lantana must have been brought to Florida during the first Spanish period, possibly from the West Indies.

**Balmy Lantana.** *Travels,* 157 (M-SJR). Shrub verbena.

**Verbena corymbosa.** *Travels,* 155, 173 (U-SJR, I-Trek). Listed as *nomen nudum*—*Verbena* sp., by Harper, 657.

Violet Family (VIOLACEAE)

**Viola.** *Travels,* 155, 173 (U-SJR, I-Trek). Undetermined violets.

Grape Family (VITACEAE)

**Vitis labrusca.** *Travels,* 136 (U-SJR). Probably Florida grape, *Vitis cinerea.* Listed as not *Vitis labrusca* but perhaps Redshank grape, *Vitis rufotomentosa* by Harper, 659.

**Monstrous grape-vines, 8 inches in diameter.** *Diary,* 27 Dec 1765 (M-SJR). Probably the Florida grape.

**Vitis vulpina.** *Travels,* 136 (U-SJR). Muscadine, *Vitis rotundifolia.* Listed as Bullace, *Vitis munsoniana,* by Harper, 660.

**Hedera quinquefolia.** *Travels,* 136 (U-SJR). Virginia creeper, *Parthenocissus quinquefolia.*

**Hedera arborea.** *Travels,* 136 (U-SJR). Pepper vine, *Ampelopsis arborea.*

Tallow Wood Family (XIMENIACEAE)

**Tallow-nut or Wild Lime.** *Travels*, 94, 114, 115 (M-SJR, U-SJR). Hog plum or Tallow wood, *Ximenia americana*.

**Pretty evergreen, which produces nuts or stones as big as acorns, and good to eat. . . . the people call them wild limes.** *Diary*, 22 Dec 1765 (L-SJR). Probably Hog plum.

Undetermined Plants

**Peanines.** *Diary*, 6 Jan 1766 (U-SJR). Unknown. Difficult to determine what plant John Bartram observed. It was obviously not the peonies in the genus *Paeonia* in the family Paeoniaceae, which are native to Asia, southern Europe, and western North America.

# ANIMALIA

## Invertebrates

### INSECTS

**Cochineal insect: (on) Cactus opuntia.** *Travels*, 163 (cactus at Salt Springs). *Dactylopius coccus* (order Hemiptera, family Dactylopiidae). This scale insect lives as a sessile parasite on the pads of cacti in the genus *Opuntia*. These insects are red in color, due to their production of carminic acid. Cactus pads, colonized by this bug, often show fuzzy gray or white coatings. The carminic acid is used to make carmine dye (called cochineal).

**Ephemera . . . clouds of innumerable millions, swarming and wantoning in the still air.** *Travels*, 80–83 (L-SJR). Listed as mayflies (order Ephemeraoptera, family Ephemeridae), and perhaps the species *Hexagenia orlando*, by Harper, 499. William Bartram's account included life history and reflections on mayflies.

**Mosquitoes, "musquetoes" or "musquitoes" or "musquitoes" (culex).** *Travels*, 88, 135, 136,158, 216, 252 (SJR, M-SJR, I-Trek). Listed as species of the family Culicidae, including such genera as *Culex*, *Anopheles*, and *Aedes*, by Harper, 567.

**Troublesome mosquitoes.** *Diary*, 15, 18, 19 Jan 1766 (U-SJR).

**Yellow wasps:** *Diary*, 24 Dec 1765 (L-SJR). Bartram's yellow wasp was probably one of the Yellow jacket wasps in the genera *Vespula* and *Dolichovespula* in the family Vespidae.

**Swarm of bees and some honey:** *Diary*, 24 Dec 1765 (L-SJR). Honey bees, *Apis mellifera* (family Apidae), were introduced to North America in the 1600s by European settlers.

## Vertebrates

FISH

**Full of large fish, as cats, garr, mullets and several other kinds:** *Diary*, 27 Dec 1765 (M-SJR).

### Mudfish Family (AMIIDAE)

**Mud fish ... large, thick or round, and two feet in length; meat ... soft and tastes of the mud.** *Travels*, (I-Trek). Bowfin, *Amia calva*.

### Sunfish Family (CENTRARCHIDAE)

**Bream:** *Travels*, 166, 168 (M-SJR). Listed as various fishes of the bass family by Harper, 456.

**Yellow bream or sunfish, Cyprinus coronaries.** *Travels*, 176 (U-SJR, I-Trek). Warmouth, *Lepomis gulosus*. Listed as Warmouth, *Chaenobryttus coronarius*, by Harper, 456.

**Great black and blue bream.** *Travels*, 153, 154, 176 (I-Trek). Bluegill, *Lepomis macrochirus purpurescens*. Listed as Copper-nosed bream by Harper, 456.

**Great yellow or particolored bream.** *Travels*, 176, 177 (I-Trek). Shell-cracker bream, *Lepomis microlophus*.

**Red bellied bream.** *Travels*, 176 (I-Trek). Red-breasted bream, *Lepomis auritus*.

**Silver or white bream.** *Travels*, 176 (I-Trek). Undetermined.

**Spotted Bass.** *Travels*, 166 (M-SJR). Perhaps Black crappie, *Pomoxis nigromaculatus*. Listed as Calico Bass by Harper, 449.

**Trout.** *Travels*, 108, 109, 117, 124, 153, 158, 159, 166, 176 (M-SJR, U-SJR, I-Trek). Large-mouth bass, *Micropterus salmoides*.

### Stingray Family (DASYATIDAE)

**Dreaded sting-ray.** *Travels*, 166 (M-SJR). Probably Atlantic stingray, *Dasyatis sabina*.

### Catfish Family (ICTALURIDAE)

**Barbed catfish.** *Travels*, 166, 176 (M-SJR, I-Trek). Probably either Yellow bullhead, *Ameiurus natalis*, or Brown bullhead, *Ameiurus nebulosus*.

Garfish Family (LEPISOSTEIDAE)

**Garfish** (or **garr**). *Travels*, 166 (M-SJR). Listed as either the Longnose gar, *Lepisosteus osseus*, or the Florida gar, *Lepisosteus platyrhincus*.

**Great brown spotted garr, accoutered in an impenetrable coat of mail.** *Travels*, 175, 176 (I-Trek). Florida gar.

Skate Family (RAJAIDAE)

**Skate.** *Travels*, 166 (M-SJR). Listed as possibly one or more species of the genus *Raja* by Harper, 627. Doubtful occurrence, no modern records.

Drum Family (SCIAENIDAE)

**Ominous drum.** *Travels*, 166 (M-SJR). Listed as either Red drum, *Sciaenops ocellata*, or Black drum, *Pogonias cromias* by Harper, 495.

Flatfish Family (SOLEIDAE)

**Flounder.** *Travels*, 166 (M-SJR). Southern hog-choker, *Trinectes maculatus*. Listed as *Trinectes maculatus fasciatus* by Harper, 507.

Seabream Family (SPARIDAE)

**Sheepshead.** *Travels*, 166 (M-SJR). Listed as Sheepshead, *Archosargus probatocephalus* by Harper, 624.

AMPHIBIANS

**Frogs.** *Travels*, 88, 89, 92, 109, 150, 152, 154, 178 (L-SJR, U-SJR, I-Trek).

REPTILES

Alligator Family (ALLIGATORIDAE)

**Alligator.** *Travels*, 78, 90, 106, 145, 150, 168 (L-SJR, M-SJR, U-SJR). American alligator, *Alligator mississippiensis*.

**Crocodile.** *Travels*, 88, 89, 90, 117–30, 134, 136, 138, 140, 153, 166, 167, 168, 174, 175 (L-SJR, M-SJR, U-SJR, I-Trek). See Harper, 487, 488. William Bartram used the names alligator and crocodile interchangeably.

Softshell Turtle Family (TRIONYNICHIDAE)

**Great soft shelled tortoise.** *Travels*, 176–78 (I-Trek). Florida softshell, *Apalone ferox*. Listed as Southern soft-shelled turtle, *Amyda ferox*, by

Harper, 647, 648. Generic names changed from *Amyda* to *Trionyx* to *Apalone*.

LIZARDS

Racerunner Lizard Family (TEIIDAE)

**Called in Carolina, scorpions: ... from five to six inches in length ... with longitudinal lines or stripes of a dusky brown colour.** *Travels*, 172 (I-Trek). Six-lined racerunner, *Aspidophorus sexlineatus*. Listed as *Cnemidophorus sexlineatus* by Harper, 554. The genus was recently changed from *Cnemidophorus* to *Aspidophorus*.

SNAKES

Pit Viper Family (CROTALIDAE)

**Rattle snake.** JB (L-SJR, Ft Picolata). Eastern diamondback rattlesnake, *Crotalus adamenteus*. William Bartram retells the encounter with a large rattlesnake during the Bartrams' first trip to Florida in *Travels* (chapter 10). *Travels*, 260–63 (M-SJR, encounter at Spalding's lower store).

BIRDS

**General Birds.** *Travels*, (L-SJR, M-SJR). Comments in *Travels*: "sweet enchanting melody of feathered songsters at end of day" [82], "chearful summons of the gentle monitors of the meadows and groves " [100], "winged inhabitants of the groves" [106], "melody of the merry birds, tenants of the encircling aromatic grove (at Salt Springs)" [116].

Eagle Family (ACCIPITRIDAE)

**Eagles.** *Travels*, 91 (L-SJR). Bald eagle, *Haliaeetus leucocephalus* by Harper, 496.

Geese and Duck Family (ANATIDAE)

**Ducks.** *Travels*, 144, 178 (U-SJR, I-Trek). Unidentified ducks.
**Geese.** *Travels*, 144. Canada goose, *Branta canadensis* by Harper, 515, or possibly Brant, *Branta bernicla*.
**Shoot geese in the pine-lands ponds.** *Diary*, 20 Jan 1766 (M-SJR).

Anhinga Family (ANHINGIDAE)

**Snake birds, a species of cormorant or loon.** *Travels*, 132, 133 (U-SJR). Florida water-turkey or Anhinga, *Anhinga*.

Heron, Egret, and Bittern Family (ARDEIDAE)

**Bitterns.** *Travels*, 124 (U-SJR). Listed as probably small species of heron by Harper, 454.

Limpkin Family (ARAMIDAE)

**Indian name ... signifies in our language the crying bird.** *Travels*, 147 (U-SJR, St. Francis). Limpkin, *Aramus guarauna*.

Goatsucker Family (CAPRIMULGIDAE)

**Shrill voice of the Whip-poor-will, Caprimulgus rufus called chuck-will's-widow.** *Travels*, 154 (U-SJR). Chuck-will's-widow, *Antrostomus carolinensis*. Listed as *Caprimulgus carolinensis* by Harper, 662.

Cardinal and Bunting Family (CARDINALIDAE)

**Nonpareil.** *Travels*, 106, 154 (M-SJR, U-SJR). Painted bunting, *Passerina ciris*. Listed as *Linaria cirus* by Harper, 575.

**Blue linnet.** *Travels*, 154 (U-SJR). Indigo bunting, *Passerina cyanea*. Listed as *Linaria cyanea* by Harper, 552.

Vulture Family (CATHARTIDAE)

**Vultures.** *Travels*, 179 (I-Trek). Either Turkey vulture, *Cathartes aura*, or Black vulture, *Coragyps atratus* by Harper, 660.

**Coped Vulture or carrion crow, Coragyps atratus.** *Travels*, (U-SJR). Black vulture, *Coragyps atratus*, see Harper, 660.

**Painted vulture, Vultur sacra.** *Travels*, 150–52 (U-SJR). Possibly the King vulture or sometimes referred as the White-tailed vulture, *Sarcoramphus papa*, a Central and South American species by Harper, 660. No modern records for Florida. Its possible presence has been an endless argument.[23]

Wood Stork Family (CICONIIDAE)

**Stork, temporary resting places.** *Travels*, 91 (L-SJR). Probably the Wood stork, *Mycteria americana*, although Harper, 636 suggested Whooping crane, *Grus americana*, as a possibility.

Pigeon and Dove Family (COLUMBIDAE)

**Dove.** *Travels*, 88 (L-SJR). Mourning dove, *Zenaida macroura*. *Zenaidura macroura* .

### Jay and Crow Family (CORVIDAE)

**Crows.** *Travels*, 90 (SJR). Listed as either the American crow, *Corvus brachyrhynchos*, or Fish Crow, *Corvus ossifragus*, or possibly both by Harper, 488.

**Ravens.** *Travels*, 179 (L-SJR). Listed as perhaps Northern raven, *Corvus corax* by Harper, 609. No modern records from Florida. Bartram made no mention of distinguishing features, only this comment, "*The vultures and ravens, crouched on the crooked limbs of the lofty Pines.*"

**Jay without a crest.** *Travels*, 172 (I-Trek). Florida scrub-jay, *Aphelocoma coerulescens*.

### Cuckoo and Roadrunner Family (CUCULIDAE)

**Cuckoo.** *Travels*, 181 (I-Trek). Yellow-billed cuckoo, *Coccyzus americanus*.

### Sparrow Family (EMBERIZIDAE)

**Chirping Sparrow.** *Travels*, 179 (I-Trek). Bachman sparrow, *Aimorphila aestivalis*. Listed as Pine-woods sparrow, *Aimophila aestivalis*, by Harper, 632.

**Towee bird (fringilla erythrophthalma).** *Travels*, 172 (I-Trek). White-eyed towhee. *Pipilo erythrophthalmus alleni*.

### Crane Family (GRUIDAE)

**Savanna cranes.** *Travels*, 146, 147, 179 (L-SJR, U-SJR, I-Trek). Sandhill crane, *Grus canadensis*. Crane resting in cypress in *Travels*, 91, was probably a wood stork or large heron. See Harper, 486.

### Oriole and Blackbird Family (ICTERIDAE)

**Golden Icterus.** *Travels*, 154 (U-SJR). Presumably Baltimore oriole, *Icterus galbula*, but record doubted, wrong season of year, by Harper, 531.

### Shrike Family (LANIIDAE)

**Bluish grey butcher bird, bluish grey (lanius).** *Travels*, 172 (probably I-Trek). Loggerhead shrike, *Lanius ludovicianus*.

### Turkey and Pheasant Family (PHASIANIDAE)

**Turkey(s) (or "turkies").** *Travels*, 75, 83, 84, 103, 109, 110, 146, 179 (L-SJR, M-SJR, U-SJR, I-Trek). Wild turkey, *Meleagris gallopavo*.

Parrot Family (PSITTACIDAE)

**Paroquets, seen hovering and fluttering in tops of cypress and their favorite food** (feeding on cypress seeds). *Travels,* 91, 92 (L-SJR). Carolina parakeet, *Conuropsis carolinensis.*

Rail, Gallinule, and Coot Family (RALLIDAE)

**Laughing coots.** *Travels,* 118 (U-SJR). American coots, *Fulica americana.*
**Coot enrobed in blue.** *Travels,* 160 (M-SJR). Purple gallinule, *Porphyrio martinica.*
**Squealing water-hen.** *Travels,* 160 (M-SJR). Probably Purple gallinule.

Owl Family (STRIGIDAE)

**Whooping owls.** *Travels,* 124 (U-SJR). Probably Florida barred owl, *Strix varia.* Listed as *Strix acclamator georgica* by Harper, 584.

Ibis and Spoonbill Family (THRESKIORNITHIDAE)

**Curlews.** *Travels,* 148, 149 (SJR). Listed as White ibis or "Spanish curlews," *Eudocimus albus* by Harper, 490.

## Mammals

Dog Family (CANIDAE)

**Rapacious wolf that stole my fish from over my head.** *Travels,* 103, 158, 159 (M-SJR). Red wolf, *Canis rufus.* Listed as Florida wolf, *Canis niger* in Harper, 664, 665. Extirpated from Florida.
**Wolves howled . . . the first time I heard them in Florida.** *Diary,* 10 Jan 1766 (U-SJR).

Deer Family (CERIDAE)

**Deer (or "dear" or fawns or roebuck or Cervus sylvaticus).** *Travels,* 103, 110, 179 (L-SJR, M-SJR, I-Trek). White-tailed deer, *Odocoileus virginianus.*

Mice and Rat Family (MURIDAE)

**Wood rat.** *Travels,* 124–25 (U-SJR). Eastern woodrat, *Neotoma floridana.* Bartram described this animal and its nest.
**Wood rat, great nest, built of long pieces of sticks, near 4 foot high and 5 in diameter.** *Diary,* 10 Jan 1766 (U-SJR).

**Wild rats.** *Travels*, 124–25 (U-SJR). Another smaller rat, probably Hispid cotton rat, *Sigmodon hispidus* suggested by Harper, 609.

## Opossum Family (DIDELPHIDAE)

**Opossums.** *Travels*, 103 (M-SJR). Virginia opossum, *Didelphis virginiana*. Listed as *Didelphis marsupialis* by Harper, 582.

## Cat Family (FELIDAE)

**Wild-cat.** *Travels*, 103, 110, 125 (M-SJR). Florida wildcat, *Lynx rufus*.

## Weasel Family (MUSTELIDAE)

**Otter(s) (or otter lutra).** *Travels*, 89 (SJR). River otter, *Lontra canadensis*. Imagined otters on floating islands along the SJR in Harper, 584.

## Raccoon Family (PROCYONIDAE)

**Raccoons.** *Travels*, 103 (M-SJR). Raccoon, *Procyon lotor*. Linnaeus originally listed the raccoon in the bear genus *Ursus*.

## Squirrel Family (SCIURIDAE)

**Squirrels.** *Travels*, 103 (M-SJR). Either the Eastern gray squirrel, *Sciurus carolinensis* Gmelin, or Sherman's fox squirrel, *Sciurus niger*, depending on whether the island featured hardwoods or pinelands.

## Bear Family (URSIDAE)

**Bear(s).** *Travels*, 103, 124, 125 (M-SJR, U-SJR). Black bear, *Ursus americanus*. Listed as Florida bear, *Euarctos americanus floridanus*, by Harper, 451.
**Bear roaring in the night.** *Diary*, 28 Dec 1765 (M-SJR).
**Hunter killed a large he-bear . . . 400 pounds, was 7-foot long.** *Diary*, 14 Jan 1766 (U-SJR).

# Acknowledgments

Sometimes it takes a village to accurately reconstruct a story about explorations, particularly when it began 250 years ago in the uncharted Florida frontier.

Francis Harper told his story of the exploits of William Bartram in his opus, *Travels: Naturalist's Edition*. This publication allowed modern Bartram enthusiasts Sam Carr, Dean Campbell, and Ken Mahaffey to tenaciously pursue Bartram sites along the St. Johns River (SJR). The outgrowth of their efforts led to the formation of the Bartram Trail Committee of Putnam County (Florida), establishment of the Bartram Trail in Putnam County, and the sponsorship of the 2015 Bartram Trails Association conference in Palatka. This national meeting attracted 167 registered attendees from ten states and Great Britain; the committee acknowledges the huge effort by Yvonne Parrish that made this conference so highly successful. This Bartram book grew out of local efforts to popularize the Bartram visits to the St. Johns River valley in the 1700s.

Numerous colleagues assisted in the preparation of this book by their support in field efforts, text reviews, and information accuracy. Their advice enabled me to interpret complex geologic, archaeological, and taxonomic issues. I acknowledge the following individuals: Tom Hallock (University of South Florida, esteemed Bartram expert), as well as Dean Campbell and Robert Virnstein (both retired scientists from the St. Johns River Water Management District) for their critiques of various iterations of the manuscript; Donna Ruhl (Florida Museum of Natural History) for providing information on St. Johns River shell middens and the cassine-black drink; Jim Macdonald for sharing his extensive knowledge of the St. Johns River, and Stephen Hale (Georgia Southern University, retired archaeologist) for open-ended discussions on natural history, Florida native peoples, and historic Florida.

The book *Ecosystems of Florida* by Myers and Ewel was probably the most valued published source for information on Florida landscapes. I highly recommend this text for those seeking a greater understanding of Florida environments.

One of the most difficult texts to construct concerned the origins of sulfur water that flows from the St. Johns River springs. I thank the following individuals who were essential in those discussions: Tom M. Scott (Florida Bureau of Geology, retired) and Guy H. Means (Florida Bureau of Geology) for local geology, and Jeff Davis (St. Johns River Water Management District, hydrologist), Bettina A. Moser (UF Clinical and Translational Science Institute, microbiologist), Robert Knight (Howard T. Odum Florida Springs Institute, springs specialist), and Claude Brown (UF Lake Watch Program, hydro-chemist) for their substantive comments on sulfur water and sulfur bacteria.

Another challenge for me was chasing Bartram plant and bird names from their original interpretations by Harper (1967) to their present-day usage. I became dependent on the Florida vascular plant book by Wunderlin and Hansen (University of South Florida) for its taxonomic clarifications, specifically changes in family and genus names for local plants; David W. Hall (Gainesville) for his painstaking review of the included plant list; Walter S. Judd (Florida Museum of Natural History) for his critique of the *Naming Plants and Animals* section; and finally Tom Webber (Florida Museum of Natural History) for his taxonomic updates for Florida birds.

I especially want to recognize our special friends, Willy The Losen (Johnson, Florida) for helping to explore possible sites of William Bartram's Halfway Pond campsite, Jim and Carol Macdonald for their informative tours on the St. Johns River in their Cape Horn boat, Sandy and Jack Kokernoot for their companionship in the field, and Andi Blount and Melanie Wegner for their diligent efforts in reviewing the page proofs. I am particularly appreciative of my wife, Melanie Wegner, who has supported my Bartram obsessions.

# Notes

## Introduction

1. John Bartram to Peter Collinson, 28 September 1755 (Berkeley and Berkeley, *Correspondence*, 387); John to William Bartram, 19 May 1765 (Hallock and Hoffmann, *Bartram*, 48).

2. Kathryn E. Holland Braund reviews the conference in "'The Congress Held in a Pavilion': John Bartram and the Indian Congress at Fort Picolata, East Florida." John's brief "Remarks" on the conference appear in his *Diary* (51).

3. See John Bartram's *Diary*, 12 December 1766; on the Davises, see *Florida History Online*, unf.edu/floridahistoryonline/Plantations/.

4. On the outfitting of William's plantation, see John to William Bartram, 5 April 1766 (reprinted in this volume); on the de Brahm claims, see the chronology by Thomas P. Slaughter in *William Bartram: Travels and Other Writings* (598–99); on the family's confusion, see the 15 July 1772 letter from John to William (Hallock and Hoffmann, *Bartram*, 82).

5. John Fothergill to William Bartram, 22 October 1772 (Hallock and Hoffmann, *Bartram*, 84–86). The route of Bartram's tour has been investigated and retraced many times over. See the Bartram Trail Conference, *Bartram Heritage Report*, prepared in 1975–79, and sources listed on the BTC website (bartramtrail.org).

6. The book is available in many forms, including online (docsouth.unc.edu). Slaughter's volume includes images, supporting documents, and the *Report to Fothergill*; the standard text is Francis Harper's *"Travels" of William Bartram: Naturalist's Edition*. A revised scholarly edition of *Travels* is long overdue.

7. Frazier, *Cold Mountain*, 15.

8. Bartram describes the "flowery Regions" in a letter to Mary Robeson, 7 September 1788 (Hallock and Hoffmann, *Bartram*, 141); his thoughts on the "Divine Monitor" are best outlined in "The Dignity of Human Nature" (Hallock and Hoffmann, *Bartram*, 348–58); on the reception of *Travels*, see Francis Harper's introduction (xxiii–xxviii).

9. Thomas Say to Jacob Gilliams, 30 January 1818 (Hallock and Hoffmann, *Bartram*, 237); the April 1792 review of *Travels*, from the *Universal Asylum and Columbian Magazine*, is quoted from the introduction of Harper's *Naturalist's Edition* (xxiv), still the definitive edition of the classic work.

10. For Bartram's account of Salt Springs, see *Travels*, 165. Bracketed page numbers in the text indicate pages in the original 1791 edition.

11. William Bartram to Lachlan McIntosh, 31 May 1796 (Hallock and Hoffmann, *Bartram*, 182); *Catalogue of Trees, Shrubs, and Herbaceous Plants, Indigenous to the United States of America*, 7.

12. *Travels*, 93.

13. The second edition of Stork's *An Account of East-Florida* (1766) included *A journal, kept by John Bartram of Philadelphia, Botanist to His Majesty for the Floridas; upon a journey from St. Augustine up the river St. Johns*, 1–35 (paginated separately). The popular *Gentleman's Magazine*, which published an engraving of William's drawing of the spotted turtle in 1758 mistakenly attributed John's *Diary* to William in "An extract of Mr Wm. Bartram's observations in a journey up the River Savannah in Georgia, with his son," 166–68.

14. *Travels*, 80.

15. From the introduction to *Travels* (not paginated).

## Part I

### CHAPTER 1. *DIARY*, BY JOHN BARTRAM

1. On the east side of the St. Johns, above Cow-ford (or Jacksonville); the Bartrams traveled the main road from St. Augustine (*Diary* 69).

2. "The Magnolia mentioned here among the trees 100 feet high, must be the Laurel-leafed Tulip-tree; and it is the most elegant evergreen tree of North-America, both for its large milk-white odoriferous blossoms, and its shining Laurel shaped leaves. It will scarcely bear this climate without shelter in severe winters, unless near the southern sea-coast. This is the Magnolia grandiflora, Lin. Spec. p. 755." [Stork's note]

3. "Liquidambar styraciflua, Linn. Spec. 1418. American gum-storax-tree, with a maple-leaf, called also sweet-gum.—Monardes, in his history of Mexico, calls this tree by the name of liquid-amber, where he says it grows to a vast height; and that upon wounding its thick spongy bark, the balsam flows out, of the same scent with storax. See Casp. 4. Bauh. Pin. p. 502. This tree grows not only in Mexico, but in the greatest part of North-America, from the Floridas to New-York; it yields its valuable balsam in proportion to the heat of the climate it grows in. Some excellent specimens of it have been collected in Georgia lately. It is found to be an admirable remedy for green wounds or bruises." [Stork's note]

4. "Guilandina dioica, Linn. Spec. 546 Bonduc or Nickar Nut.—We have two

kinds of this genus in the West-India Islands, that are climbing plants; one of them is thorny, and bears pods with round grey seeds like marbles; the other has no thorns, and bears yellow seeds of the same size with the former, and are likewise used by children to play with. The one mentioned here, may be the same that Mons. du Hamel of Paris says grows wild in Canada, and is male and female in different plants. This tree is very hardy in respect to cold, and esteemed one of the rarest and most elegant hardy trees in the English gardens, growing erect with large doubly-pinnated leaves." [Stork's note]

5. Beauclerc Bluff was an indigo plantation owned by Robert Davis. See *Florida History Online*, http://www.unf.edu/floridahistoryonline/Plantations/.

6. "Laurus Borbonia, Linn. Spec. 529. Red-Bay.—This tree makes excellent timber for the cabinet-makers, and is very little inferior to mahogany; some trees of this kind are so close-grained, that they are not to be distinguished from the best mahogany. They grow much larger near the sea-coast than in the inner parts, and will soon become a beneficial article of trade." [Stork's note]

7. "Zanthoxylon, Clava Herculis, Linn. Spec. 1455. Tooth-ach-tree.—Dr. Linnæus observes, that this is the same species that grows in Japon, and is called there Seo and Sansjo, or Japon-pepper, where they use it to season their food, as we do pepper and ginger. Vid. Kæmpfer's Amœnitates, p. 892. Besides this, the wood will afford a yellow dye." [Stork's note]

8. "The Purple-berried Bay, is called by Catesby a Ligustrum or Evergreen Privet; but Dr. Solander, who has dissected many specimens of it, both with blossoms and fruit on them, says it is a species of olive: it is a beautiful evergreen-tree, with opposite lanceolated leaves, as long as those of the Red-bay." [Stork's note]

9. "This shrub is well worth enquiring after; it is not known at present to the Botanists by this superficial description." [Stork's note]

10. In the area of present-day Palatka; the next day, the Bartrams explored nearby Rollestown, which William described in further detail (*Travels*, 93).

11. "This is the Magnolia glauca of Linnæus Sp. p. 755, and is the most valuable shrub that the gardeners import to England, both on the account of its standing the severest frost, and the delightful fragrancy of its large white flowers; there is a great demand for this shrub both at home and abroad. Here we find it grows to a large tree; which is a strong proof of the richness of the [s]oil, as well as the excellency of the climate." [Stork's note]

12. "Saururus cernuus, Linn. Spec. 418. Lizard's-tail, a creeping plant with heart-shaped leaves." [Stork's note]

13. "Iris, in English, flower-de-lace." [Stork's note]

14. "Pancratium Carolinianum, Linn. Spec. 418. Carolina sea-daffodil." [Stork's note]

15. "Convolvulus, in English, bindweed." [Stork's note]

16. "Chenopodium, in English, goose-foot." [Stork's note]

17. "Pontederia, a water-plant, with arrow-headed leaves, and a spike of blue flowers." [Stork's note]

18. Dunn's (now Murphy) Island is at the mouth of Dunn's Creek; the Bartrams returned to the site on 26 January. Spalding's lower store, at present-day Stokes Landing upriver from Palatka, served as the base of operations for William's Florida explorations.

19. Alachua? Prominent site of William's 1774 tour.

20. "Tagus Pumila, Linn. Spec. 1416. Dwarf-chesnut Chinquapin—This tree grows about 10 or 12 feet high, and produces a great quantity of small round nuts, exceeding the common chesnuts in the sweetness of their taste." [Stork's note; spelling of "Fagus" corrected in *Erratum*.]

21. "Prunus Virginiana, Linn. Spec. 677, and 3d Padus of Miller's Dictionary, American Bird-cherry or Cluster cherry.—The wood of this tree is much esteemed by the Cabinet-makers; it preserves its leaves the longest of any of the deciduous trees. There is an evergreen sort of this Bird or Cluster-cherry, which grows about 30 feet high in S. Carolina, and from the beauty of its evergreen shining leaves is called the Mock-orange; the fruit of this steeped in brandy makes a fine flavoured ratafie [ratatia]. This is the 6th Padus of Miller's Dictionary." [Stork's note]

22. Bartram describes Johnson and Satsuma and Springs, respectively.

23. Present-day Beecher Point, a small shell mound, site since removed for road fill; see *Travels* (98).

24. "Gleditsia, Linn. Spec. 1509, Three-thorn'd Acacia or Honey-locust. This tree with its elegant leaves grows up to a large size, and is said to make excellent timber. There is a very large one of this kind in the Bishop of London's garden at Fulham.—There is another species of this, with small thin oval pods, inclosing only one seed, called by Mr. Catesby Water-acacia, on account of its growing in moist places, which also comes to very good timber, and is mentioned here by Mr. Bartram." [Stork's note]

25. Mt. Royal, currently in a gated community, near the Fort Gates ferry landing on the east side of the St. Johns; see *Travels* (98).

26. "Cupressus-disticha, Linn. Spec. 1422. Deciduous Swamp, Cypress or Bald-cypress.—This most useful tree grows in great plenty in many of the swamps, and grows to such an amazing size, that boats or pettiaugres, capable of carrying a considerable burthen, are formed from the trunks of single trees. From the cones of this tree issues a most fragrant balsam like balsam of Tolu." [Stork's note]

27. "Chamærops humilis, Linn. Spec. 1657.—Dwarf-palmetta. This Dwarf-palm grows on the sea-coast, from the capes of Florida up to Charles-Town in South-Carolina, and bears bunches of berries something larger than black currants. These contain round horny seeds which are the size of small peas, and are covered with a thin pulp, which the Indians use as food. The leaves furnish them with thatch, and the soil where they grow is judged to be a middling kind between the sand and the swamps." [Stork's note]

28. Lake George.

29. "Kalmia, an elegant evergreen flowering shrub, bearing umbels of beautiful red flowers, now cultivated in the curious English gardens." [Stork's note]

30. "Vaccinium. Cranberries, four times larger than the English Cranberries." [Stork's note]

31. "Myrica cerifera, Linn. Spec. 1453. Dwarf-myrtle.—This is a dwarf kind of the common Candleberry-myrtle, of such importance to the people of North-America, by supplying them with excellent wax, with only the trouble of collecting and boiling the berries, and when the water is cold taking off the wax." [Stork's note]

32. "Andromeda. There are many shrubs of this genus now cultivated for their beauty in the English gardens." [Stork's note]

33. "Pistia Stratiotes, Linn. Spec. 1365. A Water-plant like the Water-soldier or Water-house-leek.—Sir Hans Sloane has given us a figure of this plant in his history of Jamaica, vol. 1, table 2, fig. 2, and says it is used for the same diseases as Plantain, either outwardly or inwardly, in juice, or the powder to a drachm." [Stork's note]

34. "Palma altissima, fructu pruniformi, &c. Sloan Hist. Jamaica, vol. 2, 115, 116, &c. The palm called the Cabbage-tree—It appears from this Palm growing here, (which is a native of the West-Indies,) that many others of the West-India productions may also be cultivated. From the pith with which this tree abounds, very good Sago has been made, and the long trunks of this palm serve very well for pipes to convey water under-ground, and when split in two make excellent long troughs or conduits to convey water from place to place above-ground." [Stork's note]

35. The Bartrams depart from the lower store, present-day Palatka, for the upper store in what is now Astor.

36. Lake Beresford, the branch being Hontoon Dead River.

37. Blue Springs, southern terminus of William's 1774 St. Johns explorations.

38. Rod, or 16.5 feet.

39. Peanines: Peavines.

40. Lake Monroe.

41. Duck-meat: Duckweed.

42. Lake Harney, later called Round Lake, which the Bartrams explore below; they camped on Lemon Bluff, on the west side of the river north of Mullet Lake (*Diary* 72).

43. "Juniperus Virginiana, Linn. Spec. 1471. Red-cedar, or Great Juniper.—'Tis necessary to distinguish this tree from the many that are called Cedars: It is of great use not only in the building of houses, but in ship-building: This is the wood used in making black lead pencils; the berries put into spirits make excellent geneva, and from the tree distils a resin equal to gum-sandrach, very useful in making varnish." [Stork's note]

44. William described the Florida woodrat (*Neotoma floridana*) in greater detail in *Travels* (124).

45. Puzzle Lake.

46. "Celtis, occidentalis, Linn. Spec. 1748. The Lote or Nettle-tree—This grows to be a very large tree, and the wood of it is much esteemed for being so tough and pliable; it is reckoned the best wood for the shafts of all kinds of carriages." [Stork's note]

47. Lake Loughman. The Bartrams camp on Baxter/Persimmon Mound (*Diary* 73), their southernmost campsite; on 13 January, they turn around.

48. Coffee Bluff, on the west side of the river, just below Lake Harney; the "west lake" is Lake Jesup (*Diary* 73).

49. Mineral Springs (*Report to Fothergill*, 73).

50. Lake Monroe, coasting along the south bank by present-day Sanford; "Bartram's Bluff," where they camp, sits on the east side of the river, below the lake (*Report* 73).

51. Hontoon Island. The route down the left branch, Hontoon Dead River, bypassed Lake Beresford (*Report* 73).

52. Lake Dexter; the Bartrams spent the night at the upper store, just above the "great lake," Lake George.

53. Silver Glen Springs.

54. Salt Springs, described memorably in *Travels* (165–68).

55. "By the above description this may probably be the Illicium anisatum of Linn. Spec. 664. which is the Somo or Skimmi of Kæmpfer's amænitates, p. 880.—This is the tree so much admired for its spicy quality by the Chinese and Japonese, and which has been discovered lately by William Clifton, Esq; Chief-Justice of West-Florida, to grow near Pensacola." [Stork's note]

56. Drayton Island, described in *Travels* (102).

57. Mount Royal, described in *Travels* (98). See note 25 above.

58. The Bartrams camped on Dunn's Island on 26 December; "Dunn's Lake" is today's Crescent Lake and the "small island," below, is today's Bear Island. The king awarded Lord Adam Gordon's petition in 1766.

59. Could "4" mean Rolle's Quarter? William describes Rollestown or Charlotia (JB's "Charlottensburgh") in *Travels* (93).

60. Present-day Rice Creek; the "great-orange grove" is at Forrester Point.

61. San Francisco de Pupo, on Bayard Point and opposite Fort Picolata, was an abandoned fort built by the Spanish (1714–16) to protect the crossing for the Camino Real, the road between St. Augustine and Apalachee. "Caldwell's store," reached the following day, was in present-day Middleburg, off Black Creek.

62. "Hamamelis, a shrub with leaves like the common hazel, propagated for the sake of variety by the English gardeners." [Stork's note]

63. "Tanniers, a species of Eddo's.—This is a species of Arum or Wake Robin.—There are many sorts of them cultivated in the West-Indies, and in Carolina, for the sake of the roots as well as the leaves, which latter is called Indian-Kale; for further information consult Sir Hans Sloane, Hist. Jam. vol. I. p. 166 to 170; Brown's Hist. Jam. and Miller's Dictionary, under the title Arum." [Stork's note]

64. Hester's Bluff, settled by William Hester, occupies a high point used for defense over the centuries; Richard Hazard settled an indigo plantation in 1764–65 on Fort George Island, near the St. Johns confluence with the Atlantic.

CHAPTER 2. *TRAVELS*, BY WILLIAM BARTRAM

1. Bartram carried a 15 August 1773 letter of introduction from James Spalding, owner of the upper and lower stores, to Charles [McClatchie] McLatchy: "you will receive this One Trunk & one box the property of M. W. Bertram who means to take a Tour of S. Johns River inquest of the naturall production's of Country, and as I have promised him a passage for these two Packages & that they will be taken care of by you till his arrivall which will be about the month of October nixt, I again recomend them to your Care and M. Bartram himself to your friendship when he arrives" (Hallock and Hoffmann, *Bartram*, 94).

2. Several printer's errors appear in the list of botanical Latin, including misspellings and missing parentheses and commas.

3. Fort William, on Cumberland Island, commanded by John Stuart, who was superintendent of Indian affairs and whom Bartram knew from the 1765 Fort Picolata conference and 1773 Augusta negotiations (*Travels* 34–47).

4. Stephen Egan, agent for the Amelia Island plantation owned by Lord Egmont, John James Perceval. Egan accompanied Bartram to Cowford, or present-day Jacksonville.

5. Present-day Kingsley Creek, with "Fort George's Sound" probably being today's Nassau Sound and the party's camp on the north end of Talbot Sound.

6. *Travels* sets in different sequence a trip with traders, "to hunt up some horses belonging to them," which took Bartram to the Alachua Savanna, south of present-day Gainesville, and to the town of Cuscowilla (*Report to Fothergill*, 146–50); the important events at Alachua Savanna are folded into an independent section in chapter 6 of *Travels*. In *Travels* Bartram also de-emphasizes the plantation economy; his *Report* notes how Governor Patrick Tonyn used "twenty hands" to yield "about twelve hundred [weight] of indigo the last year" (150).

7. Bartram's *Report to Fothergill* identifies the Indian as "a slave bro't from off Musqueto Shore," or present-day Nicaragua (146; Waselkov and Braund, *William Bartram on the Southeastern Indians*, 234n22). Bartram spent the night at Suttonia Plantation, near Plummers Point; Abraham Marshall was the agent for this 10,000-acre property, not the owner

8. *Putrescent* means "rotten," but it is also an agricultural term, referring to the decayed matter that assists "the melioration of the land" (*Oxford English Dictionary*).

9. The host, possibly Francis Philip Fatio, refers to a 1774 meeting between the Lower Creeks (or Seminoles), including Oconee Mico (or Cowkeeper), whom Bartram would meet on his cross-Florida journey, and the governor of East Florida, Patrick Tonyn.

10. On their 1765 journey, John and William Bartram witnessed the British and Seminole conference at Fort Picolata, near the present-day town of the same name. The 500-acre plantation that William attempted to settle in 1766 was nearby.

11. Probably on the east side of the St. Johns, between Tocoi Creek and Racy Point (Harper, *"Travels" of William Bartram*, 352).

12. "I have made use of the terms alligator and crocodile indiscriminately for this animal, alligator being the country name." [Bartram's note]

13. Present-day Palatka.

14. On Native American foods, see Bartram's *Report to Fothergill* (169–71).

15. Rollestown, or Charlotia, a failed utopian settlement founded by Dennys Rolle around 1764 and built on an indigenous site, on the eastern shore between the present East Palatka and San Mateo.

16. Murphy, or Dunn's Island.

17. Spalding's lower store (present-day Stokes Landing) was the trading house owned by James Spalding and Roger Kelsall and managed by Charles McLatchy, and it served as a base for Bartram's Florida explorations.

18. From here the record of Bartram's route grows more confusing. Although *Travels* recounts the journey from Spalding's lower store to Lake Beresford as one trip, Bartram folded material from two trips, May–June 1774 and August–September 1774, into a single narrative. He also moved overland trips to chapters 6 and 7 of *Travels*.

19. Beecher Point (see John Bartram's *Diary*, 28 December 1765).

20. Mount Royal (see John Bartram's *Diary*, 28 December 1765). In the *Report to Fothergill*, William puts emphasis on economic uses: "Mo. Royal gives name to a large Plantation belonging to L. Egmont, was formerly an Indigo Plantation, but now given up & the hands removed to Emelia [Amelia] Island on the No. of this province[,] there is about 150 Acres of Land cleared here & has been planted with Indigo, here is a handsom large Framed house, which stands about 100 Yards from the River[,] having sundry convenient out houses, placed, in regular maner" (*Report*, 150).

21. The tone to Bartram's narrative changes dramatically here. His hymn to morning marks the beginning of the draft "Travels" (Hallock and Hoffmann, *Bartram*, 302).

22. Bryan's and Drayton Island, the latter inhabited by planter and jurist William Drayton; Bartram returned to the site in fall 1774. The *Report to Fothergill* describes a rough sail, though one not so solitary: "went about 3 miles & entered the great lake George which is about twelve miles over either way; we set a course streight across for the mouth of the River. at other side, having passt Draiton Isle, the wind came about a head & blowing a fresh gale from thunder clouds rising up from the SW. we were obliged to put back for a harbour, but before we made the shore the gale carried a way our mast & Sail, which however we saved from going over board & with great danger got into a harbour on the Island where we were detailed all night" (151).

23. "Convol. dissectus." [Bartram's note]

24. "Cervus sylvaticus. The American deer." [Bartram's note]

25. Spalding's upper store on the west bank of the St. Johns, present-day Astor.

26. Because Bartram compressed journeys, it can be difficult to determine the status of his companions. The *Report* indicates that a trader accompanied him to Spalding's upper store in spring 1774 (150), whereas in *Travels*, this trader morphs into the solitary Indian who leaves the solitary explorer. Sections of the August St. Johns tour were apparently taken alone (*Report*, 162).

27. Readers of *Travels* mark the "little promontory" as a shell mound on the west shore of Lake Dexter. In the *Report to Fothergill* Bartram provides further details about alligators, with direct reference to the image: "They heave their heads and upper part of their body upright[,] opening their throats to swallow [trout], & I have seen them with two or three great Trout in their mouth at a time[,] choping them up[,] the fishes tail hanging out. the noise of their jaws choping together[,] with the water & prey in their Throats; their plunging through the water after their Prey & pursuing one another altogether exhibits a very terrifying shew; Got no rest this Night owing to the stinging of Musquitoes & Noise & confusion of the Alegators & Fish. As soon as day appeared the Thunder of the Allegators, roaring all around us, & for many Miles. Their noise is louder then the bellowing of the most furious Bull, or a Lyon, more like the latter, the water rattling in their throats, which they force out in froth & foam, & makes the earth to tremble, & our little Island shook as by an earth quake; When they roar their Body is swoln like an empty Hogshead on the water[,] their head & Neck raisd out of the water, his Tail raised 5 or 6 feet in the air[,] waving too & fro, & lashing the surface of the water in a terrible maner as they utter their terrable Voice[,] their body sinks gradually in the water[,] then swelling again rises up[,] thus alternately as they continue their bellowing. The deep swamps & banks of the river's & Forest re-echoing the dreadfull roar, the noise is communicated from one to another[,] fills the whole country with a noise like dreadfull Thunder. But this is only in the Spring of the year about the time of their incubation" (152).

28. Squamae: scales.

29. Mosquito Grove, above Lake Dexter. Harper notes that the pace had slowed considerably, as Bartram takes two to three days to cover the fifteen miles from Lake Dexter to Lake Beresford (357).

30. "Cucurbita peregrine." [Bartram's note]

31. Bartram's campsite, the "perpendicular bluff," was a Yamassee burial ground, since removed for road fill, between Lakes Dexter and Beresford.

32. Present-day Hawkinsville, on the west side of the river.

33. The seasonal squall comes uncharacteristically in the spring, a slip of detail resulting from the collation of two tours into one journey; the indigo harvest, below, sets the storm between August and September.

34. The "delightful little bluff" was probably on Hontoon Island.

35. Beresford Plantation, a 20,000-acre plot that extended from the middle of Lake Beresford to Blue Springs, overseen by Charles Bernard.

36. "New-Smyrna is built on a high shelly bluff, on the West bank of the South branch of Musquito river, about ten miles above the capes of that river, which is about thirty miles North of Cape Canaveral, Lat. 28. I was there about ten years ago, when the surveyor run the lines or precincts of the colony, where there was neither habitation nor cleared field. It was then a famous Orange grove, the upper or South promontory of a ridge, nearly half a mile wide and stretching North about forty miles, to the head of the North branch of the Musquito, to where the Tomoko river unites with it, nearly parallel to the sea coast, and not above two miles across to the sea beach. All this ridge was then one entire Orange grove, with Live Oaks, Magnolias, Palms, Red Bays and others: I observed then, near where New-Smyrna now stands, a spacious Indian mount and avenue, which stood near the banks of the river; the avenue ran on a strait line back, through the groves, across the ridge, and terminated at the verge of natural savannas and ponds." [Bartram's note]

37. Bartram reached Blue Springs, the southernmost point of his 1774 tour, with his father in 1766.

38. "Tantalus pictus." [Bartram's note]. See figure 1, page 7.

39. *Flirting* is defined as a coquettish act, but also means to move suddenly (*Oxford English Dictionary*).

40. "Tantalus albus. Numinus albus. Cat." [Bartram's note]

41. "Tantalus versicolor. Numinus fuscus. Cat." [Bartram's note]

42. "Tantalus loculator. Linn." [Bartram's note]

43. "Vultur sacra." [Bartram's note]. See "Vulture Family," chapter 4, 189.

44. "Vultu[r] aura." [Bartram's note]

45. "Cyprinus coronarius." [Bartram's note]

46. Possibly Tick Island, between Lakes Woodruff and Dexter.

47. "Caprimulgus rufus called chuck-will's-widow, from a fancied resemblance of his notes to these words: they inhabit the maritime parts of Carolina and Florida, and are more than twice the size of the night hawk or whip-poor-will." [Bartram's note]

48. "Passiflora incarnata, called May-Apple." [Bartram's note]

49. After arriving at the lower store in late April 1774, Bartram joined the group of traders, probably led by Job Wiggins, to Alachua Savanna (Waselkov and Braund, *William Bartram on the Southeastern Indians*, 149–50); see the letter to his father, this volume (124–27).

50. In *Travels* Bartram follows the "easternmost channel," between the upper store and Lake George, presumably the main river, and not the smaller Blue Creek on the west shore. His *Report* indicates that Bartram traveled the eastern shore on his first trip and the western shore on his second (Harper, *"Travels" of William Bartram*, 361).

51. Bartram visited Salt Springs on 24 January 1766 with his father and returned in August 1774 (*Report* 161). The spring is notable for William's discovery of the yellow anise (*Illicium parviflorum*), puzzlingly not described here, and for Coleridge's allusion to *Travels* in his poem "Kubla Khan."

52. Spellings here have been corrected; the original reads "obcunciformibus obsolete tribobis minoribus."

53. Salt Springs. The *Illicium Floridanum*, or purple anise, is native to West Florida and confusingly labeled here.

CHAPTER 3. CORRESPONDENCE

1. Manuscript in the Bartram Papers at the Historical Society of Pennsylvania; the document is torn and heavily interlined at the list of goods.

2. "Taniers" (coco yams, *Colocasia esculenta*, see John's *Diary* for 10 February 1766); "ground nuts" (peanuts, *Arachis hypogaea*); "hesing," either hosing or hessian, a type of burlap. The Lambolls are Thomas and Elizabeth.

3. Alexander Garden (1730–91), Charleston physician and botanist; John Moultrie (1702–71), physician trained at the University of Edinburgh, lieutenant governor and landholder in East Florida. De Brahm notes a trader named Sanders who operated a store on the St. Mary's River.

4. Gabriel Manigault (1704–81) or more likely his son Peter (1731–73), who managed several plantations. "Nairney" may be Thomas Nairne, or based on the context of a letter, a descendant. Thomas Nairne's widely circulating *Letter from South Carolina* (1710) tabulated the resources, tools, and labor force needed to clear and manage a plantation.

5. Probably Adam Bachop, who with his brother Peter captained the schooner *East Florida*, which sailed (with John Bartram aboard) from Philadelphia in 1765.

6. Kramanti, or Coramantine, from the coast of present-day Ghana.

7. Manuscript at the American Philosophical Society.

8. Manuscript at the Library Company of Philadelphia, held by the Historical Society of Pennsylvania. Benjamin Rush (1746–1813), a prominent Philadelphian and social reformer, studied medicine at Edinburgh. Bartram's description was appended to a letter from John Bartram to Rush on plant "instinct." An illustration and brief mention of the Ixia also appears in *Travels*.

9. A stained copy of the 1742 second edition of Linnaeus's *Genera plantarum* (Gen=Genera; plant=Plantarum), inscribed to "J Bartram," is at the Library Company of Philadelphia; the flower, once in the letter, is now missing.

10. Manuscript damaged, possibly "determined."

11. Manuscript in the Bartram Papers at the Historical Society of Pennsylvania; mistakenly dated 1774, the letter was written at the Charleston home of Mary Lamboll Thomas, a family friend. See note 2 above.

12. Stephan Egan was an agent for John James Perceval, the second Earl of Egmont, and his son; see *Travels* (64).

13. Ahaye, or Cowkeeper, was the Seminole chief who became famous for giving William Bartram the nickname Puc Puggy (*Travels* 184–86).

## Part II

### CHAPTER 4. THROUGH THEIR EYES: THE BARTRAMS EXPLORE THE ST. JOHNS RIVER VALLEY

1. Much of the information on Roland and Francis Harper is drawn from Shores, *On Harper's Trail*.

2. My friend Stephen Hale, a retired archaeologist, provided the information on Long Warrior and a Seminole village on the Ocklawaha. The rest of the material in this section is based on the following sources: Belleville, *River of Lakes*; Miller, "Hydrogeology of Florida," Nordlie, "Rivers and Springs," and Schmidt, "Geomorphology and Physiography of Florida," 1997.

3. General plant information in this section is drawn from Dressler et al., *Identification Manual for Wetland Plant Species of Florida,* and from Hall, Weber, and Byrd, *Wildflowers of Florida and the Southeast*.

4. Information in this section on the bluff hammock ecosystems along the St. Johns River is based on Platt and Schwartz, "Temperate Hardwood Forests." General plant information comes from Hall et al., *Wildflowers of Florida and the Southeast*.

5. Dressler et al., *Identification Manual for Wetland Plant Species of Florida*; Ewel, "Swamps."

6. The information on marsh ecosystems in this section is based on Kushlan, "Freshwater Marshes." The information on wetland plants comes from Dressler et al., *Identification Manual for Wetland Plant Species of Florida*, 1991.

7. Scott, "The Lithostratigraphy of the Hawthorn Group (Miocene) of Florida."

8. Varying archaeological interpretations of Florida's shell middens can be found in the following sources: Brinton, *A Guidebook of Florida and the South;* Milanich and Fairbanks, *Florida Archaeology;* Moore, "Certain Shell Heaps of the St. Johns River, Florida, Hitherto Unexplored"; O'Donoughue et al., *Archaeological Investigations at Salt Springs (8MR2322), Marion County, Florida;* Sassaman and Randall, "Shell Mounds of the Middle St. Johns Basin, Northeast Florida"; Stalter and Kincaid, "The Vascular Flora of Five Florida Shell Middens;" and Wyman, *Freshwater Shell Mounds*.

9. Information on Florida's upland pine sandhills in this section comes from Myers, "Scrub and High Pine," 174–93.

10. Information on Florida's scrub in this section comes from Myers, "Scrub and High Pine," 154–74.

11. The material on pine flatwoods in this section comes from Abrahamson and Harnett, "Pine Flatwoods and Dry Prairies," 103–49.

12. See Brenner, Binford, and Deevey, "Lakes," 364.

13. The information on ponds in this section is based on the following sources: Brenner et al., "Lakes"; Miller, "Hydrogeology of Florida"; Moler and Franz, "Wildlife Values of Small Isolated Wetlands in the Southeastern Coastal Plain"; Quillen, Gaiser, and Grimm, "Diatom-Based Paleolimnological Reconstruction." Speculation as to the location of Bartram's camp site on Halfway Pond comes from Harper's 1967 edition of *"Travels" of William Bartram*.

14. For more information on Florida's springs and spring-associated invertebrates, see Franz, "Cave Crustaceans"; Miller, "Hydrogeology of Florida"; Nordlie, "Rivers and Springs"; Sacks and Tihansky, "Geochemical and Isotopic Composition of Ground Water"; Scott et al., "Springs of Florida"; Thompson, *Identification Manual for Freshwater Snails of Florida*; and Waite, *Principles of Water Quality*.

15. The information on ruderal sites of human activity in this section, including the Spalding's lower store, is drawn from the following sources: Goggin, "A Florida Indian Trading Post, ca. 1763–1784"; Milanich and Fairbanks, *Florida Archaeology*, and Schafer, *William Bartram and the Ghost Plantations of British East Florida*.

16. Schafer, "New World"; see Goggin, "A Florida Indian Trading Post, ca. 1763–1784," for an archaeological report on this site.

17. Belleville, *River of Lakes*, 192.

18. See Linnaeus, *Species plantarum* and *Systema naturae*, and Wulf, *Brother Gardeners*.

19. Dressler et al., *Identification Manual for Wetland Plant Species of Florida*.

20. Putz, *Finding Home in the Sandy Lands of the South*.

21. Berry, "The Fossil Plants from Vero, Florida"; Quillen, Gaiser, and Grimm, "Diatom-Based Paleolimnological Reconstruction." See Evans, "Pistia stratiotes L. in the Florida Peninsula" for more information.

22. Dressler et al., *Identification Manual for Wetland Plant Species of Florida*.

23. For latest evaluation, see Snyder and Fry, "Validity of Bartram's Painted Vulture (Aves: Cathartidae)." In this paper, they claim that the Bartram bird was not the Northern Crested Caracara, *Caracara cheriway*, and they provide evidence "for the acceptance of Bartram's Painted Vulture as a historic resident of northern Florida."

# Bibliography

Abrahamson, Warren G., and David C. Harnett. "Pine Flatwoods and Dry Prairies." In *Ecosystems of Florida*, edited by Ronald L. Myers and John J. Ewel, 103–49. Gainesville: University Presses of Florida, 1990.

Barton, Benjamin Smith. "Some Account of the *Tantalous ephouskyca*." *Edinburgh Monthly Review* 4 (July–December 1820): 50.

Bartram, John. *The Correspondence of John Bartram, 1734–77*. Edited by Edmund Berkeley and Dorothy Smith Berkeley. Gainesville: University Press of Florida, 1992.

———. *A Description of East-Florida, with a Journal, Kept by John Bartram of Philadelphia, Botanist to His Majesty for the Floridas; Upon Journeying from St. Augustine up the River St. Johns, as Far as the Lakes*. Edited by William Stork. London: W. Nicoll and T. Jefferies, 1769.

———. *Diary of a Journey through the Carolinas, Georgia, and Florida from July 1, 1765, to April 10, 1766*. Edited by Francis Harper, 1–120. In *Transactions of the American Philosophical Society*, vol. 33, pt. 1. Philadelphia: America Philosophical Society, 1942.

———. "An Extract of Mr Wm. Bartram's Observations in a Journey up the River Savannah in Georgia, with His Son, on Discoveries." *Gentleman's Magazine* 37 (April 1767): 166–68.

Bartram, William. *Botanical and Zoological Drawings, 1756–88*. Vol. 74 of the Memoirs series. Edited by Joseph Ewan. Philadelphia: American Philosophical Society, 1968.

———. "Travels in Georgia and Florida, 1773–74: A Report to Dr. John Fothergill." Edited by Francis Harper, 121–42. In *Transactions of the American Philosphical Society* vol. 33, pt. 2. Philadelphia: American Philosophical Society, 1942.

———. *Travels through North and South Carolina, Georgia, East and West Florida, the Cherokee Country, the Extensive Territories of the Muscogulges, or Creek Confederacy, and the Country of the Chactaws; Containing an Account of the Soil and Natural Pro-

*ductions of Those Regions, Together with Observations on the Manners of the Indians.* 1st ed. Philadelphia: James and Johnson, 1791.

———. *Travels and Other Writings*. Edited by Thomas P. Slaughter. New York: Library of America, 1996.

———. *The "Travels" of William Bartram: Naturalist's Edition*. Edited by Francis Harper. Athens: University of Georgia Press, 1998.

———. *William Bartram, the Search for Nature's Design: Selected Art, Letters, and Unpublished Writings*. Edited by Thomas Hallock and Nancy E. Hoffmann. Athens: University of Georgia Press, 2013.

*Bartram Heritage Report: A Study of the Life of William Bartram by the Bartram Trail Conference, Including the Report to the Heritage, Conservation and Recreation Service, U.S. Department of the Interior*. Montgomery, Ala.: Bartram Trail Conference, 1979.

Belleville, Bill. *River of Lakes: A Journey on Florida's St. Johns River*. Athens: University of Georgia Press, 2000.

Berkeley, Edmund, and Dorothy Smith Berkeley, eds. *The Correspondence of John Bartram, 1734–77*. Gainesville: University Press of Florida, 1992.

Berry, Edward W. "The Fossil Plants from Vero, Florida." *Journal of Geology* 25 (1917): 661–66.

Braund, Kathryn E. Holland. "'The Congress Held in a Pavilion': John Bartram and the Indian Congress at Fort Picolata, East Florida." In *America's Curious Botanist*, edited by Nancy E. Hoffmann and John C. Van Horne, 79–86. Philadelphia: American Philosophical Society, 2004.

Brenner, Mark, Michael W. Binford, and Edward S. Deevey. "Lakes." In *Ecosystems of Florida*, edited by Ronald L. Myers and John J. Ewel, 364–91. Gainesville: University of Florida Press, 1990.

Brinton, Daniel G. *A Guidebook of Florida and the South, for Tourists, Invalids, and Emigrants, with a Map of the St. Johns River*. Philadelphia: George Maclean, 1869.

*Catalogue of Trees, Shrubs, and Herbaceous Plants, Indigenous to the United States of America*. Philadelphia: Bartram and Reynolds, 1807.

Coleridge, Samuel Taylor. "Kubla Khan; or, A Vision in a Dream." In *Samuel Taylor Coleridge: The Oxford Authors*, ed. H. J. Jackson, 103. New York: Oxford University Press, 1985.

Cruickshank, Helen G., ed. *Bartram in Florida: 1774*. Cocoa: Florida Federation of Garden Clubs, 1986.

Dressler, Robert L., David W. Hall, Kent D. Perkins, and Norris H. Williams. *Identification Manual for Wetland Plant Species of Florida*. Gainesville: IFAS, University Press of Florida, 1991.

Evans, Jason M. "Pistia stratiotes L. in the Florida Peninsula: Biogeographic Evidence and Conservation Implications of Native Tenure for an 'Invasive' Aquatic Plant." *Conservation Society* 11 (2013): 233–46.

Ewel, Katherine C. "Swamps." In *Ecosystems of Florida*, edited by Ronald L. Myers and John J. Ewel, 281–322. Gainesville: University Press of Florida, 1990.

Franz, Richard. "Cave Crustaceans." In *Invertebrates*, edited by Mark Deyrup and Richard Franz, 183–86, 191–94. Gainesville: University Press of Florida, 1994.

Frazier, Charles. *Cold Mountain*. New York: Atlantic Monthly Press, 1997.

Fry, Joel T. "Index of Historic Plant Names." In *William Bartram, the Search for Nature's Design*, edited by Thomas Hallock and Nancy E. Hoffmann, 553–96. Athens: University of Georgia Press, 2010.

Goggin, John M. "A Florida Indian Trading Post, ca. 1763–1784." *Southern Indian Studies* 1 (1949): 35–38.

Hall, David W., William J. Weber, and Jason H. Byrd. *Wildflowers of Florida and the Southeast*. Gainesville, Fla.: Privately published, 2011.

Hallock, Thomas, and Nancy Hoffmann, eds. *William Bartram, the Search for Nature's Design: Selected Art, Letters, and Unpublished Writings*. Wormsloe Foundation Nature Book. Athens: University of Georgia Press, 2010.

Harper, Francis, ed. *The "Travels" of William Bartram: Naturalist's Edition*. Edited with commentary and annotated index. New Haven, Conn.: Yale University Press, 1958; second printing 1967.

Hoffmann, Nancy E., and John C. Van Horne, eds. *America's Curious Botanist: A Tercentennial Reappraisal of John Bartram, 1699–1777*. Philadelphia: American Philosophical Society, 2004.

Howell, Arthur H. *Florida Birdlife*. Tallahassee: Florida Department of Game and Freshwater Fisheries and Bureau of Biological Survey, 1937.

Kushlan, James A. "Freshwater Marshes." In *Ecosystems of Florida*, edited by Ronald L. Myers and John J. Ewel, 324–63. Gainesville: University Presses of Florida, 1990.

Linnaeus, Carl. *Species plantarum, exhibentes plantae rite cognitas, ad genera relates, cum differentiis specificis, nominibus trivialibus, synonymis selectis, locis natalibus, secundum systema sexuale digestas*. Vol. 1. Stockholm: Laurentius Salvius, 1753.

———. *Systema naturae per regna tria naturæ, secundum classes, ordines, genera, species, cum characteribus, differentiis, synonymis, locis*. 10th ed. Vol. 1. Stockholm: Laurentius Salvius, 1758.

Milanich, Jerry T., and Charles H. Fairbanks. *Florida Archaeology*. Cambridge, Mass.: Academic Press, 1980.

Miller, J. A. "Hydrogeology of Florida." In *The Geology of Florida*, edited by Anthony F. Randazzo and Douglas S. Jones, 69–88. Gainesville: University Press of Florida, 1997.

Moler, Paul, and Richard Franz. "Wildlife Values of Small Isolated Wetlands in the Southeastern Coastal Plain." In *Third Southeastern Nongame and Endangered Wildlife Symposium*, edited by Ron R. Odom, Kenneth A. Riddleberger, and James C. Ozier, 234–41. Atlanta: Georgia Department of Natural Resources, 1988.

Moore, Clarence B. "Certain Shell Heaps of the St. Johns River, Florida, Hitherto Unexplored." *American Naturalist* 26 (1892): 912–22.

Myers, Ronald L. "Scrub and High Pine." In *Ecosystems of Florida*, edited by Ronald L. Myers and John J. Ewel, 150–93. Gainesville: University Presses of Florida, 1990.

Myers, Ronald L., and John J. Ewel, eds. *Ecosystems of Florida*. Gainesville: University Presses of Florida, 1990.

Nordlie, Frank G. "Rivers and Springs." In *Ecosystems of Florida*, edited by Ronald L. Myers and John J. Ewel, 392–425. Gainesville: University Presses of Florida, 1990.

O'Donoughue, Jason M., Kenneth E. Sassaman, Megan E. Blessing, Johanna B. Talcott, and Julie C. Byrd. *Archaeological Investigations at Salt Springs (8MR2322), Marion County, Florida*. Laboratory of Southeastern Archaeology Department of Anthropology Technical Report 11. Gainesville: University of Florida, 2011.

Platt, William J., and Mark W. Schwartz. "Temperate Hardwood Forests." In *Ecosystems of Florida*, edited by Ronald L. Myers and John J. Ewel, 194–229. Gainesville: University Presses of Florida, 1990.

Putz, Francis E. *Finding Home in the Sandy Lands of the South: A Naturalist's Journey in Florida*. Gainesville: Cypress Highlands Press of Florida, 2015.

Quillen, Amanda K., Evelyn E. Gaiser, and Eric C. Grimm. "Diatom-Based Paleolimnological Reconstruction of Regional Climate and Local Land-use Change from a Protected Sinkhole Lake in Southern Florida, USA." *Journal of Paleolimnol* 49 (2013): 15–30.

Sacks, Laura A., and Ann B. Tihansky. "Geochemical and Isotopic Composition of Ground Water, with Emphasis on Sources of Sulfate, in the Upper Floridan Aquifer and Intermediate Aquifer System in Southwest Florida. Water Resources Investigation Report No. 96–4146." U.S. Geological Survey and Southwest Florida Water Management District, 1996.

Sassaman, Kenneth E., and Asa R. Randall. "Shell Mounds of the Middle St. Johns Basin, Northeast Florida." In *Early New World Monumentality*. Edited by R. Burger and R. Rosenwig, 53–77. Gainesville: University Press of Florida, 2012.

Schafer, Daniel L. "New World in a State of Nature: British Plantations and Farms on the St. Johns River, East Florida, 1763–84." *Florida History Online*. http://www.unf.edu/floridahistoryonline/Plantations/.

———. *William Bartram and the Ghost Plantations of British East Florida*. Gainesville: University Press of Florida, 2010.

Schmidt, Walt. "Geomorphology and Physiography of Florida." In *The Geology of Florida*, edited by Anthony F. Randazzo and Douglas S. Jones, 1–12. Gainesville: University Press of Florida, 1997.

Scott, Thomas M. "The Lithostratigraphy of the Hawthorn Group (Miocene) of Florida." *Florida Geological Survey Bulletin* 59 (1988): 148.

Scott, Thomas M., Guy H. Means, Rebecca. P. Meegan, Ryan C. Means, Sam B. Upchurch, R. E. Copeland, James Jones, Tina Roberts, and Alan Willet. 2002.

"Springs of Florida." *Florida Geological Survey Bulletin* 66 (October 2004). http://www.dep.state.fl.us/geology/geologictopics/springs/bulletin66.htm.

Shores, Elizabeth F. *On Harper's Trail: Roland McMillan Harper, Pioneering Botanist of the Southern Coastal Plain.* Athens: University of Georgia Press, 2008.

Slaughter, Thomas P. *The Natures of John and William Bartram.* New York: Knopf, 1996.

Snyder, Noel F. R., and Joel T. Fry. "Validity of Bartram's Painted Vulture (Aves: Cathartidae)." *Zootaxa* 3613, no. 1 (2013): 61–82.

"St. Johns River." *Wikipedia.* https://en.wikipedia.org/wiki/St._Johns_River.

Stalter, Richard, and Dwight Kincaid. "The Vascular Flora of Five Florida Shell Middens." *Journal of Torrey Botanical Society* 131, no. 1 (2004): 93–103.

Stork, William. *An Account of East-Florida, with A Journal, Kept by John Bartram of Philadelphia, Botanist to His Majesty for the Floridas; Upon a Journey from St. Augustine up the River St. Johns.* London: Sold by W. Nicoll and G. Woodfall, 1766.

———. *A Description of East-Florida, with a Journal Kept by John Bartram of Philadelphia, Botanist to His Majesty for the Floridas; Upon a Journey from St. Augustine up the River St. Johns, as Far as the Lakes.* 3rd ed. London: Sold by W. Nicoll and T. Jefferies [Thomas Jefferys], 1769.

Thompson, Fred G. *Identification Manual for Freshwater Snails of Florida.* Online. Gainesville: Florida Museum of Natural History, 2004. https://www.flmnh.ufl.edu/malacology/fl-snail/snails1.htm.

Waite, Thomas D. *Principles of Water Quality.* Orlando: Academic Press, 1984.

Waselkov, Gregory A., and Kathryn E. Holland Braund, eds. *William Bartram on the Southeastern Indians.* Lincoln: University of Nebraska Press, 1995.

Wulf, Andrea. *The Brother Gardeners: Botany, Empire, and the Birth of an Obsession.* New York: Knopf, 2010.

Wunderlin, Richard P., and Bruce F. Hansen. *Guide to the Vascular Plants of Florida.* Gainesville: University Press of Florida, 2011.

Wyman, Jeffries. *Freshwater Shell Mounds of the St. John's River, Florida.* Salem: Peabody Academy of Science, 1875.

# Index

Page numbers in *italics* indicate illustrations.

*Account of East-Florida* (Stork), 8, 14
Agave family (Agavaceae), 169
Airplant, Bartram's (*Tillandsia bartramii*), 162
Alachua Savanna (Paynes Prairie), 3, 18, 43, 69, 126, 133, 135, 148, 152, 201n6
"Alegator of St. Johns," 83
Alligator, 4, 63, 64, 69, 92–93, 95, 103, 112; attack of, 83–84, 85, 87, 93; brood of, 88; description of, 89, 203n28; fish eaten by, 86; nesting place of, 88–89, 90; plunging of, 57; roaring of, 75, 81–82, 85, 89–90, 203n27; sighting of, 9, 16, 18, 19, 24, 26, 44, 99, 136; size of, 64, 202n12
Alligator family (Alligatoridae), 187
Altamaha River, 45, 46, 50, 125
Amaranth family (Amaranthaceae), 169–70
Amaryllis Lily family (Amaryllidiceae), 169–70
Amelia Island, 23, 43, 49
American Philosophical Society, 1, 2, 3
Amphibians, 187
Amphipod, cave (*Crangonyx* sp.), 164
Anhinga (*Anhingidae*, "snake bird"), 91–92, 188
Animalia, 185–92: birds, 188–89; fishes, 186–87; frogs, 187; invertebrates, 185–86; mammals, 191–92; reptiles, 187–88; vertebrates, 186–92
Animals: aquatic, 99; names of, 164
Anisetree family (Schisandraceae or Illiciaceae), 183
Annona: beautiful shrub, 170; dwarf decumbent, 170Apalachee (Apalachi) Bay, 69, 126
Apalachicola River, 133

Apple, gopher (*Licinia michauxii*), 162
Arum family (Araceae), 171
Ash: black, 180; green (*Fraxinus pennsylvanica*), 162
Aster or Sunflower family (Asteraceae), 172; Climbing (*Aster carolinianus*), 162
Astor, town of, 43. *See also* Spalding's upper store
Atlantic Ocean, 46, 51, 118, 160
Audubon, John James, 4–5

Bacteria, chemoautotrophic, 155
Bachop, Adam, 117, 205n5
Bailey, James, 45
Barton, Benjamin Smith, 5–6, 7
Bartram, John, vii–ix, 1–10, 70, 131; Botanist to King, 13; correspondence of, 116–18, 205nn1–6; letters to, 118–21, 124–27, 205n7, 205n12, 206nn13–14. *See also Diary*
Bartram, William, vii–ix, 5, 13, 14, 131; and art, 2, 6, 91, 124–25; correspondence of, 121–27, 205n12, 205nn8–11, 206nn13–14; letters to, 116–18, 205nn1–6; professional struggles, 1–3, 5, 9, 13, 116–20; spiritual views of, viii, ix, 4, 9, 45, 59–60, 72; travels of, iii, 3, 8–9, *15*, *17*, 23, 43–44, 80, 116, 124, 27; 202n18, 203n26. *See also Report to Fothergill*; *Travels*
*Bartram in Florida* (Cruickshank), vii–viii
Bartram's Bluff, 31
Bartram species, 167–92. *See also specific species*

Bartram Trail Conference (BTC), 9–10
Bass, spotted, 186
Basswood (*Tilia americana*), 162, 179
Batatas (Sweet potato [*Ipomoea batatas*]), 98
Bay and Laurel family (Lauraceae): dwarf sweet bay, 178; loblolly bay (*Gordonia lasianthus*), 163, 183; purple-berried bay, 180; swamp bay (*Persea palustris*), 162; sweet bay (*Magnolia virginiana*), 161, 178
Bayberry family (Myricaceae), 179–80
Bean, Cherokee (*Erythrina herbacea*), 163
Bear family (Ursidae), 85, 86, 192
Beautyberry, American (*Callicarpa americana*), 163
Beech, American (*Fagus grandifolia*), 162, 176
Beecher Springs, 155
Bees, 47, 186
Belleville, Bill, vii–ix, 9, 160
Bell Flower family (Campanulaceae), 173
Binford, Michael, 153
Binomial terminology, 164
Birds, 47, 188–89. *See also specific birds*
Blackbird, 190
Black Creek, 133
Black Creek Holes, 133
Blackgum (*Nyssa sylvatica*), 162, 174
Blue Cypress Lake marsh, 133
Blue linnet, 189
Blue Pond, 154
Blue Springs, 8, 24, 44, 99, 204n37
Bluff hammock (landscape), 138–39, 206n4
Brahm, William Gerard de, 3, 205n3
Bream (*Lepomis* sp.), 107, 164, 187
Bream: great blue and black, 186; great yellow or particolored, 186; red bellied, 186; silver and white, 186; yellow, 103–4, *104*, 186, 204n45
Brenner, Mark, 153
Broughton Island, 45
Buckthorn family (Rhamnaceae), 181
Buckwheat family (Polygonaceae), 181
Buffalo Bluff, 134
Bulrushes (*Scirpus* sp.), 162, 174
Bunting, 189
Butcher bird, bluish grey, 190
Buttonbush (*Cephalanthus occidentalis*), 163

Cabbage-bluff, 25
Cabbage Creek, 152
*Cacalia*, 172
Cactus family (Cactaceae), 173
Cactus, prickly-pear (Ocala scrub form [*Opuntia humifusa* var. *ammophila*]), 163
Caldwall's store, 38
Cane, 180
Canna Lily family (Cannaceae), 173
Cannibalism, 145
Cardinal and Bunting family (Cardinalidae), 189
Cardinal flower (*Lobelia cardinalis*), 161, 173
Cassine, 170–71
Catesby, Mark, 5, 101
Catfish family (Ictaluridae), 186
Catfish, barbed, 186
Cat family (Felidae), 192
Cattail (*Typhaceae*), 162, 183
Cedar family (Cupressaceae), 168
Cedar, Atlantic white (*Chamaecyparis thyoides*), 163
Cedar, red (*Juniperus virginiana*), 161, 168
Cedar Point, 76, 106, 142
"Celtis" Sugarberry (*Celtis laevigata*), 161
Chalmers, Lionel, 126
Chamaerops, dwarf creeping, 171
Charleston (Charles-Town), 2, 32, 41, 43, 44, 69, 124, 160
Charlotia (Charlottenburgh), 37, 66, 67, 69, 142, 202n15
Cherokees, 125, 126
Chinquapins, 177
Citrus family (Rutaceae), 182
Clades, 166
Cladistics, 166
Cladograms, 166
Clark, William, 5
Classification system (organisms and minerals), 164–65
Clement's Bluff, 22
Clifton Springs, 155
Cluster-cherry (*Prunus* sp.), 181
Coffee, wild (*Psychotria nervosa*), 163
Coffee-bluff, 29, 200n48
Coleridge, Samuel Taylor, 5, 205n51
Collinson, Peter, 1, 8

Cook, James, 5
Coontie (*Zamia pumila*), 163, 168–69
Coosawhatchee Formation (Hawthorn Group), 144
Coot, 191
Cordgrass, sand (*Spartina bakeri*), 162
Corn, 72, 98, 136
Cotton, 51, 72, 98, 160
Cowkeeper (Oconee Mico), 126, 201n9
Cowpen Lake basin, 154
Crane family (Gruidae), 190
Crane, savanna, 100, 190
Crayfish, cave (*Procambarus* sp. and *Troglocambarus* sp.), 164
Creeks (Muscogee), 2, 102–3, 125, 126. *See also* Native Americans; Seminoles
Creeks, 38, 95, 102–3, 159
Crescent (Dunn's) Lake, 36, 67
Crèvecoeur, Hector St. John de, 5
Croaker Hole, 133
Crocodiles, 187. *See also* Alligator
Crow, 103, 190; carrion, 103
Cruickshank, Helen G., vii–viii
Cuckoo and Roadrunner family (Cuculidae), 190
Cumberland Island, 48, 201n3
Curlew, Spanish, 101, 191
Cuscowilla, 43, 149
Cutgrass, southern (*Leersia hexandra*), 163
Cypress, 168; bald (*Taxodium distichum*), 162; pond (*Taxodium ascendens*), 163

Darlington, William, 13
Darwin, Erasmus, 5
Davis, John, 2, 13, 14, 16
Davis, Robert, 2, 14, 16, 39–40, 41, 197n5
Deep creek (landscape), 135, 152
Deer family (Ceridae), 77, 191, 203n24. *See also* Venison
Deevey, Edward, 153
DeLand, 155
Devil's Hole, 153
*Diary* (Bartram, John), vii, 6, 8, 13–42, 44, 132, 167; of Bartram species, 167–92; Dec. 1765, 135, 136, 137, 139, 141, 146–47, 150, 156, 158; Jan. 1766, 135, 137, 138, 139, 141, 143–44, 147, 154, 156–57, 160. *See also specific locations*

"Divine Monitor," 4. *See also* Quakerism
Doctor's Lake, 39–40
Dog family (Canidae), 191
Dogwood family (Cornaceae), 174
Dove, 105, 189
*Dracontium*, 171
Drayton (Bryan's) Island, 34–35, 36, 136, 141, 144, 202n22
Dropseed, pineywoods (*Sporobolus junceus*), 163
Drum family (Sciaenidae), 187
Drummer's Pond, 154
Duck-meat, 178–79
Ducks, 188
Duckweed family (Lemnoidaceae or Araceae), 178–79
Dunn's Creek, 133

Eagle family (Accipitridae), 188
Ebony family (Ebenaceae), 175
Econlockhatchee River, 133
*Ecosystems of Florida* (Brenner, Binford, and Deevey), 153
Edgar (Florida), 154
Egan, Stephen, 50, 52, 54, 201n4
Egmont (Perceval) plantation, 49, 50, 125
Egret, 188
Elder-trees, 169
*The Elements of Botany*, 5
Elm family (Ulmaceae), 184; Florida elm (*Ulmus floridana*), 162
Ephemera (mayflies), 8, 58, 59, 185
Ephouskyca. *See* Limpkin family

Fetterbush (*Lyonia lucida*), 163
Ferns (Pteridophytes), 168; golden polypody (*Phlebodium aureum*), 162; shoestring (*Vittaria lineata*), 162
Fish, 51, 86, 98, 99, 112–13. *See also specific fish*
Flatfish family (Soleidae), 187
Floating mats and islets of vegetation (landscape), 137–38, 206n3
Florida Aquifer, upper, 155. *See also individual springs*
Flounder, 187
Flowering plants (Angiosperms), 169–85
Forbes's Bluff, 40

Forests, 48, 49–50, 52, 60, 72
Fort George's Sound, 52
Fothergill, John, 3, 44, 124, 125
Fowl: aquatic, 75; sea, 18; wild, 98
Franklin, Benjamin, 1
Frazier, Charles, 3
Frederica, 45, 47, 48, 49, 125. *See also* St. Simons Island
French and Indian War, 1
Frog, Florida gopher (*Lithobates capito*), 164
Frogs, 63, 164, 187
Frog's-bit family (Hydrocharitaceae), 177
Ft. Gates Ferry Road, 149

Gainesville, 43. *See also* Alachua Savanna
Gallberry (*Ilex glabra*), 163
Gallinule, 191
Garberia (*Garberia heterophylla*), 163
Garden, Alexander, 117, 118
Garfish family (Lepisosteidae), 187
Garr, great brown spotted, 187
Gemini Springs, 155
*Gentlemen's Magazine*, 8, 14
George III (King), 2, 14
Georgia, 2–3, 43, 45–50, 118, 125, 126
Ginseng family (Araliaceae), 171
Gleditsia, shortpoded, 176
Goatsucker family (Caprimulgidae), 189
Goose and Duck family (Anatidae), 188
Gopher, pocket (*Geomys pinetis*), 163
Gordon, Adam, 36
Gourd family (Cucurbitaceae), 174
Grape family (Vitaceae; *Vitis* sp.), 163
Grass family (Poaceae), 180. *See also specific grass*
Great Lake. *See* Lake George
"Great Yellow Bream called Old Wife," 104
Greenbriers (*Smilax* sp.), 163
Greenwood (home), 14, 40

Hackberry family (Celtidaceae), 173
Halfway Pond, 148, 149, 153–54
Harper, Francis, 8, 13, 131–32, 153–54, 167, 206n11
Harper, Roland, 131
Hawkinsville, 95, 203n31
Hawthorn, green (*Crataegus viridis*), 162

Hazard, Richard, 41, 201n64
Heath family (Ericaceae), 175–76
Hemp-vine, climbing (*Mikania scandens*), 162
Heron, Egret, and Bittern family (Ardeidae), 188
Hesler's Bluff, 40
Hibiscus, scarlet (*Hibiscus coccineus*). *See* Mallow family
Hickory (*Carya* sp.), 161; Florida (*Carya floridana*), 163; pignut (*Carya glabra*), 162, 178
High pine (landscape), 147–49
Historical Society of Pennsylvania, 13
Hog Island, 136
Holly family (Aquifoliaceae), 170–71
Holly, dahoon (*Ilex cassine*), 161
Hontoon (Huntoon) Island, 31, 142, 200n51, 203n34
Humboldt, Alexander von, 5
Hurricane, 8, 55, 97–98
Hyacinth, water (*Eichhornia crassipes*), 161
Hydrobes or siltsnails (*Aphaostracon* sp. and *Floridobia* sp.), 164
Hydrogen sulfide, 155–56

Ibis and Spoonbill family (Threskiornithidae), 191
Icterus, golden, 190
Indigo, 2, 54, 56, 72, 98, 160
Insects, 58–60, 185–86
Insects, cochineal, 185
Invertebrates, 185–86
Iris family (Iridaceae), 177
Isle of Palms, 106, 141–42
Isopod, cave (*Caecidotea* sp.), 164
Ivy, poison (*Toxicodendron radicans*), 162
Ixia, Bartram's (*Calydorea caelestina*), 115, 121–23, 122

Jacksonville (Cow-ford), 14, 40, 50, 53, 54, 125, 133, 135
Jay and Crow family (Corvidae), 190
Jefferson, Thomas, 5
Jekyll Island, 48
Johnson, town of, 154
Johnson's Bluff, 19
Johnson's Spring, 18, 34, 155, 156
Julington Creek, 133

Kingsessing, 1, 2, 6
Kingsley Creek (Amelia Narrows), 52, 201n5
Kingsley, Zephaniah, 144
Kinsley (Kingsley) Point, 144

Lake Beresford, 24, 97–99, 200n51
Lake Dexter (East Lake), 32, 43, 81, 105–6, 136, 204n46
Lake George, 19–21, 32, 43, 70–73, 106, 107, 111, 141–42, 144, 155, 204n50; fish in, 113; little ocean of, 73, 106; pools in, 133–34; swamps in, 90
Lake Harney (Round-lake), 26, 29, 200n48
Lake Jessup, 155, 200n48
Lake Loughman, 2, 13, 28
Lake McMeekin, 154
Lake Monroe, 25–26, 30, 155
Lake Okeechobee, 133
Lamboll, Elizabeth, 116, 124
Lamboll, Thomas, 116, 117, 118, 124
Lantana (*Lantana camara*), 74, 106, 137; balmy, 184
Large-mouth bass, 138
Latchaway, 18
Laurel, 178, 179
Laurens, Henry, 9, 45, 115, 117, 118–21, 205n7
*Letters from an American Farmer* (St. John de Crèvecoeur), 5
Lettuce, water (*Pistia stratiotes*), 161
Lewis, Meriwether, 5
Lily, rain (*Zephyranthes atamasca*), 169
Lily, string (*Crinum americana*), 161, 169
Lily, white water (*Nymphaea odorata*), 162
Limestone springs and spring runs (landscape), 154–58
Limpkin family (Aramidae): "Ephouskyca," 6, 7, 100–101, 189, 204nn38–41
Linnaeus, Carl, vii, 8, 164, 205n9; binomial terminology, 164; classification system for organisms and minerals, 164–65; taxonomy related to, 165, 166–67; *Species plantarum*, 196n2–200n63
Liquid-amber, 177
Little Lake George, 133, 141
Little Orange Creek, 152
Little St. Simons, 49, 201n3

Lizard, scrub (*Sceloporus woodi*), 163
Lizard-tail family (Saururaceae), 183
Long Lake, 98
Long Warrior, 135, 206n2
Lotus family (Nelumbonaceae), 180
Lower Creeks, 57, 201n9. *See also* Native Americans; Seminoles
Lupines, pink-flowered lady (*Lupinus villosus*), 163
Lyonia, rusty (*Lyonia ferruginea*), 163

Maclure, William, 4
Madder family (Rubiaceae), 182
Magnolia family (Magnoliaceae), 179; southern magnolia (*Magnolia grandiflora*), 161, 179
Maidencane (*Panicum hemitomon*), 162
Mallow family (Malvaceaerat): saltmarsh mallow (*Kosteletzkya pentacarpos*), 161, 179; scarlet hibiscus (*Hibiscus coccineus*), 161, 179
Mammals, 191–92
Manigault, Gabriel, 117
Maple, red (*Acer rubrum*), 162, 182
Marshall, Abraham, 56, 135
Marshes, ix, 74. *See also specific marshes*
Middens. *See* Mounds/mounts, Indian; Shell mounds
Middle Lake, 30–31
Mineral Springs, 30
Mint family (Lamiaceae), 178
McLatchie (M'Latche), Charles, 69, 159
Mississippi River, 3, 61, 116, 127, 173
Mock-bird, 105
Moultrie, John, 117
Morning-glory family (Convolvulaceae), 174
Moschatel and Elderberry family (Adoxaceae), 169
Mosquitoes, musquitoes, 93–94, 185
Mosquito Grove, 203n29
Moss, sphagnum (*Sphagnum* sp.), 163
Mounds/mounts, Indian, 67, 70, 73, 204n36; middens, 136, 135, 141, 145, 146, 206n8; Mount Hope, 19, 70, 146, 147, 202n19; Mount-joy, 25, 31; Ogeechee mounts, 50; Mount Royal, exploration of, 43, 113–14, 202n20; Mount Royal, landing at, 19, 35, 70, 71, 73, 113–14, 144, 145, 147, 198n25, 202n20. *See also* Shell mounds

Mount Hope. *See* Mounds/mounts, Indian
Mount-joy. *See* Mounds/mounts, Indian
Mount Royal. *See* Mounds/mounts, Indian
Mouse, old field (*Peromyscus polionotus*), 163
Mouse and Rat family (Muridae), 191–92. *See also* Mouse, old field; Wood rat
Mudfish family (Amidae), 186
Mulberry family (Moraceae), 179
Murphy (Dunn's) Island, 18, 36, 67, 133, 136, 198n18, 200n58
Musquito River, 99
Myrtle, 180
Myrtle, wax (*Myrica cerifera*), 162, 179
Mystery Snail family (Viviparidae), 145
Mystery snail, banded (*Viviparus georgianus*), 146, 206n8

Nairne, Thomas, 117
Nashua Spring, 155
Native Americans, 4, 19, 67, 73, 79, 95, 125; encounters with, 55, 78–80, 201n7; Florida, 34–35, 40, 41, 45, 136–37; stereotypes of, 79; trade of, 1, 55, 57–58, 67; trading houses plundered by, 48–49; villages of, 65–66, 67, 69–73, 158, 202n13. *See also* Cherokees; Creeks; Seminoles
*Natural History of Selborne* (White), 5
New-Smyrna, 99, 204n36
Newt, striped (*Notophthamus perstriatus*), 164
Nonpareil, 189
North Carolina, 2–3, 13, 78. See also *Travels*
*Notes on the State of Virginia* (Jefferson), 5
Nymphaea, floating, 180

Oak and Beech family (Fagaceae), 176–77; Chapman's oak (*Quercus chapmanii*), 163; evergreen shrub oak (*Quercus myrtifolia*), 162, 185; laurel oak (*Quercus laurifolia*), 161, 176; sand live oak (*Quercus geminata*), 162; sand post oak (*Quercus margaretta*), 162; turkey oak (*Quercus laevis*), 163; Virginia live oak (*Quercus virginiana*), 161, 176; water oak (*Quercus nigra*), 161, 165, 177; white swamp oak, 177
"Observations on the Creek and Cherokee Indians" (Bartram), 71

Ocklawaha River, 133, 134–35, 152
Ogeechee River, 50
Oglethorpe, James, 45, 48
Oglethorpe's Bluff, 40
Olive family (Oleaceae), 180
Ominous drum, 187
Opossum family (Didelphidae), 192
Orange, 182; as animal food, 73–74; bitter-sweet and sour, 20, 22, 31,33; in Bartrams' meals, 86, 93, 107; in Florida Indian agriculture and cuisine, 16, 36, 65; groves, 56, 70; notable mentions in Bartrams' landscape descriptions, 18, 19, 20, 22, 33, 37, 54, 95, 103, 106, 108, 111, 147, 157, 182
Orange point shell mound, 146
Orangery, 56
Orange Springs, 135
Orange tree (*Citrus* sp.), 161, 182
Ord, George, 4
Oriole and Blackbird family (Icteridae), 190
Otters, 192
Ovid (Publius Ovidius Naso), 92
Oviedo, town of, 155
Owl family (Strigidae), 93; whooping owl, 191

Palatka, 2, 43, 65, 133, 134, 142
Palm family (Arecaceae), 171–72
Palm, Florida royal (*Roystonea regia*), 162
Palm forests, riverside, 141–42
Palm, cabbage (*Sabal palmetto*), 161, 172
Palmetto: dwarf creeping, 171; saw (*Serenoa repens*), 162; very dwarf species of, 172
Parrot family (Psittacidae), 191, Paroquets, 65, 191
Pawpaw family (Annonaceae), 170; big-flowered pawpaw (*Asimina obovata*), 163
Paynes Prairie. *See* Alachua Savannah
Pea family (Fabaceae), 176
Peale, Titian, 4
Peanines, (undetermined plant), 185
Pelican, 52, 101–2, 204n42
Pensacola, 116, 126, 200n55
Pennywort (*Hydrocotyle* sp.), 161, 171
Pheasant, 190
Philadelphia, 43, 44, 118
Phlox family (Polemoniaceae), 181
Phylogenetics, 166–67

Pickerelweed family (Pontederiaceae), 162, 181
Picolata, Fort, 2, 16, 18, 38, 43, 58, 202n10
Pigeon and Dove family (Columbidae), 189
*Pilgrim's Progress*, 44
Pine family (Pinaceae), 168; longleaf pine (*Pinus palustris*), 162, 168; Ocala sand pine (*Pinus clausa*), 163; pond pine (*Pinus serotina*), 163; slash pine (*Pinus elliottii*), 163
Pineapple family (Bromeliaceae), 173
Pine flatwoods (landscape), 150–52, *151*
Persimmon (Pishamins), 175
Pit Viper family (Crotalidae), 188; rattle snake, 188
Plant groups (Gymnosperms) 147–49, *148*, 161, 162, 163, 168–69; (Pteridophytes) 168; (Angiosperms) 169–85
Plantations, 1, 43, 48, 55, 57, 97, 158; Beresford, 44, 204n35
Plants: names of, 164; undetermined, 185. *See also* Flowering plants; *specific plants*
Plants, cone-bearing: (cedar) 161, 163, 168; (pine), 147–49, *148*, 162, 163, 168; (zamia or coontie), 163, 168–69
Plum-tree, 181
Ponds. *See specific ponds*
Popash (*Fraxinus caroliniana*), 162
Possum Bluff Hole, 133
Prehistoric wetlands, 133
Pupa (Popa), Fort San Francisco de, 38, 200n61
Puzzle Lake, 28

Quakerism, viii, 4, 9, 72, 78–79
*Querci*, dwarf, 176

Raccoon family (Procyonidae), 192
Racerunner Lizard family (Teiidae), 188
Rail, Gallinule, and Coot family (Rallidae), 191
Rat, 192
Ravens, 190
Redbay (*Persea borbonia*), 163, 178
Reeds, tall water, 174
*Report to Fothergill*, 3, 44, 203n27. *See also* Fothergill, John
Reptiles, 187–88
Revolution, American, 4
Rice: in Bartrams' letters, 117, 118, 119; in Bartrams' meals, 86, 107; in Florida Indian agriculture and cuisine, 33, 61; plantations, 65, 102; wetlands and swamps as rice-grounds, 20, 42, 50, 67, 98, 116
Rice (Gray's) Creek, 37, 133, 200n60
River islands (landscape), 136–37
River marshes (landscape), 142–44, *143*, 206n
Riverside palm forests and Isle of Palms (landscape), 141–42
River swamps (landscape), *140*, 140–41
Rivers. *See specific rivers*
River's End, 160–61
Rocky Point, 113, 141, 144
Rocky shores (landscape), 144–45
Rodman, town of, 152
Rodman Pool, 152
Rolle, Dennys, 37, 66–67, 200n59
Roll's town, 18, 36–37, 38, 43, 67, 69, 142, 200, 200n59, 202n15. *See also* Charlotia
"Rope Island," 142
Rose family (Rosaceae), 181
Rosemary, Florida (*Ceratiola ericoides*), 162
Royal Fern family (Osmundaceae) 168
Ruderal (landscape), 158–60
Rush, Benjamin, 3, 115; letters to, 121–24, 205nn8–11

Salt marshes, 51–52
Salt plains, 46, 51
Salt ("Six mile") Springs, 34, 108, 142, 144, 149, 154, 205n51
Sand Hills, 149
Sandweed (*Hypericum fasciculatum*), 163
Sapodilla family (Sapotaceae), 183
Satsuma Spring, 18, 155, 198n22
Savanna, 45, 49, 50
Sawgrass (*Cladium jamaicense*), 162
Saxifrage, 177–78
Say, Thomas, 4
Science, progressiveness of, 167
Scientific and common names, 165–66
Scorpions, 188
Scrub (landscape), 149–50
Seabream family (Sparidae), 187
Sedge family (Cyperaceae), 174
Seminoles, 1, 57, 69, 76–77, 125–26, 135, 159

Senna family (Caesalpiniaceae), 173
Seven Years War (French and Indian War), 1
Sheepshead, 187
Shellfish, 46, 51
Shells, 146, 206n8
Shelly banks, shelly knolls, shelly provinces (landscape), 145–46
Shell mounds (landscape), 136, 145–46, 146, 198n23, 203n27, 206n8. *See also* Mounds/mounts, Indian
Shrike family (Laniidae), 190
Silvery perdicium, 172
Silver Springs, viii
Silver Glen (William's) Spring, 33, 154
Skate family (Rajaidae), 187
Skink, sand (*Neoseps reynoldsi*), 163
Slavery, 2, 14, 52, 55, 98, 116–21, 125
Sloane, Hans, 1
Smartweed (*Polygonum* sp.), 161, 181
Snail, aquatic, 156, 163
Soapberry family (Sapindaceae), 182
Softshell Turtle family (Trionychidae)
Softshell, Florida (*Apalone ferox*), 164, 187–88
*Some Account of the Tantalous ephouskyca* (Barton, Benjamin Smith), 6, 7
Spalding, James, 43, 45, 48, 69, 125, 201n1
Spalding's lower store, 18, 35, 38–39, 43, 106, 114, 125, 199n35, 204n49, 207n17
Spalding's upper store, 22, 32–33, 48–49, 69, 78, 95, 106, 160, 203n25
Sparkleberry (*Vaccinium arboreum*), 162
Sparrow family (Emberizidae), 190
Spatterdock (*Nuphar advena*), 161, 171, 180
Spider, red widow (*Latrodectus bishopi*), 163
Spoonbill, 191
Springs, viii, ix, 134. *See also specific springs*
Squirrel family (Sciuridae), 192
St. Augustine, 2, 13–14, 22, 41, 50, 57–58, 67, 125, 196n1; treaty at, 67
St. (Saint) Johns River (landscape), *v*, viii, 2, 15, 17, 23, 43, 56–57, 66–67, 69, 86, 98–99, 134, 135, 149; banks of, 138–39; bottom of, 134; boundaries of, 133; history and diversity of, viii; management of, 132, 136; pools formed by, 133; remarks on, 42; sand bars in, 134; S.E. Branch of, 28; springs along, 134, 156

St. Johns River maps: lower, 23; middle, 17; upper, 15
St. Marks, 66–67. *See also* Apalachee Bay
St. Marys River, 50, 125
St. Simons Island, 45, 46, 48, 125. *See also* Frederica
Stingray family (Dasyatidae), 186
Storax family (Styracaceae), 183
Stores, 38–39. *See also specific stores*
Stork, William, 8, 14, 160
Stork family (Ciconiidae), 189; wood stork, 189
Sugar-cane, 98
Sunfish family (Centrarchidae), 186
Suwannee River, 3, 133; as Little St. Juan, St. Juane, or San Juanito, 69, 126
Sweetgum (*Liquidambar styraciflua*), 162, 177
Sweet Leaf family (Symplocaceae), 183
Sweetspire or Virginia Willow family (Iteaceae), viii, 177–78
*Systema Naturae* (Linnaeus), 165

Talahasochte, 69
Tallow-nut, 185
Tallow Wood family (Ximeniaceae), 185
Tapegrass (*Vallisneria americana*), 161, 177
Tarflower (*Bejaria racemosa*), 163
Taxonomy. *See* Classification system
Tea family (Theaceae), 183
Thoreau, Henry David, 5
Tick Island, 142, 143
Tidal wedges, 133
Titi family (Cyrillaceae), 163, 175
Tobacco, 65, 202n14
Tortoise, gopher (*Gopherus polyphemus*), 163
Towee (Towhee) (*Fringilla erythrophthalma*), 190
Trade networks, 1, 43, 45. *See also* Native Americans; Trading houses
Trading houses, 48–49, 54, 69, 95, 158, 160. *See also* Spalding, James; Spalding's lower store; Spalding's upper store
*Travels through North & South Carolina, Georgia, East & West Florida, the Cherokee Country, the Extensive Territories of the Muscogulges, or Creek Confederacy, and the Country of*

the Chactaws: Containing An Account of the Soil and Natural Productions of those Regions, together with Observations on the Manners of the Indians (Bartram, William), vii, ix; 3–10, 43–114, 201n6; reviews of, 4
Tree-moss, long bed of, 173
Trout. See Bass, spotted
Trout Creek, 41
Trumpet Creeper family (Bignoniaceae)
Turkey and Pheasant family (Phasianidae), 190
Turkey Island, 136
Turnbull, Andrew, 99
"Two Beautifull Species Annona," 68

Upland ponds and lakes (landscape), 153–54

Vegetation, 45–46, 52–54, 59–65, 66, 105; on islands, 136; islets of, 137–38, 206n3; rocky shores, 144
Venison, 16, 29, 47, 48. See also Deer family
Vertebrates, 186–87
Vervain family (Verbenaceae), 184
Viburnum, Walter's (*Viburnum obovatum*), 162
Violet family (Violaceae), 184
Volusia Blue Spring, 155
Vulture family (Cathartidae), 102, 204nn43–44
Vulture, coped, 103, 189
Vulture, painted, 189

*Walden* (Thoreau), 5
Walnut family (Juglandaceae), 178
Wasps, yellow, 185
Water-grass, 180
Water-hen, squealing, 191

Water Lily family (Nymphaeaceae), 180; white water lily (*Nymphaea odorata*), 162
Water-numularia, 171
Weasel family (Mustelidae), 192
Wekiva River, 133
Welaka, 146
Welaka Spring, 155
Whip-poor-will, 105, 204n47
White, Gilbert, 5
White Alder family (Clethraceae) 173
"White Captain," 78–79, 80
White or Black River, 38
Whitlow's Bluff, 24
Wiggins, Job, 78–79, 106, 126, 160
Wild-cat, 192
Wild Petunia family (Acanthaceae), 169
*Wildflowers of Florida and the Southeast* (Hall et al.), 168
Wildlife, 45, 48
Willow family (Salicaceae), 182
Willow, Carolina (*Salix caroliniana*), 163
Willow, Virginia (*Itea virginica*), 162
Wilson, Alexander, 5
Wiregrass (*Aristida stricta*), 162
Witch Hazel family (Hamamelidaceae), 177
Wolves, 85, 107–8, 191
Wood rat, 87, 191–92

Yam family (Dioscoreaceae), 175
Yeats, David, 2, 13, 14

Zamia family (Zamiaceae), 168
Zanthoxilon, Hercules club (*Zanthoxylum clava-herculis*), 161

RICHARD FRANZ is retired faculty of the Florida Museum of Natural History, University of Florida, Gainesville. He has spent most of his career exploring the landscapes and species of north Florida and the Caribbean. These experiences are described in more than 160 professional publications. He now lives with his wife, Melanie Wegner, at the edge of the Ordway-Swisher Biological Station in western Putnam County, Florida.

THOMAS HALLOCK teaches English at the University of South Florida St. Petersburg. He is the author of *From the Fallen Tree: Frontier Narratives, Environmental Politics, and the Roots of a National Pastoral 1749–1826*, coeditor (with Nancy Hoffmann) of *William Bartram, the Search for Nature's Design: Selected Art, Letters, and Unpublished Writings*. He is currently working on a collection of essays about why he loves teaching the American survey, called *A Road Course in American Literature*. Hallock lives in St. Petersburg with his wife, Julie Armstrong, and their teenage son, Zackary.

www.ingramcontent.com/pod-product-compliance
Lightning Source LLC
Chambersburg PA
CBHW020836160426
43192CB00007B/682